Gate Arrays

Gate Arrays

Design Techniques and Applications

Edited by

John W. Read

McGRAW-HILL BOOK COMPANY

New York St. Louis San Francisco Auckland Bogotá
Hamburg Johannesburg London Madrid Mexico
Montreal New Delhi Panama Paris São Paulo
Singapore Sydney Tokyo Toronto

Library of Congress Cataloging in Publication Data

Main entry under title:

Gate arrays.

Includes index.
1. Integrated circuits — Design and construction.
I. Read, John W.
TK7874.G373   1985   621.381'73   85-11708
ISBN 0-07-051286-8

First published in Great Britain by
Collins Professional and Technical 1985

1234567890   KGP/KGP   898765

ISBN 0-07-051286-8

Printed and bound by Kingsport Press

Contents

Contributors' Biographies

Geoff Bostock was educated at Christ's Hospital, Horsham & Wadham College, Oxford, where he obtained an honours degree in Physics in 1962, and Southampton University where he obtained an MSc in Microelectronics. In 1970 he joined Mullard, Southampton as a Product Engineer before moving to Texas Instruments, Bedford in 1973 in a similar role. In 1975 he joined Cranfield Institute of Technology as a Senior Research Officer in Electronics before returning to Mullard in 1977 where he was a Technical Support Engineer for Signetics integrated circuits. Geoff moved to the Integrated Circuit Product Group in 1979, at first looking after CMOS circuits before taking up his current post of Product Manager for Bipolar Memory and LSI Circuits.

Bill Alexander obtained his 1st class honours in Physics at the University of Kent, Canterbury in 1973 and continued there doing research to obtain his PhD in 1976. After that he worked at the Advanced Development Division of Racal Electronics Ltd, planning and establishing a clean room facility to support the commitment for a single level metal CMOS gate array designed at Racal. After successfully establishing the commitment and passivation process for the gate arrays, he moved into system research and development concentrating on aspects relevant to integration and VLSI. In 1980 he transferred to Racal Microelectronics Ltd, working on several gate array and cell array designs.

In 1982 he joined National Semiconductor (UK) Ltd, to establish and manage the design centre for gate arrays in Northern Europe.

Derek Bray obtained a BSc in Physics at Manchester University in 1955 and an MSEE from Santa Clara, California in 1969. He has gained nearly twenty years' experience in industry, working on many aspects of semiconductor technology and applications in both linear and digital products with EMI, Westinghouse and Fairchild Semiconductor, where he was Consumer and Communications Applications Manager. He has also worked in IC design at National Semiconductor and Motorola, and was Consumer IC Design Manager at Fairchild Semiconductor from 1974 to 1976. He has had many articles and papers published.

He is currently Vice-President of Engineering at Interdesign, Inc., responsible for analog semi-custom and digital gate array engineering.

Graham Hetherington studied Physics at the University of Sussex, England obtaining a PhD in 1976. Since then he has worked in the Design Automation Department at Texas Instruments, based in England, where he has worked on symbolic layout aids and workstation schematic entry systems. His current work is with Texas Instruments Transportable Design Utility; a software suite which provides the logic design facilities required for logic array and standard cell design.

Stephen McMinn obtained a BSEE from Louisiana State University in 1977 and an MBA from Santa Clara, California in 1981. He worked on discrete bipolar transistors as a product engineer at Fairchild Semiconductor. In 1978, he joined American Microsystems Inc., Santa Clara. He started off as development engineer, responsible for matching customer-generated designs to AMI processes and transferring the circuits into manufacturing. He has since been department manager, working with customer-owned tooling products, and a test product manager for Gate Array/-Standard Cell Group. At present he is director of a customer-owned tooling (silicon foundry) business. He is responsible for all engineering operations, and marketing for the silicon foundry business.

Dave Tonge joined what is now British Telecom as an apprentice in 1966. After serving his apprenticeship and working for a time, first in London and later in Tunbridge Wells telephone area, he undertook a sandwich degree course at the Hatfield Polytechnic. Graduating during 1973, he moved to BTRL at Martlesham to join the Microelectronics Applications Group which he now heads. During this time he has been responsible for the development of a number of semi-custom integrated circuits for a variety of telecommunications applications.

Mervyn Jack is a lecturer in the Department of Electrical Engineering at the University of Edinburgh where he is engaged in teaching and research in the design and application of microelectronic systems. His current research interests include VLSI and signal processing architectures, primarily in the areas of FFT processors, self-testing VLSI structures, and speech processing.

He is co-author of the text 'Introduction to MOS LSI' (Addison-Wesley, 1983) and editor of the text 'The impact of micro-electronics technology' (Edinburgh University Press, 1983)

A member of the IEE, he received his BSc in Electrical Engineering from Heriot-Watt University, Edinburgh in 1971, an MSc from the same University in 1975 and a PhD from the University of Edinburgh in 1978.

Robert Heaton graduated from Surrey University, England with an Electronics degree in 1979. During 3 years with Texas Instruments Inc. he worked on a number of internal and customer logic array implementations, as well as writing much of TIs soft macro-library. He was a prime mover in TIs low power Schottky logic array programme in the UK.

Robert also spent one year with Philips AG in Zurich where he was responsible for the design of a fully custom CMOS display controller.

He is now with Acorn Computers Ltd in Cambridge, England where he is a section leader in the VLSI group.

Steve Clarke obtained a degree in Electronics and Electrical Engineering from UMIST and joined ICL in 1974. He has been involved in the testing of printed circuit boards and in the design and maintenance of automatic test equipment. For the last three years he has been involved in the application of gate arrays within the Mainframe System Development Division at ICL.

Acknowledgements

I would like to thank the various authors of the individual chapters for their contributions to the book and their secretaries for their patience and hard work. For my part I would like to thank my wife and family for putting up with the extra-curricular effort and activity involved in co-ordination of the manuscript and my various secretaries for their efforts in preparation and typing of the various drafts and amendments.

John W. Read

Preface

Interest in semi-custom design of integrated circuits has grown significantly over the last few years. This is because an ever increasing proportion of the functionality and performance of electronic end equipment is embedded in the silicon circuitry. Cost effectiveness and development times for the realisation of customised integrated circuits are key factors in giving electronics manufacturers the competitive edge in world markets. Conferences and magazines specialising in semi-custom design have sprung up but the rapid pace of technological change and the ever-increasing frequency with which new products are introduced make it impossible to prepare a book representing the latest state of the art.

Any statement or overview of today's products and capabilities will be out of date before it reaches the bookshelves. For that reason this is not so much a book for current practitioners of semi-custom design but more a primer for those who are considering the use of arrays, logic or linear, in their equipment designs. The contributors to the book have provided basic background information on the general types of array, the technologies available, their benefits and where each type may be most effectively used. Design tools and techniques are covered with particular reference to the question of design for testability. A summary of the manufacturing processes is provided together with an outline of the packages available.

One chapter is devoted to applications considerations viewed from a user's point of view with sections relating the experiences of two companies in the design and procurement of semi-custom devices. A short review of the future of semi-custom techniques concludes the book.

References have been provided to allow the reader to dig deeper into those aspects of most interest and to prevent the book from becoming cluttered with unnecessary detail.

Gate Arrays is thus intended to be a primer in the use of semi-custom array techniques for the potential or first-time user with some technical background and perhaps with previous experience of designing systems with standard semiconductor products.

John W. Read

Gate Arrays

Chapter 1

Introduction and Basic Technology

JOHN W. READ

STC Telecommunications Ltd

1.1 Introduction

Logic arrays, otherwise known as gate arrays, are a type of programmable or semi-custom semiconductor component made possible by the rapid advances in integrated circuit design techniques and manufacturing technology. Where an electronic system may be implemented using TTL or CMOS logic then a logic array can typically replace twenty to fifty SSI/MSI packages and effect considerable cost, weight, size and power savings in the end equipment. Although logic arrays as such perform digital functions, similar arrays of analog components exist and, despite its title, this book contains information on both types of array. For various reasons the complexity of analog arrays, in terms of device-count per chip, is lower than for logic arrays and their design presents somewhat different problems. Chapter 4 is devoted to the subject of analog/linear master slices and is by an author from a company that has made a significant name for itself in that area, namely Interdesign, a subsidiary of Ferranti. With the primary exception of that chapter, this book is devoted to digital, logic arrays. Further information on analog arrays can be found in the references given in chapter 4 and in reference 1.1.

The concept of having a fixed base pattern of logic gates on a silicon integrated circuit (IC) which is then programmed or 'wired-up' by customised metal patterns is not new. It was first proposed in the mid-1960s and used by several companies where the development costs of custom IC design were not justified for the relatively low volumes of each variant desired.

It is this trade-off of development cost, unit cost and prototyping time that is addressed by the use of logic arrays and other types of programmable components, notably microcomputers. Such components are called semi-custom integrated circuits as they are part standard (the base diffusions) and part custom (usually the interconnect and contacts). The term semi-custom is not usually applied to microcomputers, which are personalised or programmed by the ROM program mask, although conceptually they too are semi-custom. Another class of semi-custom product are cell-based designs where blocks of predesigned elements are drawn from a library, the data assembled via computer to meet the required systems function, and a total design requiring unique masks for all processing levels, instead of just a few, is generated. While cell-based techniques are not the main subject of this book, the importance of this approach must not be overlooked and an attempt will be made to show the relative advantages and disadvantages of each approach for different requirements.

1.2 About the book

The rest of this chapter will first briefly overview the background to the IC technology trends that have made semi-custom ICs, and particularly logic arrays, possible and desirable. Secondly it will cover some of the basic IC processes required to understand the design and manufacture of logic arrays. This section can be skipped by anyone with a basic understanding of semiconductor fabrication techniques.

Chapter 2 is about bipolar arrays of various kinds and where and why they would be used. Although there is a strong trend towards the use of CMOS wherever possible in order to keep power consumption and dissipation low, bipolar arrays still offer the ultimate in speed, outside of gallium-arsenide (GaAs) arrays, and advantages in off-chip drive capability and interface flexibility.

MOS and CMOS arrays are dealt with in chapter 3. Detailed information on the design of the basic cells for the array is also given. While a knowledge of this is not a requirement for the systems designer using such arrays, it can hopefully assist where usage outside the manufacturer's documented design guidelines is envisaged. Such a background is also helpful in understanding cell-based design techniques. Examples of a complete array are given together with an outline of the interfaces between semiconductor manufacturer and supplier. The chapter ends with a forecast of the general direction of CMOS technology.

Chapter 4 has already been mentioned and is a comprehensive

overview of analog/linear master slices from the leading company in this field.

Following chapters 2, 3 and 4 which discuss the different process and device technologies available, chapter 5 then focusses on the computer-aided design tools required to ensure that the manufactured product meets the required specification. This is an important subject. The advantages of short design cycle and low development costs compared with those for full custom designs are lost if the total prototyping process from design through initial samples has to be repeated one or more times. Full custom designs also require comprehensive CAD tools of course, but the importance of the tools to support semi-custom is that they can and should be subsets of the full-custom CAD suite. This allows them to be run on relatively inexpensive engineering workstations rather than large mainframes. In this way the cost benefits of semi-custom can be realised perhaps with systems designers using upper-end PCs as the advances in semiconductor technology cost reduce and enhance the capability of these machines.

Chapter 6 is an overview of the manufacturing processes involved in both wafer (slice) processing and assembly of tested chips into packages for interconnection to the outside world in printed circuit boards. A summary of the different tasks that make up the prototyping cycle time is given with a comparison of production cycle times. Package options are discussed briefly, but comprehensively.

Chapter 7 deals with the generally underestimated problem of testing of the finished array and approaches this from the important viewpoint of design for testability, a subject also used in the CAD chapter. The 'cut and strap' modifications possible when design errors are detected with PCBs are not possible (yet, if ever) with integrated circuits. If errors are present it's a case of going back to the drawing-board – or perhaps I should say back to the terminal. In any case valuable time is lost and money spent unwisely. Not only must the design be functionally right the first time, but it must also be fully testable to ensure that any devices with process defects can be fully tested out to prevent costly problems with field repairs due to inadequate test coverage at device level testing.

Chapter 8 has 3 parts. The first part is an overview of the general considerations in deciding when, where and why to use a logic array, what to use and who to engage as supplier. Some valuable pointers for first-time users should be found to avoid the pitfalls and potholes already stumbled over by others. It is hoped that many will find the additional two sections particularly useful. These are contributions from two companies that have had considerable experience in the design-in and use of logic arrays.

The final chapter gives the editor's view on future trends in the semi-custom area and attempts to put into perspective the role over the next few years of logic arrays compared with other semi-custom approaches.

1.3 The semiconductor industry

With the invention of the transistor at the end of 1948 and its subsequent commercial exploitation in the 1950s in portable radios, computers and avionics, the impact of electronics on our daily lives began to accelerate. Trends in the semiconductor industry have seldom been linear with time; rather, they have been exponential, and seem set to continue that way for a while at least. From the fabrication of individual transistors, it was a seemingly large step to the invention of the integrated circuit in 1958 where several such transistors were connected together in a single piece of silicon – a chip or die. Initial small-scale integration (SSI) of single logic gates was commercially feasible in the early 1960s. It was not until the mid-60s that the technology was well enough understood to provide the stability and reproducibility that was required for analogue or linear functions such as operational amplifiers and voltage comparators.

By that time, the complexity of digital functions achievable had further increased and the late 1960s was the era of MSI (medium-scale integration) functions and the standardisation of TTL (Transistor-Transistor-Logic) as the main bipolar digital logic family emerging from the proliferation of logic types such as RTL, DTL and DCTL which were available. Integrated circuits began to impact more industrial and computer applications replacing relays, switches and other electromechanical apparatus. The late 1960s also saw the emergence of a new type of transistor, the Metal-Oxide Silicon transistor (MOS). This type of transistor was fundamentally different from the earlier bipolar transistor and offered higher densities and lower-power circuits due to its high impedance characteristics. To make this type of transistor successfully, a better understanding was required of the silicon dioxide layer itself, its interface with the silicon surface and the effect of small amounts of mobile sodium ions in the oxide. This knowledge in turn led to improvements in bipolar transistors. Advances in complexity of both MOS and bipolar products were pursued in parallel – indeed much debate went on as to which technology was superior in meeting the needs of the customer and still continues to this day when an increase of two to three orders of magnitude in complexity has been achieved in each technology. The truth is that each technology has its place. Indeed, some modern processes combine both types of device at the expense of additional processing complexity and cost to achieve products otherwise requiring separate chips.

1970 saw the launch of the first semiconductor dynamic random access memory (DRAM) which seriously challenged and eventually eroded the dominant position then held by ferrite cores for computer mainframe storage. This was the renowned '1103' containing 1,024 (1K) bits of binary memory. With improvements in technology this has been followed every few years by devices with four-fold increases in storage capacity and ever-decreasing cost per bit. The demand for semiconductor memories has grown dramatically and in 1984 the 256K was shipped in volume quantities. 1 Meg and 4 Meg devices are in the early stages of development at a number of manufacturers. These increases in complexity have been made possible by improved process control, giving a higher yield of good chips per wafer, and ever finer photolithographic capability allowing smaller geometries and alignment tolerances and increased density of components. Typical production line widths achievable have shrunk from 10 μm in 1970 to around 3 μm in the early 80s with 2 μm (and below) processes on-line in production now in late 1984, early 1985.

Memories have always been considered as the cutting edge of the technology because memory demand is almost insatiable; hence, the volumes and commercial opportunities are enormous. The technology developed for memory manufacture can then be applied to logic devices. Similar outstanding progress has been made with the advent of 4-bit, 8-bit, 16- and now 32-bit microprocessors, microcomputers and a whole range of special-purpose devices. In the linear, analog and power areas progress has been made with higher precision components, higher voltage capability and improved stability and sensitivity. Perhaps one of the greatest impacts has been made by the progressive advances of digital signal processing techniques towards replacing analog signal handling. The codec and filter for PCM coding and the digital transmission of speech are good examples. With innovative design techniques single ICs can be designed to replace complex multi-component electronic functions and also many currently non-electronic functions.

To understand this better, we need to quantify the increasing complexity of devices available. If we characterise this complexity in

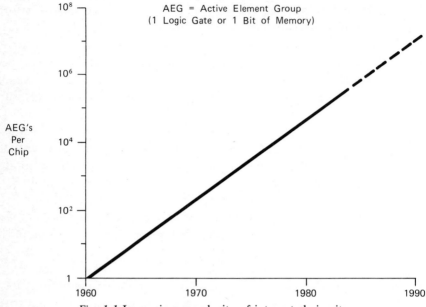

Fig. 1.1 Increasing complexity of integrated circuits

Active Element Groups (or AEGs) where 1 AEG is a single memory bit or logic gate (switch) then we can plot the complexity of available devices against time as shown in fig. 1.1. The 4 M-bit memory is expected to be in production by the early 1990s. Such a chip will probably continue to follow Gordon Moore's second law that 'all ICs will eventually cost $5 except those which cost less' and as a result will break the 0.0001 cent/bit level and be four orders of magnitude cheaper than core memories were in the early 1970s. The same cost benefits will apply to other ICs also and decreased cost for increased functional complexity (hence improved end-product features and performance) will continue to be a way of life. Looking at the products at each level of increasing complexity we can see that in general the next generation of integrated circuits has been definable from an analysis of the sub-systems or modules built using the previous generation of ICs (see fig. 1.2). In the same way that the use of discrete transistors to build simple logic gates led to the definition of logic gates as the first small-scale integration (SSI) ICs so SSI-based modular designs led to the definition of the most often used latches, registers and decoder-trees as MSI functions, and so on.

At each level of integration and technology breakthrough 'new' product ideas (often previously uneconomical 'old' ideas) have burst upon the market. Increasing levels of integration have then made cost, size and weight reductions possible together with improvements

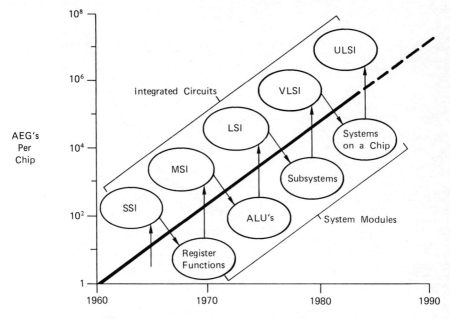

Fig. 1.2 Evolution of component families

in performance. A good example of this is the evolution of the hand held calculator.

1.4 Semi-custom techniques

All of the examples of standard products given so far have been for high volume requirements – typically millions of units. The cost benefits of ICs are dependent on the ever-increasing volume (or area) of silicon processed. The increasing complexity of ICs means they cost more to design and the increasing complexity increases until, in time, it surpasses a given set of system requirements (fig. 1.3). A single purpose-designed chip could then fulfil all the system requirements. However, except in special cases, such a purpose-built design, only low volumes (up to 500–1000, say) might be required. [1.2] Additionally the design cost and time per part increase exponentially with complexity. The economics are against us unless a solution can be found in which components have a generally applicable basic structure which can be slightly modified during, or immediately after, processing to produce a customer 'special'. Microcomputers and logic arrays are two ways of achieving these programmable systems components. [1.3] In each case it is possible

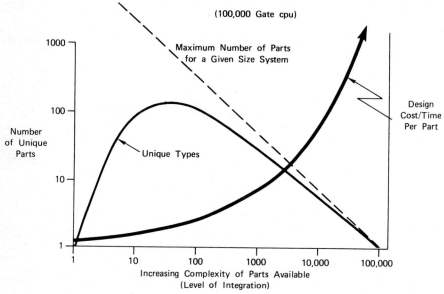

Fig. 1.3 System/part type/circuit complexity evolution

to achieve a design at lower cost and faster than for a complete custom circuit but the silicon area utilisation may be poorer giving potentially higher units costs than for an optimised custom design. However, because several different programmations are being produced the learning curve comes to the rescue and unit costs lower than for full custom designs, which are completely different in each case, can be achieved. Fast turn-around prototyping of a programmable or semi-custom design allows earlier market trials and market entry than full custom and this is of course central to a competitive position in a features-dominated end equipment market. The beneficial impact on reliability of producing customised designs based on a standard base design are also very important as the common production volumes allow progression down the learning curve on quality as well as unit cost.

The cost benefits of microcomputers have been realised for many years. A modern, say, 30 000 gate microcomputer with on-chip ROM/RAM costs upwards of two million dollars to prototype, consumes twenty man-years of design effort and takes two to three years to develop. Such costs and times are prohibitive for most individual applications and the engineering manpower does not exist to meet all the different designs that would be required on such a basis. The same microcomputer can be application-programmed with a few man-months of effort with prototypes available four to six weeks later at a cost of tens of thousands of dollars.

Not all electronic systems require the flexibility of a micro-processor or microcomputer solution. In some cases the required system can be more easily or effectively implemented with a straightforward, hard-wired logic gate design. In particular a 'micro' solution may not be able to meet the system speed requirements. This is one area where a logic array becomes important. Many systems currently using low levels of integration can be re-implemented and improved with logic arrays. New systems can be prototyped with conventional TTL or CMOS logic and then turned into production equipment with logic arrays.

Several technologies are available to satisfy a spectrum of needs from low to high speed, a range of complexities and widely different input and output interfaces. Not only are straightforward logic arrays available but some have analog capabilities also. In addition there are field-programmable logic arrays for extremely fast prototype develop-ment and standard – or poly – cell design approaches with slower turn-around, but offering enhanced cost-effectiveness for production costs.

Fast availability of prototypes is of key importance to most equipment manufacturers in order to be able to introduce new items to the market place as early as possible. It is therefore very important that semi-custom circuits work properly first-time and do not have errors. To ensure this, CAD (Computer-Aided Design) tools are required and various levels of these exist to check logic design, autoroute arrays and verify the layouts. Such programs should interface directly with the manufacturer's equipment for tooling masks and for testing the final components. They must also allow the system designer to simulate the end-equipment performance to check all aspects of the design before committing to the expense of prototype fabrication.

Present logic arrays are only the beginning of a new era of integrated circuits. As IC fabrication technology and design tools improve, function arrays with wide ranges of capability and interfaces will become available allowing easier customisation of systems design requirements. Techniques and design methodologies (such as Carver-Mead VLSI at Caltech) [1.4] are already being developed to allow complete tops-down design of integrated circuits by systems engineers. It will be strongly advantageous for design engineers to have a basic grounding in current technology not only for immediate designs but also to be able to understand and use these future design tools.

1.5 IC technology

The purpose of this section is to introduce some of the key concepts of the process technology particularly relevant to the subject of gate arrays and other semi-custom ICs. Chapters 2 and 3 on bipolar and MOS arrays cover the basic technology for these devices. It is also necessary to make the point that a detailed understanding of IC processing and device technology is not required in order to use gate arrays. In fact, this is one of the reasons that semi-custom techniques in general are so important – they represent a trend towards the day when electronic system designers can get the purpose-built ICs which they need without a costly and time-consuming sub-contract exercise to the IC designers.

There are many good text books on semiconductor devices and processing [1.5–1.8], some current magazines reflecting in a more timely manner, perhaps, changes in technique and equipment [1.9] and survey articles covering the basics of gate array technology. [1.10, 1.11]

1.5.1 Batch processing

Integrated circuits are fabricated on thin, high purity, extremely flat and highly polished (because of the flatness required) single crystal, circular, slices or wafers of silicon. These range from 100 to 150 mm in diameter on today's production processes and 0.5 to 1 mm thick. Each wafer will have a number of usually identical ICs on it. Typically a gate array IC chip is 0.5 to 1 cm on a side. For most of the steps in silicon wafer processing a large number of silicon slices are handled together in a batch, some 50 to 100, to achieve production economies of scale. The fixed cost per process step is a large percentage of the total cost. It is easy to see, therefore, that even with an overall process and test yield of 50%, 10 000 or more ICs can result from one production batch. However, some key processes are done on each wafer singly. In particular for the masking steps which determine the patterns on the silicon prior to each diffusion or implantation and after each polysilicon or metal-layer deposition the wafers are handled individually then re-batched for subsequent processing. If different masks are used on different silicon slices in a batch then the circuits on each of those slices will of course be different. In the limit with some advanced techniques such as e-beam direct slice writing, it is possible to vary the pattern on each die or chip on a wafer. This is presently only used for advance prototyping. In general, whole slices are fabricated to a single pattern resulting in many hundred identical (except for faults) devices from each slice. It is the variation of some or all of the masking steps with otherwise common diffusion and metallisation processing that forms the basis for semi-custom capability.

1.5.2 The masking process

The pattern on an IC is formed by a photolithographic process using a photomask embodying the basic design of each layer. This process is basically very similar to that used for printed circuit boards (PCBs) and is shown in fig. 1.4 for the case where an oxide pattern is being cut to define the areas to be diffused or doped with controlled amounts of impurities which will define the electrical properties of the devices on the chip. This process is known as the Planar process and has many advantages, particularly in that the oxide layer protects the silicon surface from unwanted impurities and 'seals' the junctions providing lower leakage currents and higher voltage breakdowns than possible, in general, with unpassivated surfaces.

The sequence of events is as follows. First, a layer of silicon dioxide is grown on the silicon slice by subjecting it to an oxygen rich environment at 1000–1200°C. The actual temperature and time for this will be very accurately controlled as with all other semiconductor processes. Typically the temperature will be controlled to within 0.5°C of the desired value and the time to within 1–2% of a set amount. Depending on the stage of the process the resultant oxide thickness from an oxidation step may range from 1000 to 10 000 Å (Angstroms) thick.

Next the slice is coated with a layer of ultraviolet light-sensitive photoresist, somewhat similar to that used in PCB work. This is done in a room where the uv content of normal lighting has been filtered out – a 'yellow' room. The mask containing an image of the desired pattern is then brought into contact with the slice which is exposed to uv light for a short time. This polymerises the exposed areas. Unexposed photoresist can then be washed off with organic solvents leaving a negative image of the mask on the wafer. Exposure of the photoresist can also be done by soft contact printing where there is a small gap between slice and mask, by projection printing, or by direct step on wafer (DSW) where an enlarged image is photo-reduced and stepped directly on to the slice in the same way as masks are made (see chapter 5). These techniques increase the mask life and provide increased image definition, they do not alter the basic

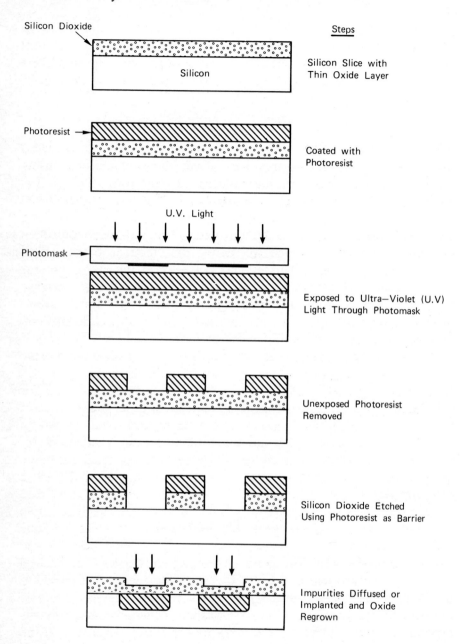

Fig. 1.4 Masking steps in IC processing

principles of the process.

The next step is the selective removal of the exposed silicon dioxide using the remaining photoresist as an etch mask. Buffered hydrofluoric acid is used for this and the silicon dioxide is taken away down to the silicon surface.

Finally the patterned photoresist is removed again using organic solvents, or more usually an rf sputter technique. The slices are then cleaned and diffused with the required dopants. This is again a well controlled, high temperature process. Typically the dopant material will only penetrate a few microns into the silicon, except for some of the deep diffusions required for bipolar isolation or high voltage breakdown devices. Simultaneously with the diffusion a new layer of silicon dioxide is grown to passivate the surface and prepare for the next masking step.

High density processes now use ion-implantation to dope the various regions of CMOS devices. This provides better control for the very small amounts of impurity required, in particular where control or adjustment of the threshold voltage is the objective. To prepare for subsequent processing a high temperature annealing/-oxidation step must be done or a chemical-vapour deposition process is used to provide an oxide layer.

Patterning of the polysilicon and metal conductor layers is performed using essentially the same photoresist process as described above with variations in types of photoresist or etchant as required.

Since a number of photographic reversals happen during the photoresist and etching process it is important to get the polarity of the image on the photomask correct. The semi-custom user does not have to worry about this as the semiconductor manufacturer should normally have all of this worked out.

Testing of the completed wafer and subsequent packaging are dealt with in chapter 6.

Photoresist processing and etching forms the basis for determining the functionality of a silicon device. Typically twelve to fifteen such steps will be used in a total process. For a gate array one to three of these levels will be varied for each customisation. Since the slices are exposed to mask patterns individually before being grouped together for diffusion, implantation, poly or metal deposition or oxide etch, it is possible to see how different wafers can be customised separately to provide a few hundred or a few thousand of devices for separate customers in a batch containing twenty to fifty separate customis-ations. This is the basis for the cost benefits of low-volume prototyping and production of semi-custom circuits.

1.6 References

1.1 Jung, Walter G. (1980) *IC Array Cookbook*. Hayden Book Company Inc: Rochelle Park, New Jersey

1.2 Fubini, E.G. and Smith, M.G. (1967) 'Limitations in Solid-State Technology.' *IEEE Spectrum* 4, No. 5, pp 55–59.

1.3 Fischer, J.L. (1979) 'VLSI Programmation in the 1980s'. *Address to the Ninth Annual Morgan Stanley Semiconductor Forum*: New Orleans, May 4, 1979.

1.4 Mead, C. and Conway, L. (1980) *Introduction to VLSI Systems*. Addison-Wesley: Reading, Mass.

1.5 Grove, A.S. (1967) *Physics and Technology of Semiconductor Devices*. J. Wiley & Sons Inc: New York

1.6 Sze, S.M. (1969) *Physics of Semiconductor Devices*. Wiley-Interscience: New York

1.7 Till, William C. and Luxon, James T. (1982) *Integrated Circuits: Materials, Devices & Fabrication*. Prentice-Hall Inc: Englewood Cliffs, New Jersey

1.8 Elliott, David J. (1982) *Integrated Circuit Fabrication Technology*. McGraw-Hill.

1.9 *Semiconductor International* Cahners Publishing Company: Denver, Colorado

1.10 *Designing with ULAs – Electronic Engineering* (Joint course with AMI) March to June issues 1982. (4 parts)

1.11 Beresford, R. (1984) 'Evaluating Gate Array Technologies.' *VLSI Design*. Jan. 84 pp. 48–52 and Feb. 84 pp. 34–39

Chapter 2

Bipolar and High Speed Arrays

GEOFF BOSTOCK

Mullard Ltd

2.1 Bipolar technology for high speed

2.1.1 The perfect logic element

2.1.1.1 Definition of a logic element

All real systems are necessarily a compromise compared with the ideal or perfect system, but one function of scientists and engineers is to achieve as nearly as possible perfection. In terms of electrical logic circuits there have been many different routes taken to approach perfection, some of them are applicable to semi-custom logic and a subset of these will be described in this chapter, together with the techniques used to put the logic elements together into a finished circuit. In order to judge how closely a particular route approaches the ideal, the perfect logic element must first be defined.

A logic element may be considered as the lowest order of logic with which a system is built. Very often this will be a 'gate' which is an element with one output signal whose value depends on the logical combination of two or more input signals, usually the logic function is AND or OR, or a simple combination of these with possibly an inversion. Another common logic element is the 'flip-flop' which is used to ensure that all signals in a logic function are defined at a certain instant of time (usually a transition of synchronising signal, or 'clock') and stored unchanged until a later instant of time when they will take new values according to the inputs of the flip-flop at that time.

2.1.1.2 Parameters of a perfect logic element

Some common parameters of logic elements are defined in fig. 2.1 but all perfect logic elements will have the following features:

Supply voltage	– the element will function with no lower or upper limit to the supply voltage.
Supply current	– the element will draw no current from the supply under all conditions of operation.
Input voltage	– the element will recognise all input voltages over half of the supply voltage (the threshold voltage) as logic HIGH, and all input voltages below the threshold voltage as logic LOW.
Input current	– connection to a driving logic element will cause no current to be drawn from the driving element in either the static or dynamic state.
Output voltage and current	– when the output is logic HIGH its voltage is equal to the supply voltage irrespective of any attached load. When the output is logic LOW its voltage is equal to zero volts (ground) irrespective of any attached load.
Propagation delay	– the output will change state simultaneously with the input causing that change of state passing through the threshold voltage.
Clock characteristics	– the output will reflect the state of the inputs as they are at the moment when the clock passes through the threshold voltage, irrespective of their state immediately before or after that moment; any output change will also occur at that moment.

In other words, for all V_s, $I_s = 0$.

$$V_{il} \text{ (max)} = \tfrac{1}{2}V_s \qquad V_{ih} \text{ (min)} = \tfrac{1}{2}V_s$$
$$V_{ol} \text{ (min)} = 0 \text{ V} \qquad V_{oh} \text{ (max)} = V_s$$
$$t_{plh} \text{ (min)} = t_{phl} \text{ (min)} = 0$$
$$t_{is} \text{ (min)} = t_{ih} \text{ (min)} = 0$$

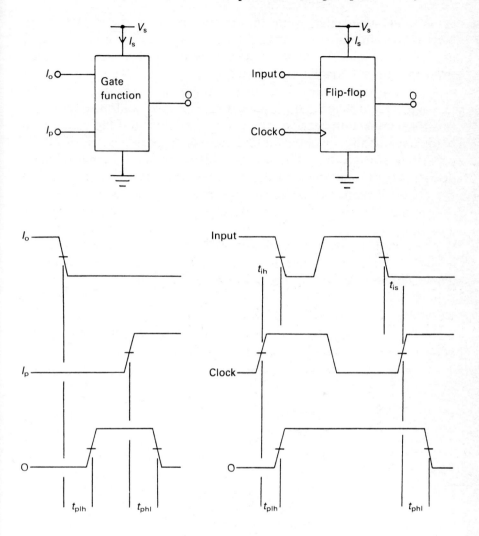

Fig. 2.1 Definitions of parameters of logic elements

2.1.2 *Constraints of real systems*

2.1.2.1 Electronic switches

Logic elements in real electronic systems use electronic switches, the most common in current use and the ones considered in this book being bipolar and MOS transistors manufactured by the silicon planar process.

The perfect logic element would contain perfect switches, which have no electrical resistance when closed, permit no electrical conduction when open and when connected together have no capacitance associated with the nodes or connection points. An electronic switch also has a third terminal which determines whether it is open or closed and this, ideally, is totally isolated electrically from the other two switch terminals.

Real transistors, however, have a finite 'ON' resistance, exhibit leakage current when 'OFF', have a capacitative, and in some cases, resistive connection between the control terminal and the conduction path and finally, possess interelectrode capacitance as well as capacitance to ground. The source and magnitude of some of these deviations from perfection will be examined in the next section, but the effect of them can be considered in general terms here.

Consider the case of a switch which is turned off by a low voltage and on by a high voltage. It is possible to turn this into a logic gate if the outputs from two or more switches are connected to its input. In order to supply a voltage reference, one active side of each switch is connected to 0 V or ground, while the other side of each switch is connected through a load to a positive voltage as shown in fig. 2.2. Very often this load will itself be a switch connected in antiphase, but it does not have to be and it makes only a minor difference to the results of the argument.

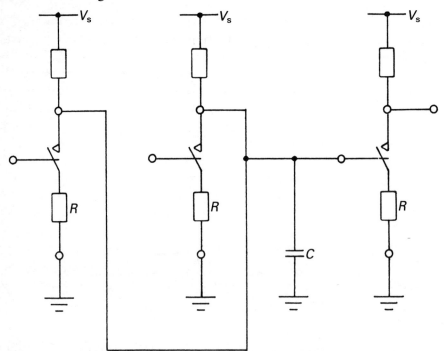

Fig. 2.2 Real switches connected to form a logic gate

2.1.2.2 DC considerations

Consider first, all the driving switches turned off; the node connecting these to the gating switch will therefore be at a high voltage level so the switch will be turned off. Although logic gates have some form of isolation between the inputs, a small current will usually flow into the input because of imperfections in the devices used to make the logic elements. This has two effects; first, it causes power to be dissipated in the gate, and secondly, it limits the number of logic elements which can be connected to one load. A voltage drop will appear across the load and beyond a critical number of connections, called the 'fan-out', this will cause the voltage on the node to fall below the voltage sufficient to keep the switch turned on. Another problem arises in real systems. In any environment where electrical signals are being transmitted, a conductor such as the connection node will act as an aerial and pick up these signals which will then appear as small voltage spikes on the node. In practice a safety margin, known as the noise margin, is added to the input voltage needed to turn the switch on or off which limits the fan-out even further.

Notice also that if the load on the gating switch is constant (i.e. not a switch) then current will flow between the positive supply voltage and ground giving a second, potentially much larger, source of power dissipation in the gate. Thus in the static state we have already violated some of the conditions of the perfect logic element since our real switch will draw current from the supply, can support only a fixed number of outputs and will have actual output voltages below the supply voltage or above ground because of the finite resistance of the switch.

2.1.2.3 AC considerations

What of the dynamic case then? What happens if one of the switches driving the node is turned ON? First it must be realised that the node itself will possess capacitance, that is the ability to store electrical charge. Any electrical conductor must have capacitance relative to ground and in a real system, probably with copper track on a printed circuit board, this capacitance will not be negligible. Because the switch has a finite resistance it will take a finite time to remove sufficient charge from the capacitor to reduce the node voltage to the point where the gating switch is turned OFF. If the capacitance and resistance are independant of voltage the delay time will be:

$$t_d = RC \ln\frac{(V_H - V_L)}{(V_T - V_L)} \tag{2.1}$$

where V_H = the initial voltage of the node
V_T = the voltage need to turn off the switch
V_L = the final voltage of the node.

Moreover, a charge of $C(V_H - V_L)$ is removed from the node capacitance and will have to be replaced every time the node is taken high again. Because current is the rate at which charge flows, if the node is switching at a frequency of f Hz, a current of $fC(V_H - V_L)$ will have to be supplied to the node. Thus even if a perfect switch was physically possible a real logic element would have to draw current from the supply and delay signals passing through it.

2.1.3 *Real electronic switches*

2.1.3.1 Bipolar transistors

As mentioned earlier the majority of logic circuits use either bipolar or MOS transistors to perform the switching function. While we are concerned with bipolar logic circuits, it is also worthwhile considering some of the properties of MOS transistors so that the limitations of each class can be seen and thus the appropriate areas of application defined.

Using the terminology of the previous section, assuming that our switch is a bipolar silicon planar NPN transistor, the control terminal is the base, the load is connected to the collector while the emitter is grounded. The static behaviour of the transistor can best be seen from a family of curves known as the common emitter characteristics in which the collector current is plotted against the collector–emitter voltage difference for a number of different base currents (incremented in equal steps). Figure 2.3 shows a common emitter characteristic for a typical transistor together with the base characteristic which shows how the input current to the control input (base) varies with input voltage.

2.1.3.2 Limitations of bipolar transistors

When operated as a switch the transistor will normally be in either the saturation region on 0A, or the cut off region on 0B. The characteristics of fig. 2.3 together with the simplified structure shown

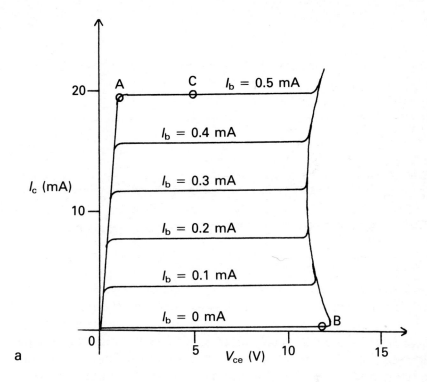

a

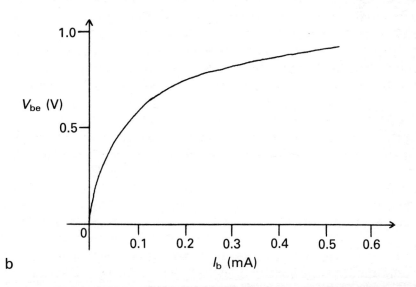

b

Fig. 2.3 a) Typical common emitter characteristics for NPN planar transistor;
b) Typical base characteristic for NPN planar transistor

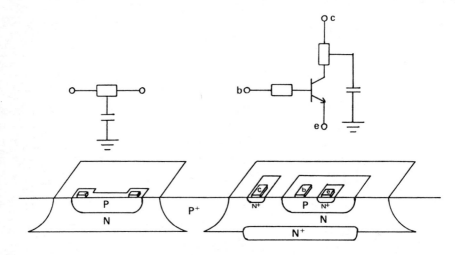

Fig. 2.4 Diffused resistor and NPN transistor in the silicon planar process

in fig. 2.4 give an indication of the magnitude of the various parasitic components which prevent a real transistor having the properties of an ideal switch. First it should be realised that any manufacturing process is a series of tradeoffs or compromises between the various competing factors, subject to the limits of the technology. As an example consider the most basic parameter, which is transistor size. It has already been shown that a serious limiting factor concerning the delay time of a signal through a logic element is the capacitance associated with each node. From the structural drawing it may be seen that one major capacitance contribution is the collector–ground junction. To minimise this the junction area should be made as small as possible. However, it is also desirable to keep the series resistance in the collector as low as possible to minimise voltage drops in the ON state. A major contributor to collector resistance is the buried N layer which is the path which enables a lateral connection to be made to the active collector region of the transistor. Clearly, the wider this path is made the lower will be the resistance, but this of course increases the capacitance. There are other factors involved; for example, the efficiency of the emitter at a given current is reduced below a particular perimeter length. The technology effects must be of paramount importance though; whichever technique is used for defining the features of a transistor, the alignment of adjacent patterns, the control of etch rates and sideways diffusion, all limit both the minimum feature size and the necessary clearance between features. It is certainly feasible to talk of a minimum emitter size of 6 μm × 3 μm; allowing 3 μm clearance all round for the base plus a 3 μm wide base contact hole gives a minimum base size of 15 μm × 12 μm. Because the isolation and base diffusions spread towards each other, a 12 μm clearance may well be needed, which together with an allowance for the collector contact gives a final transistor size of 45 μm × 36 μm. In practice, the processes typically used for manufacturing logic circuits will give a parasitic capacitance of 1–2 pF, a collector resistance of 20–50 Ω and a useful working current of less than 5 mA for the minimum geometry described above. A logic circuit may well use two or three different transistor geometries depending on their exact circuit function.

2.1.3.3 Operating regions of bipolar transistors

There is another important capacitive effect in bipolar transistors which is due more to the way in which they operate than to any parasitic effects and applies particularly to the saturation region of operation. A bipolar transistor contains two semiconductor PN junctions, either of which may be forward biased or reverse biased depending on the conditions of the circuit in which it is being used. Table 2.1 summarises four possible modes of operation.

Table 2.1 Bipolar transistor operating modes

Emitter–base junction	Collector–base junction	Operating mode
Forward biased	Forward biased	Saturated
Forward biased	Reverse biased	Normal
Reverse biased	Forward biased	Inverse
Reverse biased	Reverse biased	Cut-off

The inverse and normal modes are similar in that one junction is forward biased and the other reverse biased. In each case the forward biased junction injects charge carriers into the base, the charge diffuses across the base to the reverse biased junction where it is collected. There is no electric field in the base region as all the voltage drops are across the actual PN junctions, so the current is due entirely to diffusion with a high concentration of charges near the emitter and a low concentration near the collector. A number of the charge carriers (electrons in an NPN transistor) combine with holes which are naturally present in the P-type base region and form one component of the base current. The other major component is holes which are injected into the emitter from the base. For efficient operation as a transistor both these must be small compared with the number of electrons collected at the collector. For normal operation the transistor geometry and processing is arranged for maximum efficiency and the collector current is usually a factor of fifty or so greater than the base current. This number is defined as the gain of the transistor and usually given the symbol β. In the inverse mode the gain is normally less than ten and may be less than unity.

2.1.3.4 Saturation region of bipolar transistors

When the collector–base junction becomes forward biased it will start to inject electrons into the base and have holes injected by the base in addition to collecting the electrons being injected by the emitter; the net collector current is the difference between these two injected currents. Because the emitter is not very efficient at collecting electrons, the emitter current will remain relatively unchanged and the net difference is made up by an increase in base current. In practice the collector current is often limited by a fixed resistive load connected to the supply voltage and increasing the base current merely increases the amount of forward bias on the collector–base junction to enable the collector to balance the effect of increased injection from the emitter. The net result then of increasing base drive in saturation is to cause both emitter and collector to inject more electrons into the base thereby increasing the total number of electrons present in the base at any one time. If the transistor is now turned OFF, collector current will continue to flow until the electrons have been removed from the base. Figure 2.5 shows the charge distribution in the base for the three modes of operation. The effect of this in circuit operation is to cause a delay between removing drive from the base and actually switching off the collector current.

2.1.3.5 Circuit impedance of bipolar transistors

The other relevant parameters of the bipolar transistor may be reviewed by referring back to fig. 2.3. When the transistor is ON, base current must be supplied in order to permit load current to pass through the transistor. The higher this is in relationship to the collector current, the more will the collector be forward biased and therefore the lower will be the collector voltage if the emitter is grounded. There is of course a penalty to pay in terms of increased delay time at turn off; a factor of one tenth is often chosen as a

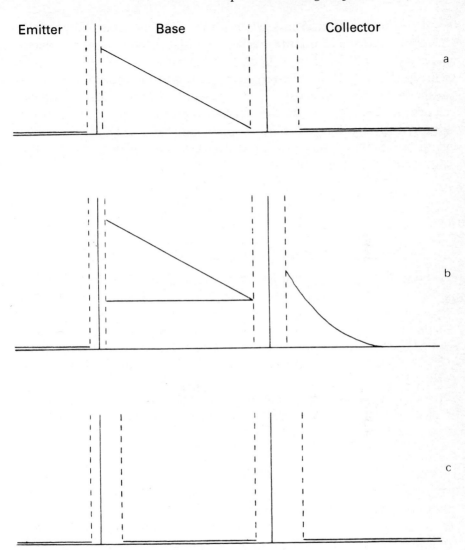

Fig. 2.5 Charge distribution for three modes of bipolar transistor operation:
a) active; b) saturated; c) cut-off

reasonable compromise if the gain is fifty for the normal operating mode. Thus driving logic switches have a fairly high load to drive and fan-out is often limited by static current considerations in bipolar logic circuits.

Output impedance is determined largely by the available base drive and by the parasitic collector resistance. If the transistor of fig. 2.3 is being used in a 5 V logic circuit with a 1 kΩ load it will sink a

load current of about 5 mA when turned ON and thus will probably
have a base drive of 0.5 mA. When it is first turned ON the collector
capacitance will hold its collector voltage momentarily at 5 V so it
will sit at point 'C' in its characteristic. It will therefore have 25 mA
available to discharge its collector current and this current will not
change until point 'A' on the characteristic when the capacitance is
almost fully discharged. Rather than equation (2.1) then which is
valid for passive, or resistive discharging, for active, or constant
current discharging we have:

$$t_d = \frac{C(V_H - V_T)}{\beta I_b} \qquad (2.2)$$

2.1.3.6 Breakdown voltages of bipolar transistors

Another limit of operation is shown by fig. 2.3; as the voltage on the
collector is increased the electric field in the collector–base junction
increases to the point where secondary ionisation occurs. The result
of this is a large increase in current for a small increase in collector
voltage, a phenomenon known as voltage breakdown. This limits the
supply voltage which can be used with the transistor. Once again
processing compromises have to be reached; for example the
breakdown voltage is increased by increasing the resistivity of the
bulk N-type region in the collector (the epitaxial layer), but this also
increases parasitic collector resistance.

2.1.3.7 Operation of MOS transistors

A brief resumé of the properties of MOS transistors will show how
they compare with bipolar transistors and thus indicate where bipolar
logic circuits are more suitable than MOS circuits. Figure 2.6 shows a
typical characteristic and fig. 2.7 the physical structure of an MOS
transistor. The most obvious difference is that conduction between
the active terminals of an MOS transistor switch is via an inversion
layer of charges induced into the surface of the bulk material (P-type
in an N-channel device). The resistivity of this surface layer depends
on the charge density in the channel, but for a given voltage on the
control terminal (gate) the charge is proportional to the capacitance
between gate and ground; in other words there is a trade-off between
input capacitance and channel resistance. The channel resistance is
also proportional to the width of the channel but both the gate
capacitance and drain capacitance, assuming that the source is
grounded, are also proportional to channel width and so a

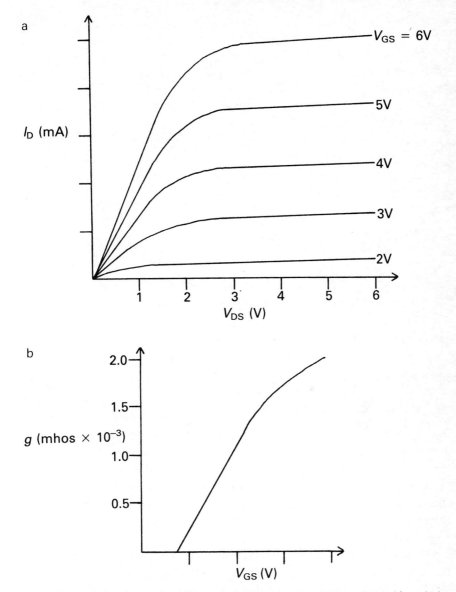

Fig. 2.6 a) common source characteristics of N-channel MOS transistor; b) variation of transconductance with gate voltage

compromise between switch resistance and node capacitance must be realised in actual transistor designs.

2.1.3.8 Characteristics of MOS transistors

With current technology it is quite feasible to make the length of the conducting channel 3 μm (as for the emitter of the bipolar transistor).

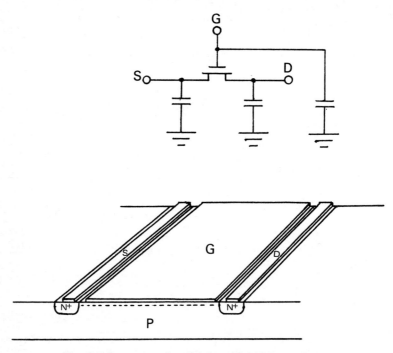

Fig. 2.7 Structure of an N-channel MOS transistor

In order to obtain a reasonable transconductance or channel resistance, the aspect ratio of the transistor must be around ten, giving a channel width of 30 μm. This leads to a junction of 30 μm × 3 μm for the drain node, assuming a 3 μm wide diffusion. The node capacitance can therefore be made an order of magnitude smaller but the channel resistance will be an order of magnitude higher. This does not matter much when all connections have a negligible capacitance to ground, but will make delay times longer when MOS transistors are driving a load with more than a few tenths of a picofarad.

Because the input gate is isolated from the channel by the silicon oxide gate dielectric the input will pass virtually no current, moreover a calculation of capacitance between the gate and the channel gives a result of less than 0.01 pF, so the input and output are virtually isolated. The switch resistance when ON has been discussed; when OFF the junction between drain and channel will be reverse biased, so only leakage current will pass through the switch.

2.1.3.9 Comparison of bipolar and MOS transistors

We are now in a position to compare the main switching features of bipolar and MOS transistors, which are summarised in table 2.2.

Table 2.2 Comparison of bipolar and MOS transistors

	Bipolar transistors	MOS transistors
Input current	~ 0.1 mA	< 1 pA
ON resistance	10–100 Ω	100–1 kΩ
OFF leakage current	1 μA	1 μA
Output capacitance	1–2 pF	0.1–0.2 pF

As also implied above, interconnections form another important source of parasitic capacitance in logic circuits. In an integrated circuit the interconnections are made by aluminium tracks insulated from the active silicon areas by thermally grown silicon dioxide. Making assumptions about the dimensions enables an approximate value of the capacitance to be calculated. For example a 10 μm wide track of 1 mm length on 1 μm thick oxide will have a capacitance of about 0.04 pF. This will clearly have a more noticeable effect on MOS transistors than on bipolar. Going to the outside world gives an even worse result; 10 cm of 1 mm wide copper track on 1.6 mm circuit board will look like 2 pF if there is a ground plane backing the track. In addition a similar value of capacitance is associated with the packaging in which integrated circuits are commonly used, so that node capacitance is only a small part of the load seen by a logic switch.

For that reason, bipolar logic switches will usually show a smaller delay than MOS switches if the same technology is used for each in terms of transistor size and interconnection technique. This leads to the commonly held conclusion that bipolar logic circuits are most suitable when high speed operation is required. Certainly with today's technology the upper limit for MOS is about 20–30 MHz, while bipolar circuits can operate at an order of magnitude higher in speed.

2.1.4 Techniques to improve switching speed

2.1.4.1 Direct charge removal

As discussed in the previous section the main restrictions on switching speed in a bipolar transistor are saturation capacitance and collector capacitance. In order to optimise the switching speed of a bipolar transistor when it comes out of saturation it is necessary to remove the excess base charge as efficiently as possible. If the base is left open circuit when the base drive is removed the only route by which the charge can escape is across the collector–base junction. However, in the silicon planar process the collector is more lightly doped than the base region so most of the current due to the forward biasing of the collector–base junction will be due to the injection of holes into the collector region. When the transistor is turned off the excess concentration of holes in the collector region will begin to drift back across the collector–base junction. This two-way flow of carriers across the junction will obviously be helped if the base is made as negative as possible. Put simply, this will repel the electrons and attract the holes and remove the excess charge more quickly. In practice this is usually achieved by having a resistor connected between the base and the most negative point, or in some designs a transistor is used to pull charge actively out of the base. These techniques are shown in fig. 2.8.

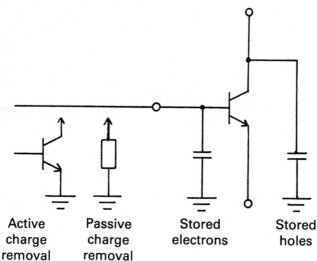

Active	Passive	Stored	Stored
charge	charge	electrons	holes
removal	removal		

Fig. 2.8 Techniques for removing excess charge from saturated transistors

2.1.4.2 Internal charge removal

In practice there is another way in which excess charge will disappear. As holes drift one way across the collector–base junction and electrons the other way, some will collide and the electron fills the hole causing both to disappear. This recombination effect is normally kept to a minimum in semiconductor manufacture since it represents a current loss or leakage and reduces the efficiency of normal transistor operation. It is minimised by keeping the silicon crystal structure as perfect as possible and as free as possible from contaminating impurities. This is because lattice defects and impurities act as recombination centres or traps and increase the recombination rate compared with perfect silicon. However, in order to speed up removal of excess base charge it would clearly help to encourage recombination. Gold is particularly good at helping recombination as it provides trapping centres which will attract both holes and electrons; it is therefore often used in logic circuits, in carefully controlled amounts, to speed up recombination without making leakage current too high or transistor gain too low.

2.1.4.3 Non-saturating circuit techniques

Of course, the best way to reduce the effects of saturation is to prevent the transistor from saturating in the first place. There are two common ways of doing this; limiting the emitter current means that the collector load can be set to a value such that the collector voltage never falls below the base voltage. This technique is dealt with in section 2.3 which describes current mode logic. The second method is to limit the base current so that the transistor is never driven hard enough to reach the saturation state. The usual way of achieving this is to connect a diode between base and collector as in fig. 2.9.

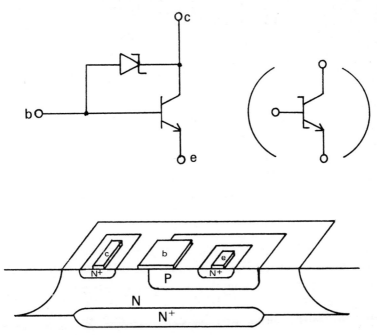

Fig. 2.9 Bipolar transistor with Schottky clamping diode

As the collector voltage falls with increasing base drive, the diode will start to conduct and any additional base current will be diverted to the collector, which is clamped at a voltage sufficient to prevent the collector–base junction from becoming forward biased. To be successful, the diode voltage when conducting must be lower than the voltage across the collector–base junction. Also it is no use putting in a diode if it holds a high stored charge similar to the base as that is just transferring the problem instead of removing it. One type of diode which meets these requirements is the 'Schottky' diode which is formed when one side of the junction is very heavily doped and is commonly made by alloying a metal into lightly doped silicon of the opposite polarity. In integrated circuit manufacture, aluminium is normally used to make the interconnection between circuit elements and when alloyed with silicon make a P-type material. Thus some care has to be taken when connecting to N-type regions on the silicon surface, to avoid making rectifying contacts. A heavily doped N-type diffusion is made wherever contact has to be made to an N-type region so that the connection is essentially a diode with a breakdown voltage of only a few millivolts. In a Schottky clamped transistor the base connection is deliberately overlapped into the lightly doped collector region to form the clamping diode. Sometimes other metals such as platinum or palladium are also deposited to optimise the characteristics of the Schottky diode.

2.1.4.4 Oxide isolation

As described earlier, the parasitic collector to substrate capacitance is determined largely by transistor size which in turn is related to the process characteristics, particularly the fact that the base and isolation diffusions move sideways towards each other during processing and therefore set a limit to their minimum separation.

During the early 1970s an alternative method of isolation was developed jointly by Philips and Fairchild in which silicon dioxide is used as the isolating material rather than a reverse biased junction. This had the dual advantage of largely eliminating the capacitance between the collector sidewall and isolation, and enabling the collector region to be made smaller. The process consists of masking the actual logic element areas with silicon nitride and converting the whole of the N-type epitaxial layer in the intervening spaces into silicon dioxide. This leaves N-type regions sitting on the P-type substrate and surrounded completely by silicon dioxide. A cross section of a bipolar transistor fabricated in the Philips 'SUBILO' process is shown in fig. 2.10. It may be seen that the emitter and base regions are butted up against the isolating oxide region, which effectively cuts the transistor area in half compared with a conventional geometry. As approximately half the parasitic capacitance can be associated with the sidewall, this design will exhibit only a quarter of the parasitic collector capacitance which would be found with a conventional junction-isolated transistor.

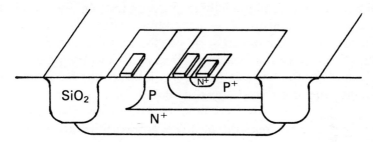

Fig. 2.10 Oxide isolated bipolar transistor structure

2.2 Description of bipolar gate structures

2.2.1 The background to semi-custom logic

2.2.1.1 Introduction of standard logic circuits

Any description of bipolar semi-custom logic circuits must be based on a description of the standard bipolar logic families, the first of which were developed some twenty years ago in integrated circuit form. The printed circuit itself was still relatively new so that in the space of about fifteen years state of the art logic design had progressed from thermionic valves connected with wiring looms to single packages containing half a dozen logic gates or flip-flops interconnected on a mass-produced wiring board. The first logic circuits were merely monolithic versions of standard discrete logic elements, but these evolved into the logic families we know today by making use of the advantages of the silicon planar process while minimising the disadvantages. The complexity of the early logic circuits was limited by the process; the silicon planar process comprises a number of processing steps to define the various layers in the integrated circuit, and each step will introduce a number of defects to the silicon wafer. Any logic circuit which contains a processing defect is likely to be inoperative and clearly the greater the number of components in the circuit the greater the chance of that circuit containing a defect. Thus as skill and techniques improved the opportunity arose to make more and more complex circuits.

To start with it was fairly easy to define the functions which could usefully be made as most logic designers will want adders, multiplexers, shift registers, counters, etc., and these were incorporated into the well-known MSI (medium-scale integration) devices, available in all logic manufacturers catalogues. At the same time some integrated circuit users were looking for functions which were not standard. The reasons might be economic, by integrating several logic functions into one package the costs of integrated circuit assembly and printed circuit board assembly could be reduced, or commercial, proprietary designs could be safeguarded by using customer special integrated circuits. Unfortunately for most users, the economics of scale meant that it was not worthwhile either for the producer or user to consider a customer special unless the quantity to be manufactured was 100 000 pieces or so. This was largely because of the amount of skilled labour needed to design the circuit, a process which might involve hand drawing the eight or ten photomasks used during the processing plus the effort in test program generation, reliability, assessment, etc., needed to bring the device to production.

2.2.1.2 Introduction of semi-custom logic circuits

However, it was equally realised that nearly all pure logic circuits are simply an assembly of logic gates, the difference between the individual circuits being the pattern of interconnection of the various gates. Thus a new technique for producing customer specials was devised; a fixed array of logic gates was designed and fabricated leaving only the upper aluminium interconnection layers undefined. Users were then invited to design their own interconnection patterns which could then either be hand drawn or, as the problem was only one of joining points on a fixed grid, drawn by a computer thus relieving the integrated circuit designers of the tedium of a fairly elementary chore. By programming the computer with design rules, reliability can be assured by testing a single design, and testability is assured by using a computer to simulate the function of the interconnected network and to ensure that all the gates are tested during the proposed test program. It may now be economic to manufacture as few as 1000 circuits by using this semi-custom approach and enables many more users to enjoy the economic and commercial benefits of their own 'specials'. Thus semi-custom circuits are derived from the standard logic families and their features are best understood by first considering the features of the standard logic families.

2.2.2 Saturated transistor logic

2.2.2.1 Resistor transistor logic (RTL)

The simplest logic switch is the single transistor, see fig. 2.11. Provided the output is not loaded too heavily, a voltage of about 0.7 V applied to the base will make it saturate and its output voltage will fall to about 0.2 V (these values will depend on the design of the transistor, the value of load current and the temperature). When the voltage on the base falls well below 0.7 V the transistor will be cut off and the voltage will rise to V_{CC}. Thus a chain of these transistors will have their collectors sitting alternately at 0.7 V and 0.2 V and will therefore form a series of inverters. In order to form a logic element such as a NAND gate the transistor must have two or more inputs into the base. In practice this would not operate satisfactorily for the following reason – consider the case where the two inputs are from a high and low gate respectively, the low gate will pull the high output low and cause it to be in the wrong state for any other inputs to

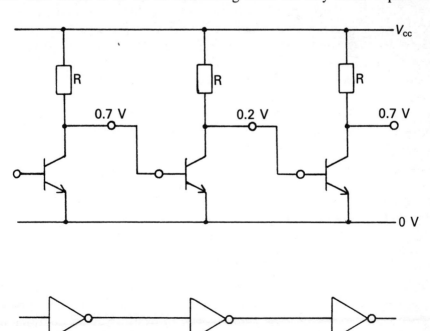

Fig. 2.11 Single transistors connected as an inverter chain

which it is connected. The cheapest solution for discrete components is to buffer each input with a resistor. A possible scheme is shown in fig. 2.12.

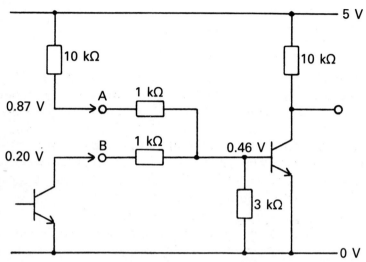

Fig. 2.12 Possible RTL 2-input NAND gate

Input A is connected to a HIGH output, input B to a LOW output and the input buffer resistors from a voltage divider so that the base is at 0.46 V and the HIGH output at 0.87 V, which is just enough to drive another transistor. If both inputs are HIGH (at say 0.87 V), and the transistor requires 0.7 V on its base to enable it to conduct, then each input will supply 0.17 mA, a total of 0.34 mA. The 3 kΩ resistor from base to ground will take 0.23 mA leaving 0.11 mA available as base current, which is sufficient to drive the transistor into saturation with about 0.5 mA collector current.

2.2.2.2 AC performance of RTL (t_{plh})

Thus with both inputs HIGH the output is LOW and for any other condition the output is HIGH since a base voltage of 0.46 V is insufficient to allow conduction and the transistor will be cut off. An estimate can also be made of the switching times between the HIGH and LOW states. If we are looking at this structure as a contender for use in semi-custom circuits some assumptions must be made about the capacitances associated with the various nodes. The collector ground capacitance has been estimated as 1–2 pF and track capacitance as 0.4 pF/mm, while resistors will also have distributed capacitance to ground; this capacitance depends on resistor geometry and processing but we can assume it is approximately equal to 0.3 pF at each terminal for each 1 kΩ of resistance. Thus an assumption of 2 pF for the base terminal and 6 pF for the collector terminal can be made. We also have to make an assumption about the threshold voltage; this is the input voltage at which the output voltage will start to change. The choice is somewhat arbitrary as long as it lies somewhere between the HIGH and LOW voltage levels and often the 50% point is chosen; for the sake of argument we will choose 0.6 V.

When the transistor is being switched off the main delay is caused by the transistor having to come out of saturation, the amount of excess base charge depending on the transistor design. An order of magnitude calculation based on a collector current of 0.5 mA, a base width of 1 μm and a base current of 0.1 mA suggests an excess base charge of about 3×10^{-9} C which will be discharged in 3 ns if the current pulled out of the base is 1 mA. Once the charge has been removed, the collector will be pulled up by the 10 kΩ load resistor; using equation (2.1) the delay time will be $10^4 \times 6 \times 10^{-12} \ln(4.8/4.4)$ since the 'aiming voltage' will be 5.0 V. This gives 5.2 ns for the rise time, so the total switch-off time or t_{plh} will be 8–9 ns.

2.2.2.3 AC performance of RTL (t_{phl})

In the other direction, first the base node has to be charged from 0.46 V to 0.7 V. In practice this is complicated by the fact that the input is also a rising voltage and a DC analysis shows that the base voltage will reach 0.7 V by the time the input has reached 0.6 V. If the assumption is made that both input and base voltage rise linearly, then it can be shown that the transistor will turn on by the time that the input reaches 0.6 V. The only delay then is in pulling the output node down to 0.6 V. The starting voltage depends on what other nodes the output is driving, but will be in the range of 0.8 V to 1.1 V. At the point at which the input reaches 0.6 V there will be 0.06 mA of base drive available, so if the gain of the transistor is fifty, equation (2.2) can be used to determine the delay time. This comes to 1 ns for the worst case, so the main factor in determining turn-on time will be the internal capacitance and transit time limitations within the transistor itself, which are likely to be the same order of magnitude.

To complete an assessment of the performance it is necessary to estimate the power consumption of our basic gate. When turned on, a transistor will sink about 0.48 mA through its load resistor, when turned off the current will flow into the input of the gate it is driving and will be about 0.40 mA, so the mean current is 0.44 mA assuming equal numbers of transistors are ON and OFF respectively. The mean power is thus 2.2 mW and the mean delay 6 ns giving a speed power product of 13 pJ. (The product of average propagation delay and power consumption is often used as a figure of merit for logic circuits.)

2.2.2.4 Circuit limitations of RTL

This simple analysis of the circuit has overlooked some shortcomings, which would make the performance inadequate except under ideal conditions. First, only a fan-in of two and a fan-out of two were considered, secondly, no allowance was made for changes in temperature and thirdly, only nominal values of device parameters were used. A full worst case treatment is beyond the scope of this chapter, but some indications can be given of the likely results, particularly if this circuit configuration were to be used in an LSI application. A minimum useful fan-in/fan-out would be three or four, otherwise frequent buffering is necessary in most logic designs. Consider the case where a gate with a high output drives one gate with all inputs high and three gates where three of the inputs are low. If all the high inputs come from gates in a similar situation, the output voltage from each gate will be dragged down to 0.38 V by the three outputs associated with the low inputs and so the circuit will fail as 0.38 V is not enough to turn on the transistor.

Temperature has a significant effect on transistor parameters, the most noticeable effects being the decrease in base–emitter voltage (at a rate of about 2 mV/°C) and the increase in leakage current with temperature. In an LSI chip, the temperature can easily rise by more than 50°C which will give rise to a junction temperature of 125°C, even in a 'commercial' environment of 70°C. The base–emitter voltage will thus fall to about 0.5 V, perilously close to the 0.46 V on the base of the transistor in the example of fig. 2.12. Leakage current of 0.01 µA at 25°C will increase to about 10 µA at 125°C; this will cause an extra 0.1 V drop in the 10 kΩ load resistor to input A, in fig. 2.12, reducing the drive available from that output.

The effects of device parameter variation are also numerous. The most obvious are absolute values of resistance and transistor current gain. Careful design of integrated circuit resistors will enable them to keep a fairly constant ratio (better than 5%) and so the node voltages are unlikely to be affected greatly. However, device performance is closely related to absolute resistor values so the final speed and power consumption are the most likely to vary with changes in device parameters.

2.2.2.5 Diode transistor logic (DTL)

Resistor transistor logic was chiefly used in discrete component logic circuits before integrated circuit logic elements became widely used. It was therefore possible to adjust the resistor values to cater for the fan-in and fan-out of the various logic gates in the system. Clearly the main problem is one of isolating the transistor switch from the effects of the possible changes in load in its environment. Referring back to section 2.1.1 we argued that the ideal logic switch should be unaffected by any loading on its inputs or outputs. Using a diode instead of a resistor to isolate the inputs from each other gives a much improved performance in that respect. Consider the circuit of fig. 2.13. In (a) T1 can be driven by R1 provided that no current flows in D1 or D2, which will be the case if both the input terminals are above the base voltage of T1, which will keep both diodes reverse biased. Once again the circuit performs the function of a two-input NAND gate. However, in practice one of the inputs will have to fall below 0 V to divert current from the base of T1, since the voltage drop across the diode when it conducts is approximately the same as the base–emitter voltage.

This situation would not lead to a practical logic circuit, but the addition of D3 and R3 as in fig. 2.13(b) overcomes these problems. In this case a voltage of 0.7 V on either input will be sufficient to start diverting base current from T1 due to the extra 0.7 V voltage drop across D3. R3 provides the discharge path for the excess charge when T1 is switched off since D3 will then be reverse biased and no charge will be able to pass through it. This configuration is called 'diode transistor logic' or DTL and is more suitable for integration than RTL.

2.2.2.6 DC performance of DTL

In the first place, high inputs to a gate are not noticeably affected if low inputs are also connected to the same gate. Even if the node connecting R1, D1, D2 and D3 is at 0.7 V due to one input being at ground, the other input can be at 5 V as its diode will be reverse biased and only a very small leakage current (probably less than 1 µA) will flow. Secondly, diodes D1, D2 and D3 share a common terminal. The usual way of making a diode in an integrated circuit is to connect the collector and base of a transistor together, most of the forward current then flows in the collector with only base current in the base–emitter junction. This gives a relatively low forward resistance. The breakdown voltage is then determined by the

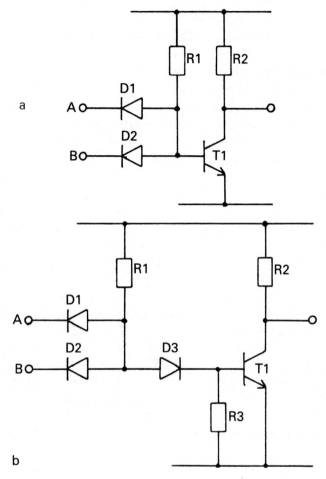

Fig. 2.13 Development of simple DTL NAND gate

base–emitter breakdown voltage which is typically 6–7 V, quite adequate for circuits operating from a 5 or 6 V power supply. All the diodes can then be made in the same collector region which means that even with the extra components the circuit can be fitted into as small an area as the RTL circuit. Parasitic capacitance will then be no higher. In order to give the same dynamic performance as the RTL circuit R1 and R2 will have to be the same value as the RTL load resistor. This will cause some increase in power dissipation. When either input is low, about 0.4 mA will flow in R1 but no current in R2. If all inputs are high, 0.36 mA will flow in R1, and 0.48 mA in R2, so the average current, as calculated before, will be 0.62 mA. Although this is 50% higher than the RTL gate, the DTL gate will support a much higher fan-in and fan-out so the 'amount' of logic which can be performed per gate is also higher.

2.2.2.7 AC performance of DTL

Because the circuit arrangement of DTL is different from RTL there will be some changes in the 'aiming' voltages and threshold points, which will affect the delay times in the circuit. An important difference occurs when the gate is being switched on; in DTL the output will have to be pulled down to 0.6 V from 5 V. The available base drive is 0.13 mA if R1 is 10 kΩ and R3 3 kΩ, so there will be 6.5 mA of current available for charging up the output capacitance (assumed to be 6 pF, as before). Equation (2.2) may be used again to give a result of about 4 ns. Together with the delays inherent in the transistor and diode D3 a total t_{phl} of about 6 ns will result. The t_{plh} case is slightly improved however; neglecting the diode resistance there is now at least one extra resistor apart from the 10 kΩ load to pull up the output capacitance. The worst case will be 5 kΩ pulling up 8 pF, assuming the node capacitance is still 2 pF. Equation (2.1) gives a delay time of 3.5 ns, or 6–7 ns including the transistor storage time. Thus overall the DTL gate will be marginally slower than the RTL circuit and with the extra power consumption the speed power product comes to 20 pJ. As already stated this reduced performance is more than compensated for by the wider gating possibilities of DTL.

2.2.2.8 Performance limitations of DTL

The change in device parameters with temperature will affect the DTL but not to the same extent as the RTL circuit. First of all the diode voltage drops across D3 and the input diodes will cancel, so even if chip temperature rise reduces the forward voltage to 0.5 V, the input will have to rise above 0.5 V to cause the output to turn on erroneously. Leakage current across the input diodes will increase with temperature, of course, but this will only add to T1's base current perhaps causing a marginal increase in switch-off time but no other noticeable effects, unless input A is HIGH and input B LOW for instance, when there will be a small increase in the voltage across D2.

Of course, in a discrete logic family, the fan-in, fan-out, input and output currents and voltages have to be accurately specified, and tested, in order to ensure compatibility between the different logic elements which may be connected together to form a logic system. These parameters are well enough controlled in a DTL circuit to show how the various parameters are interrelated and specified.

2.2.2.9 Specifying a logic family

The first step in specifying a logic family is to define the HIGH and LOW logic levels, the fan-in and fan-out and the working range of supply voltage ensuring at the same time that these are compatible with the fabrication process and, of course, the electrical design. The logic levels for inputs must be 'inside' the logic levels for outputs so that any perturbations in the way of noise pickup, voltage drops in supply lines, capacitative coupling of adjacent signal lines, etc., may be absorbed. The difference between these figures is the 'noise margin'. For example, the LOW input voltage for the DTL circuit may be set at 0.5 V, as this will keep the output transistor turned off even at high chip temperatures; the LOW output voltage may be specified at 0.3 V, provided the process and transistor design are good enough to keep the saturation voltage this low. Let us then specify the fundamental parameters of this particular DTL family.

LOW voltage: 0.5 V at input; 0.3 V at output
HIGH voltage: 0.9 V at input; 2.0 V at output
Supply voltage: 5–6 V
Fan-out: 4; fan-in: 4
Tolerance on internal resistors: ± 30%; matching to ± 10%
Minimum transistor current gain: 40
Maximum leakage current: diodes 10 µA; transistors 100 µA
Resistor values: R1 = 10 kΩ; R2 = 10 kΩ; R3 = 3 kΩ (fig. 2.13(b))

The parameters which need to be specified (to ensure that all the logic circuits in a family are compatible) are input currents, at the specified logic levels, and output voltages at full loading; this will ensure that, provided connection rules are observed, all device outputs will be capable of driving all device inputs in the correct state for all combinations of supply voltage and junction temperature. The convention for naming parameters is to use three letters: the first, usually V or I for voltage or current; the second, subscript i or o for input or output; and the third, subscript h or l for high or low.

2.2.2.10 Specifications of DTL

I_{il} (LOW input current) is worst for V_{cc} at 6 V, V_{il} at 0.3 V, maximum temperature (diode voltage = 0.5 V), 30% low resistors and a fan-in of four (three HIGH, one LOW). The value is thus 5.2/7 mA through R1 and 0.04 mA diode leakage (including D3), totalling 0.783 mA. I_{ih} is just the diode leakage current, 0.01 mA. For a fan-out of four, the worst case I_{oh} is 3.15 mA and we must check that T1 has enough base drive to maintain it in saturation. The worst case will be when V_{cc} is 5 V, temperature is minimum (diode drop is 0.75 V), R1 is 30% high and R2, 20% high. The current through R1 will be 3.5/13 = 0.27 mA and the current through R3, 0.75/3.6 = 0.21 mA leaving only 0.06 mA of base drive; 0.16 mA is the minimum necessary to achieve reasonable saturation with a current gain of forty. Thus we can only afford to allow 0.11 mA to flow in R3 which means its value must be doubled to 6 kΩ. The worst case for I_{oh} is four diode leakages, 0.04 mA, while T1 can have a leakage current of 0.1 mA, so the worst value of V_{oh} is 5.0 − (13 × 0.14) = 3.18 V. The specification could therefore be improved from 2.0 V to 3.0 V.

The above analysis has shown, for a simple case, how logic family specifications may be defined and how it may be necessary to modify design to cater for processing spreads and variations in the 'environment'. The same rules have to be applied in defining logic elements in semi-custom circuits although there will be easier trade-offs. For example the situation of an element with 30% high resistors driving four elements with 30% low resistors will not occur on a semi-custom circuit, because process variation across a single integrated circuit should not cause resistor values to spread by more than 10%. Also, careful design of internal power buses should ensure that supply voltage to all elements will be more tightly controlled than in our discrete logic example.

2.2.2.11 Transistor-transistor-logic (TTL)

Although several semiconductor companies in the 1960s brought out families of DTL circuits, none could claim to have become an 'industry standard'; however this was not the case with the next improvement in saturated transistor logic which was 'transistor-transistor-logic' or TTL. Improvements were made in three areas to the basic DTL design. The noise was improved by a modification to the input structure, the fan-out capability was increased by changing diode D3 to a transistor and t_{plh} was reduced by replacing R2 with an active pull-up transistor. Also gold doping, as described earlier, became a standard feature of the process to speed up recombination of the excess base and collector charge in saturation. The basic TTL NAND gate circuit is shown in fig. 2.14(a); this configuration became the standard for a whole family of logic parts called the '74 series' which was introduced in the late 1960s and early 1970s by Texas Instruments and became an industry standard with many manufacturers also supplying the family.

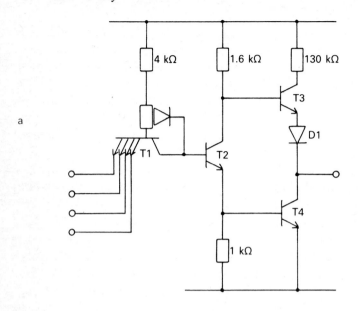

a

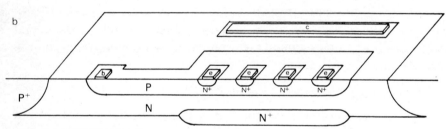

b

Fig. 2.14 a) TTL NAND gate circuit configuration; b) TTL multi-emitter input structure

2.2.2.12 TTL performance

From fig. 2.14(b) it may be seen that the multi-emitter input transistor is merely the DTL input diode cluster merged into a single transistor structure. There is however, one important difference in the resulting DC levels; in the DTL circuit with one or more inputs low, the voltage at the node connecting the diodes is $V_{il} + V_f$, in the TTL circuit this voltage is $V_{il} + V_{sat}$, which will be at least 0.2 V lower, even at the high temperature limit. The noise margin can therefore be improved from 0.2 V for DTL to 0.4 V for TTL. As usual though in integrated circuit technology this improvement is not obtained without taking a loss as well. In this case the problem is I_{ih}. Any of the emitters taken high will act as a collector of an inverse transistor with either another emitter held low as the emitter or the collector acting as emitter if all the true emitters are high. The gold doping also increases the leakage current. The inter-emitter transistor is a lateral transistor so its characteristics are not as easily controlled as the normal vertical transistor, being affected by over-etching of the emitter diffusion windows, sideways diffusion of the emitter and surface effects of the silicon–silicon dioxide interface. The latter is particularly important in long-term operation; before the stabilisation of surface states was properly understood, drift of mobile charges in the silicon dioxide caused changes in I_{ih} which led to failures due to parasitic MOS transistors, so, perversely it was the development of the stable MOS processes which led to reliable operation of bipolar circuits.

T2 is called the phase split transistor and performs the dual role of providing increased drive to the output transistor and controlling the two halves of the output stage, ensuring that they do not turn on simultaneously. In fact for a short period during each output transition they do both conduct while T2 is passing through the active region between cut-off and saturation. Diode D1 reduces the region for which this occurs but cannot prevent it completely. When T2 is cut off no base current is available to drive T4, but T3 can be supplied with base current by the 1.6 kΩ resistor, so the upper half of the output stage can supply current to the high input stages which it is driving, or to charge load capacitance in the dynamic case when it is changing state. The pull-up resistor is now nominally 130 Ω since there will be enough base drive to keep T3 saturated for any voltage applied to the output.

2.2.2.13 The totem-pole output stage

When T2 is fully driven into saturation, T4 will be supplied with base current but the voltage on T3 base will be 1.0 V or less, so T3 will be held off as it needs $1.4 + V_{ol}$ to conduct. The operation of T4 is just as the output transistor in the DTL circuit and needs no further description. This output stage is called a 'totem-pole' output because of the way in which the active devices are stacked on top of each other, but although both halves are capable of supplying a large current to charge and discharge the output capacitance they do not load each other significantly and so do not waste power in driving each other. The only exception to this is during the changeover period; this causes a momentary current spike to be drawn from the supply which means that the power supply and its layout have to be considered carefully.

By using an extra active stage to improve drive both for the DC and AC conditions, additional internal delays and power consumption have been introduced. However, having worked through a simple dynamic and DC analysis of RTL and DTL circuits, I will leave it to the reader to perform the same calculations for TTL.

The extra drive capability of the totem-pole output makes it ideal for driving loads off the integrated circuit, when capacitances of tens of pF may be encountered. However, for complex circuits on the chip, whether dedicated or semi-custom, it is not usual to incorporate the full output circuit and many leave off the totem-pole completely relying on the saturation voltages of the input transistor and driving gate output to keep the output turned off. This means a reduction in noise margin, but noise is not usually such a problem within an integrated circuit.

2.2.2.14 Enhanced TTL families

Various enhancements have been made to the 74 series family starting in the early 1970s with Schottky TTL. The enhancement consisted of replacing saturating transistors with non-saturating Schottky diode clamped transistors. Two families emerged from this process, standard Schottky (74S) with slightly higher power than the 74 series, but about a quarter the delay time, and low power Schottky (74LS) with the same spread as the 74 series, but one fifth the power. Later still the junction isolated process was replaced by oxide isolated processes with the Fairchild Advanced Schottky TTL (FAST®) and Advanced Low Power Schottky (74ALS). (FAST is a trademark of the Fairchild Camera and Instrument Corporation.) FAST® has aimed at a slight improvement on 74S speeds with a substantial power reduction, while ALS has made moderate improvements to both speed and power compared with 74LS. A summary of the performance of the various families described in this section is given in table 2.3.

Two factors should be borne in mind when comparing semi-custom parameters with discrete logic parameters; first, discrete logic is normally specified with an external capacitative load, whereas semi-custom is specified for driving 'on chip' and interfacing to the outside world will cause additional delay. Secondly, a glance at a discrete logic families circuit schematic in a standard data book will show that the actual circuit configuration is more complex than the simple four-transistor circuit described in this section. Additional components are added to provide fast AC paths for the pulse edges and to speed up charge removal from switching transistors. These techniques reduce

Table 2.3 Comparison of bipolar logic families

Technology	Family	Maximum gate delay (ns)	Average gate power (mW)	Speed–power product (pJ)
Junction isolation Saturated transistors	RTL	50	3	150
	DTL	35	5	175
	74 series TTL	18.5	40	740
Junction isolation Schottky transistors	74LS	15	8	120
	74S	5	70	350
	Signetics EPL (semi-custom)	4.5	2.6	25
	TI TAL (semi-custom)	5.0	1.25	6
Oxide isolation Schottky transistors	FAST®	5	16	80
	74ALS	10	4	40
	NSC/Motorola ALS (semi-custom)	4.0	1	4

circuit delay at the expense of power consumption and silicon area, factors which are not so important in SSI or MSI circuits where power consumption is generally low and packaging is a large proportion of device cost. In an LSI circuit, junction temperature, and hence power dissipation, and chip cost are far more important, and output loads are more easily defined and controlled, so circuit structures tend to be more basic.

2.2.3 Current switch logic

2.2.3.1 Current mode logic (CML)

The previous section described logic families where the switching transistors are either fully saturated, or held on the edge of saturation by clamping diodes. Saturation occurs because the collector voltage and current are not limited, so when the transistor is supplied with enough base drive the current drawn from the collector load increases to the point where the collector voltage is so low that the base–collector junction becomes forward biased. Clearly if the collector current were limited in some way it would be possible to prevent the collector voltage falling low enough to allow the transistor to saturate. One way of doing this is to limit the emitter current. A constant current source connected to the emitter will limit the current flowing in the transistor when it is switched on, and a suitable choice of collector load will prevent the collector voltage from falling below the base voltage. The simplest implementation of this technique is the current mode logic (CML) used by Ferranti in their uncommitted logic array (ULA) families. Ferranti also use a simplified version of the standard planar process which they call collector diffusion isolation (CDI). CML and CDI are shown in fig. 2.15.

2.2.3.2 Collector diffusion isolation (CDI)

The CDI process starts in the same way as the standard process by diffusing low resistivity collector regions into a P-type substrate. The CDI process then diverges by laying down P-type epitaxy which will become both the isolation and base regions. Two N-type diffusions then follow, a deep diffusion in a rectangular frame enclosing a P-type base region followed by a shallow diffusion into the base. The deep diffusion connects the surface to the buried collector and the shallow diffusion forms the emitter; as may be seen in fig. 2.15(c), the transistor structure thus formed is surrounded by the P-type epitaxy and is thus isolated from adjacent components.

2.2.3.3 DC Performance of CML

Several different speed power versions of the CML gate in fig. 2.15(a) are in use. The one which most nearly equates to TTL performance uses a 1.7 kΩ load (R_L), a 0.21 mA current source (I_S) and 0.95 V voltage rail (V_S) – all nominal values at 25°C. If all inputs are below 0.7 V, no current will flow in R_L so the output will be at 0.95 V. If the output is connected to an input of a similar gate the

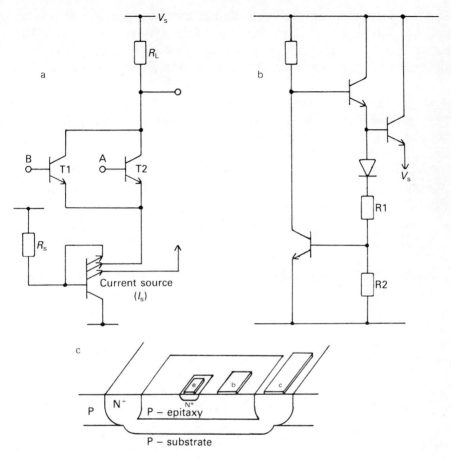

Fig. 2.15 a) basic CML gate and current source; b) voltage source; c) CDI transistor structures

0.21 mA will flow in R_L and its output will drop to 0.59 V, sufficiently low to keep any gates connected to it turned off, but not low enough to saturate the transistor. Naturally, base current has to be supplied by the load resistor of OFF gates. If the minimum current gain is twenty, each driven gate will cause a drop of less than 20 mV in output voltage, so a fan-out of at least five is possible. It should also be noted that if either input is HIGH the output will be LOW, so that the logic function is a NOR gate.

The design of current and voltage sources is crucial to the successful operation of CML over a full range of temperature, supply voltage and process variation. In fig. 2.15(a), R_S is the same value as R_L to ensure good tracking between the source current and load. The current source uses an inverse transistor, the current through each emitter depending on the area of that emitter because the inverse current gain with the CDI process is relatively high (>10). Thus the actual source current may be accurately defined by R_S and the ratio of emitter areas and variation in absolute resistor values and transistor current gain will not affect the voltage levels at the output. The voltage source shown in fig. 2.15(b) is equal in value to $(R1 + R2)/R2V_{be}$, and thus depends both on temperature and transistor forward base–emitter voltage. However, the threshold voltage of the gate transistors will also depend on temperature and base–emitter voltage so the design of the voltage source provides built-in compensation for these factors. The only problem could be that V_S will fall faster than V_{be} as temperature rises, so the transistors will approach more nearly to saturation at high temperature.

2.2.3.4 AC performance of CML

Dynamic performance may be estimated as for the other cases we have considered previously using equations (2.1) and (2.2). Device geometries can be made smaller than standard planar devices because no allowance needs to be made for sideways diffusion of isolation and base regions, but doping levels tend to be higher with CDI and a standard two-input cell needs two transistors, so node capacitance at the output will still be about 6 pF. Putting in the values for R_L, I_S and the voltage levels previously calculated gives 7.0 ns for t_{plh} and 5.2 ns for t_{phl}.

In a typical ULA, one current source supplies two gates and it may be assumed that half of the gates are OFF at any one time, so the mean power is 0.185 mW giving a speed–power product of just over 1.1 pJ. This figure is an order of magnitude better than for saturating logic and is partly accounted for by the non-saturating aspect of the logic, but also by the reduced voltage swing of the logic, meaning that a much lower current can be used to obtain a comparable switching time.

2.2.3.5 Emitter-coupled logic (ECL)

Although this version of CML has been successfully applied to semi-custom circuits, the traditional current switching logic which has been used for both discrete and semi-custom high speed designs is emitter-coupled logic (ECL). This also uses a current source to define emitter and collector current, but the switching threshold is defined by a fixed voltage derived from the supply and is not directly related to the base–emitter voltage. The design of ECL, fig. 2.16(b), is based on a standard circuit called a long-tailed pair amplifier shown in fig.

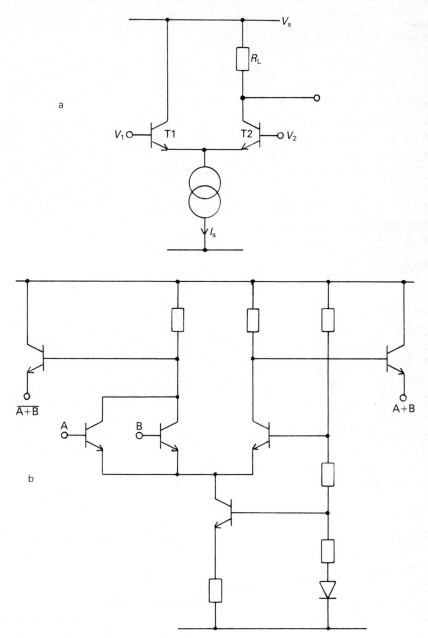

Fig. 2.16 a) long-tailed amplifier; b) ECL OR/NOR gate

2.16(a). If two identical transistors are connected as shown, the source current will be divided between them according to the difference in V_1 and V_2. If V_1 and V_2 are equal then nominally one half of I_s will flow in each transistor, but if they are different the currents in T1 and T2 are related by:

$$\ln \frac{I_1}{I_2} = \frac{q}{k_T} (V_1 - V_2)$$

For small differences in V_1 and V_2 such that $\ln (I_1/I_2)$ is close to 1, $\ln (I_1/I_2) \approx I_1/I_2$ and the output is approximately a linear function of the input. This is only true if $(V_1 - V_2) < 2.5$ mV or so, but in these cases the circuit may be used as a linear amplifier whose voltage gain is $(qR_L I_S)/(2k_T)$. If, on the other hand, $q/k_T (V_1 - V_2) > 4.6$, $I_1 > 100 I_2$; in other words all the source current will flow in T1. At room temperature this requires $(V_1 - V_2) > 0.115$ V, so if V_2 is held at a fixed voltage and V_1 swings below $V_2 + 0.115$, the output will swing from V_S to $V_S - I_S R_L$.

In this system it makes sense to make V_S the ground and provide a negative supply rail as the power supply. This means that the supply does not have to be defined as accurately as it does for the ULA since all voltages are effectively referenced to the HIGH logic level. In a semi-custom circuit a simple long-tailed pair is quite adequate by itself as a gating element, provided V_S is the system ground. For example, the RTC (Philips) advanced customised ECL (ACE) uses I_S of 1.5 mA and R_L of 300 Ω. The HIGH logic level is thus 0 V, and low is 0.45 V. A reference voltage of 0.25 V gives nearly 200 mV of noise margin while allowing for 50 mV of voltage drop in R_L to provide base current for load gates. While adequate for driving loads internally, some circuit modification is required for coping with external loads.

2.2.3.6 ECL characteristics

Because ECL is non-saturating it is capable, with the appropriate design, of much lower delays than TTL. This means that printed circuit layouts have to be designed with more care to avoid signal reflections and losses. In TTL, signal reflections may occur but because of the slower circuit response may not be 'recognised' because they arrive so soon after the original signal. ECL is fast enough to see these reflections and treat them as if they were real signals, so the usual technique is to design the interconnections as transmission lines, which means that the outputs have to be capable of matching into impedances as low as 50 Ω. ECL standard logic circuits then use an emitter follower output circuit with sufficient base drive to enable the appropriate impedance to be connected externally to match the interconnection characteristic impedance. The emitter follower also provides a level shift which allows the voltage swing to be increased to 0.8 V. The industry standard ECL family is the 10 000 series which was introduced by Motorola, and the basic OR/NOR gate diagram is shown in fig. 2.16(b).

2.2.3.7 ECL circuit techniques (wired-OR and series gating)

Because the long-tailed amplifier is symmetrical, outputs of either polarity with negligible skew are obtained by putting a load in each 'side' of the amplifier, and other benefits may be obtained from this circuit technique. The most obvious is the ability to connect two outputs to the same load, then either output going HIGH will take the load HIGH. This configuration is called wired-OR and it enables functions to be gated together with very little penalty in terms of added propagation delay, while power is saved because the load is shared and one gate is not needed. Another circuit technique which is used to reduce overall delay and power is series gating. In this case, long-tailed pairs are placed in the collector circuits of the basic long-tailed pair to provide an additional level of gating. Often a diode or emitter follower is used in the bottom level to provide a DC offset which prevents these transistors from saturating. Figure 2.17 shows how an exclusive-OR/NOR function may be implemented in a single stage; normally two stages of logic are required for this function. If A and B are both HIGH, source current flows through T1 and T3 from R1; even though T6 is also ON it does not pass current because T2 is OFF. If A and B are both LOW, T2 and T5 conduct and R1 is again the load which passes current, thus the exclusive-OR function is implemented.

2.2.3.8 ECL performance

One further benefit of ECL is that the supply current to an ECL gate is virtually constant, except for charging current for node capacitance, although the output buffers will take varying current depending whether they are HIGH or LOW. Discrete ECL devices therefore usually have separate ground pins for the logic and the buffers so that common earth impedance is reduced and the logic is isolated from possible movements in the absolute ground level. Some ECL semicustom designs use the full ECL circuit with on-chip buffers, while others sacrifice some noise immunity and fan-out capability for an improved speed–power product by leaving off the buffers and using CML with an on-chip reference voltage. Just as TTL performance has been improved by using oxide isolation so the 10 000 series of

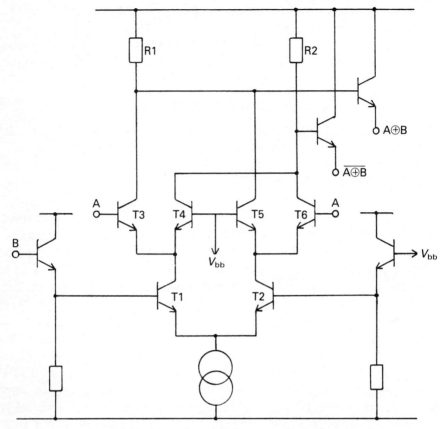

Fig. 2.17 Series gating used for exclusive-OR/NOR

ECL has been upgraded into the 100 000 series, at the same time making the logic levels practically independent of supply voltage and temperature. The performance of discrete ECL logic and some of the semi-custom approaches may be seen in table 2.4.

2.2.4 Current steering logic

2.2.4.1 Integrated injection logic (I²L)

Unlike TTL and ECL which use voltage levels to determine HIGH or LOW state, some logic designs work on the principle of diverting current from bult-in current sources to switch the gating transistors on and off. The original technique was integrated injection logic (I²L), developed by Philips in the late 1960s. The basic I²L cell, shown in fig. 2.18, uses a multi-cmitter transistor in the inverse mode as the gating element with a lateral PNP transistor as the current source. In a semi-custom or LSI design the current sources are

Table 2.4 Comparison of current switching logic families

Technology	Family	Maximum gate delay (ns)	Average gate power (mW)	Speed–power product (pJ)
Junction isolation	10 000 series	3.5	40	140
	ULA R series (Ferranti)	2.5	0.3	0.75
	Q700 (AMCC)	1.3	1.8	2.4
	Microgate E (Plessey)	0.55	10.4	5.8
Oxide isolation	100 000 series	0.95	140	133
	MCA series, Motorola/NSC	1.3	4.4	5.8
	UPB 6300, NEC series	0.5	5.4	2.7
	ACE, RTC/Philips	0.5	6.8	3.4

supplied from a common I_{bb} supply, so the working current of the individual cells may be defined externally.

Logic is performed by wire-ANDing outputs at an input node. Thus if output collectors from several cells are connected at an input they must all come from OFF cells if the driven cell is conducting; this is a NAND function. Although an I^2L cell is fabricated in a single isolation 'pocket', thereby achieving high packing density and low capacitance it does suffer from a number of disadvantages which make it unsuitable for high speed operation. It is basically a saturating logic and therefore suffers from the same stored charge problem as TTL, although as the transistors are operating in inverse mode, the excess charge is largely in the base and will take longer to recombine with holes supplied by the current source. Although the outputs are largely isolated by the multi-emitter structure, they show the same transverse gain properties as the TTL input structure, so leakage is a potential hazard. The use of NPN and lateral PNP on the

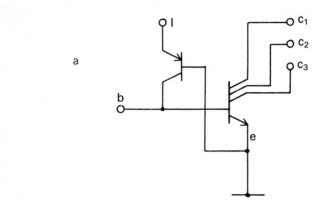

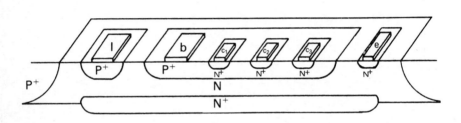

Fig. 2.18 a) I²L cell schematic; b) I²L cell structure

same chip lead to incompatible requirements, namely that for efficient operation the emitter doping level must be higher than the base, so careful process specification is necessary. In any case lateral PNP transistors are very inefficient at high current levels where the increase in carrier density reduces emitter efficiency because the doping level of the base is so low. This means that I²L will normally operate at low current levels and therefore low speeds.

2.2.4.2 I²L performance

The input capacitance of the I²L cell will be relatively low as the normal collector region is tied to ground, so just the base diffusion capacitance plus interwiring capacitance amounting to no more than 3 pF need to be switched. However, a typical source current of 0.1 mA is used and the typical voltage swing is 0.6 V. Using equation (2.2) gives a t_{plh} of 9 ns but storage time of say 3 ns must be added to give a total of 12 ns. If the inverse gain is ten and there are three output collectors, then 0.3 mA will be available for discharging the input capacitance but the cell will not start to turn on until the input voltage reaches 0.7 V, a further 9 ns. The actual fall time from 0.7 V to 0.4 V will be 3 ns giving a total again of 12 ns. The power taken by the cell is quite low, of course, the 0.1 mA being supplied at about 1.5 V usually, so the speed–power product is 1.8 pJ.

Because the processing used for I^2L is similar to that used for linear devices, it is often used in combined digital and linear circuits to provide the logic area. The standard techniques to improve performance would not be feasible for I^2L. Oxide isolation would not reduce the capacitance because it is the base diffusion capacitance which is important for I^2L, and this is not affected by oxide isolation. Also it is not possible to make Schottky diodes on the collector sites because these are too heavily doped to make rectifying junctions. Improved versions have been made, however, in the form of integrated Schottky logic (ISL) and Schottky transistor logic (STL); both use a transistor cell in the normal mode and isolate the outputs by means of Schottky diodes. Both also use a fixed resistor to a low voltage supply as the current source, but the method of preventing saturation is different for each design. STL uses a Schottky transistor, which leads to certain complications; if the forward voltage of the clamping diode and output diode were the same it would be impossible to switch off the transistor, since with no input applied, the input and output voltages would be equal. The forward voltage of a Schottky diode depends on the work function of the metal from which it is made, so by using two different metals the forward voltage of the output diode and the gate will function with a logic swing equal to the difference in forward voltages.

2.2.4.3 Integrated Schottky logic (ISL)

The design of ISL is based on a different approach as illustrated in fig. 2.19. All NPN transistors made in the planar process have potential parasitic transistors, which are normally biased off or designed to have negligible effect. In ISL two parasitic PNP transistors are deliberately enhanced to steal some of the base current and keep the NPN transistor just out of saturation. The two parasitics are the vertical T2 and lateral T3. T2 is normally made to have very low gain by extending the buried collector region completely under the NPN base. This highly doped region in the PNP base drastically reduces the minority carrier lifetime making the gain negligible. In ISL the buried layer extends under only part of the base, the remaining portion acts reasonably well as a PNP. T3 normally has its gain held low by making the base-isolation separation much longer than the minority carrier diffusion length. In ISL the gain

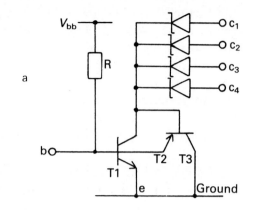

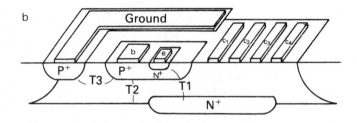

Fig. 2.19 a) ISL gate schematic; b) ISL transistor structure

is enhanced by making a horseshoe-shaped diffusion around the true base and partly covering the isolation diffusion to make a true lateral PNP transistor. The collector–emitter voltage of T1 is the difference between the base–emitter voltage of T1 and that of the T2–T3 composite. Because the geometry of T2–T3 is much larger than T1, this difference is large enough to prevent T1 saturating even when they are passing similar currents. The output voltage of an ON transistor will therefore be about 0.5 V, 0.3 V drop across the collector–emitter terminals and 0.2 V forward voltage across the Schottky diode. In the OFF state the voltage will be held at about 0.65 V by the base–emitter junction of the load transistor.

2.2.4.4 ISL performance

The effect of internal loading or fan-out may be illustrated by ISL. Each cell has a parasitic capacitance of about 1.5 pF associated with its output, while 6 pF will load the input due to the 7 kΩ base resistor and enhanced PNP devices. The fall time when the cell is turned ON is once again given by equation (2.2) and comes to just over 0.2 ns assuming a current of 5 mA. The actual fall time will therefore be determined by the internal switching time of the transistor itself and affected very little by any increase in load capacitance because of additional fan-out. The t_{plh}, on the other hand, is dependent on the pull up by the base bias resistor, and is calculated from equation (2.1). With an aiming voltage of 1.5 V for the rising waveform, the rise time from 0.5 V to 0.65 V is 8.5 ns. In this case, each additional cell connected to the input will add 1.5 pF to the load to be pulled up and hence 1.7 ns to the rise time. These delays reflect only diffusion capacitance so allowance also has to be made for capacitance of interconnections; this can add up to 50 ps to the delay per thousandths of an inch of track.

2.2.4.5 Enhancements to ISL and STL

These effects can be minimised by making use of other features of the circuit and layout. Usually ten or twelve per cent of gates will not be used in a design so the base resistor may be used to provide additional pull up, at the expense of increased power dissipation. Some ISL arrays and STL arrays incorporate a pull-up resistor into the cell to minimise fan-out effects. Another possibility is to increase the bias voltage; raising V_{bb} to 2.0 V decreases the calculated rise time to 5.5 ns. All these additional measures increase the power dissipation of the cell and are normally used only when speed is a really critical factor. For example, OFF state current is 0.12 mA and ON state current is 0.14 mA for the basic cell, giving an average dissipation of 0.2 mW and a speed–power product of 1.0 pJ. Increasing V_{bb} to 2.0 V doubles the power dissipation but only improves the delay from 5 ns to 3.5 ns so the speed–power product increases to 1.4 pJ.

The other method of improving performance is to use an improved process; for example Signetics has recently introduced an ISL gate array using oxide isolation with an average propagation delay of 1.5 ns, while maintaining power dissipation at 0.2 mW per gate.

There are no standard logic families using this structure so the array is usually surrounded by interface cells which translate inputs from TTL levels to ISL/STL and *vice versa* for outputs. For this reason there is nothing to be gained by tabulating performance of the different arrays; the performance described in this section may be assessed by comparing it with the performance of TTL logic families and semi-custom circuits.

2.3 Semi-custom techniques

2.3.1 Mask programmable semi-custom techniques

2.3.1.1 Requirements of semi-custom techniques

Having seen that there are several different techniques available for implementing logic functions it is now possible to describe the several ways in which these designs can actually be built on to a silicon wafer. These methods must obey some simple criteria:

(a) they must give predictable performance;
(b) they must be capable of being designed without specialist integrated circuit design knowledge;
(c) the customising masks must be made on an automatic or semi-automatic basis;
(d) the functional performance of the finished device must match the design.

A full-custom circuit, in which design is due at individual component level, may not meet the first three criteria since performance will depend on parasitic effects between adjacent components, specialist integrated circuit design expertise is essential and each diffusion mask has to be individually defined. The matching of device function to design requirement is usually a function of the computer-aided design (CAD) tools used for the design. In a semi-custom circuit the problems of layout expertise are usually overcome by fixing the positions of logic elements in advance. The logic elements themselves may then be designed by the integrated circuit expert so that all the diffusion areas and part of the interconnection area are predefined, the remaining area is then available for connecting the logic elements together into the required logic function. This task is analogous to printed circuit board layout and may be performed by either a skilled draughtsman, or more usually now, by a routing program on a minicomputer or graphics system.

2.3.1.2 Principles of gate arrays

The simplest logic element to design is a logic gate and the simplest semi-custom circuit is a gate array. The logic gates are arranged in a regular pattern, usually in fixed locations on a grid, the grid lines may then be used to define the positions of the interconnections. The 'difficult' parts of the layout such as ensuring adequate cross-sectional area of aluminium to distribute power supplies reliably, need be done only once for each array. The task for the circuit designer is then to prove a good electrical design, usually with the help of logic simulation software and finally, to transfer this design into a layout on the array corresponding to the electrical circuit, probably using an automatic placement and routing program.

This approach has been used successfully by many manufacturers to allow their customers to develop customised logic circuits. The main disadvantage lies in the provision of only a single type of logic element. For example, if the standard gate is a four-input NAND (a minimum of four inputs are required in practice in order to be able to build up more complex circuits), then these must be combined to form other functions. This is not such a problem with high order functions such as registers or multiplexers, but may be a problem when trying to create a NOR gate for instance. If the complements of signals are not readily available it might take three or four NAND gates to implement a single gate function. This is obviously wasteful of silicon area, but will also increase propagation delay and power consumption, leading to an inefficient design. The higher order functions are usually available to the designer as predefined functions called 'macros', in a library forming part of the logic simulation software. However, since layout is done at gate level, care needs to be taken that the components of the macro are positioned close together with short interconnections, otherwise such hazards as internal races in flip-flops may occur causing the device to malfunction. A good logic simulator will allow the interconnection capacitance to modify the simulation result after an attempt at layout, and this should show up potential hazards, but it will still cause extra work and delay in the design process.

2.3.1.3 Macrocells

An alternative approach which can prevent this type of problem is the 'macrocell'. In this case the array is not composed of basic gates, but cells containing anything from four or five components (i.e. transistors, diodes, resistors, etc.) up to fifty or more. Cells may all contain the same numbers of components or an array may contain minor cells with only a few components and major cells with many components. In some designs a large number of I/O cells are provided on the periphery of the device with the possibility that cells not used for I/O can be used for logic functions. Other possibilities include blocks of ROM or RAM etc., embedded in the area. Each cell is capable of being layed out to perform any one of the several different functions which are described in the macro or cell library.

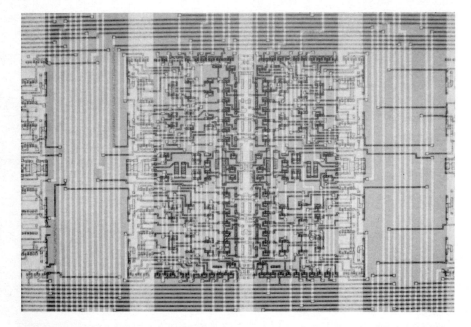

Fig. 2.20 Enlargement of four ACE macrocells (advanced customised ECL, Philips)

The design process is now more akin to designing with a standard logic family and has the advantage that the performance of each function is very well defined because the layout is invariant. This technique is very often used in ECL arrays so that use can be made of series gating and wire-ORing and thus make optimum use of the components. Figure 2.20 shows four ACE macrocells (Advanced Customised ECL).

Although the cell array offers some advantages over the gate array there are also some drawbacks. The 'pinout' of each cell is fixed, so that although inversions and rotations may be possible, layout is not as free as in the gate array. Also silicon area may not be optimised; if the cell contains sufficient components to make a complex function such as a multiplexer, then cells used to make basic gate functions will either contain several gates, which may not all be needed, or have a restricted I/O so that not all the components in the cell are needed to make the number of gates supported by the I/O. In either case the need to 'visit' a particular cell location to find a basic gate can lead to some extended track lengths.

2.3.1.4 Cell libraries

An alternative to the fixed array, either of gates or cells, is the cell library approach. Again the design is made with a library of standard cells but in this case the cell may be any size, from a single inverter to a complete ALU. Each macro in the cell library has a corresponding physical equivalent whose every parameter, including shape and size, is predefined and precharacterised. Only those cells actually used in the electrical design are used in the layout and they may be placed for optimum layout to minimise track length of critical paths and avoid wasting space with unused routing and unused gates or cells. The layout is usually structured by having two or three standard widths for the cells so they may be laid end to end which simplifies routing of power supplies. Additional space can be saved by making all cells with a single input and expansion node and providing diode expansion cells to add as many inputs as the logic dictates.

The greatest benefit of this approach is to be seen in designs where a non-standard configuration of gates or I/Os is required, particularly as the trend is now to arrays with ever-increasing numbers of gates, while small arrays tend to have a correspondingly small number of I/Os. The designer with low gate count and high I/O count or merely a small circuit, well below the smallest array offered, may well find it advantageous to look at a cell library design. The main disadvantage is that the device has to be made from the 'bottom up', meaning masks have to be made for all diffusion layers as well as the interconnection; this is liable to add to the cost and time taken for the design. However, once complete, the design is likely to be cheaper than any other approach, except full custom, and will probably give the best electrical performance for the technology used.

This technique is sometimes referred to as the 'silicon compiler' comparing it with the design of software in high level languages.

2.3.2 Field programmable logic

2.3.2.1 Comparison of mask and field programming

One inescapable aspect of the design techniques described so far is that it is mandatory that the physical task of customising the finished circuit has to be performed by a specialist manufacturer who at least must be able to deposit thin metal films, etch silicon dioxide and aluminium and package the finished device. This assumes he is able to buy diffused silicon wafers and subcontract the mask making to another specialist. The most successful suppliers are generally those who are able to do the whole fabrication and testing process themselves. The impact of this on the user of semi-custom circuits is that it usually costs at least £10 000 to pay for layout, mask making, test generation, sample manufacture, etc., and a wait in excess of four weeks is often entailed before the samples are available to test the design in the whole circuit. Clearly it would be preferable if the designer could use a device whose logic function could be modified or programmed without sending it to a specialist manufacturer for processing.

Techniques have been devised whereby users can modify the contents of integrated circuits, and were first used to make programmable read only memories (PROMs) or erasable PROMs (EPROMs) depending on the type of technique employed. Both devices have a memory type structure with up to fifteen inputs (at the current state of technology) defining 2^{10} addresses, each address having an associated output, usually of four or eight bits. These devices are intended generally for uses such as program storage in microprocessor systems, look-up tables, character generators and so on. EPROMs use a 'field-effect capacitor' to store the information. One plate of the capacitor is embedded in insulating oxide on the silicon surface, a high voltage pulse applied to a charging electrode will charge the capacitor enabling one bit of information to be stored. Clearly an EPROM with fifteen inputs and eight outputs would require 262 144 capacitors; such a device is called a 256 kbit EPROM because a kilobit is defined as 1024 (2^{10}) bits. The information can be erased by exposing the silicon surface to ultraviolet radiation, this lowers the resistance of the insulator sufficiently for the capacitors to be discharged in a few minutes.

2.3.2.2 Using bipolar PROMs for logic

EPROMs are MOS devices and therefore relatively slow with access times in excess of 100 ns. Access time is the equivalent of propagation delay, being the time taken for an output to change in response to a change in address. PROMs made in a bipolar process are faster but cannot use field-effect capacitors to store information as different processes are involved. The original method of storing information is to use a matrix of fuses made from some alloy such as nichrome or tungsten–titanium. When a sufficiently high current pulse is passed through the fuse the alloy and the surrounding glass passivation melt together to form an insulating gap. The presence or absence of a fuse link can clearly be detected when the fuse location is addressed and the relevant output driven high or low accordingly. Unlike the EPROM, PROMs are fixed once the fuses are blown and although they may be modified by blowing previously unblown fuses they cannot be repaired and re-used. A new technique called Avalanche Induced Migration has recently been introduced; this consists of destroying one junction of an open base transistor, so an unblown transistor will exhibit high impedance whilst a blown transistor will appear as a diode and may be used directly as a gating element in the PROMs logic.

Any combinatorial logic system may be defined in a memory format, since every possible combination of inputs has a completely defined set of outputs associated with it. For example a 256 × 4 PROM could be used to implement the same function as a 74LS00 (quadruple two-input NAND gate) each possessing eight inputs and four outputs. The difference is that the 74LS00 has a truth table of sixteen lines because the inputs of one gate are completely independent of the other three, while the PROM has a truth table of 256 lines because all eight inputs must have all possible combinations completely defined. Of course the much greater complexity of the PROM allows more complicated logic functions to be realised in a single device. It could be used to detect four 8-bit addresses in a memory mapped I/O processor system; this would need five packages in a standard logic family design (an octal inverter and four eight-input NAND gates). However, even this application uses only four lines out of 256 to defined outputs actively, the other 252 lines corresponding to inactive states. This inefficiency in the use of active states has led to the development of a number of families of field programmable devices directly aimed at realising logic functions.

2.3.2.3 Field programmable logic devices

The two most commonly available families of field programmable logic are integrated fuse logic (IFL) and programmable array logic (PAL®) both being supplied by several manufacturers. (PAL is a trademark of Monolithic Memories Incorporated.) Both families have common features which are best illustrated by the simplest IFL device, the field programmable gate array (FPGA) whose structure is illustrated in fig. 2.21, and is available as type number 82S103. Inputs to the device are connected to the gates via a true/complement buffer enabling both input functions and their inverts to be available for implementing logic functions. The internal gate is a thirty-two-input AND gate formed by conventional diode logic using Schottky diodes. In any one application no more than half the inputs can be used, otherwise at least one input will have both its true and complement connected to the AND gate which will cause it to be held permanently LOW. Inputs or their complements which are not

contained in the logic being implemented have the fuse in series with
their input diode blown, effectively removing that input from the
gate.

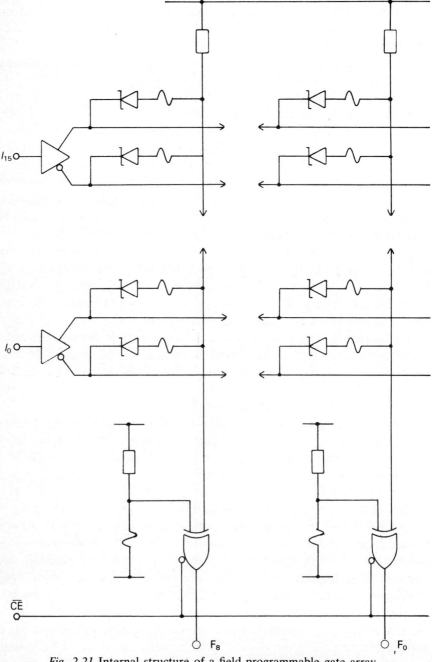

Fig. 2.21 Internal structure of a field programmable gate array

The AND function formed could be output via a totem-pole driver stage and provide a useful gating function, but on some ranges an additional feature is added. The output is taken to one input of an exclusive-OR gate whose other input is grounded via a fuse. As long as the fuse is blown, the other input will be held HIGH and the output inverted. This feature means that by using De Morgan's Theorem and selecting true or complement of inputs and outputs as appropriate, any of the functions AND, NAND, OR or NOR may be implemented. As with the PROM an address decoder can be realised directly by blowing either true or complement fuse for each address bit depending whether the bit is HIGH or LOW. With the FPGA nine different 16-bit addresses can be decoded, over four times the complexity of the PROM, but only 297 fuses are in the FPGA compared with 1024 in the PROM.

2.3.2.4 Field programmable logic arrays (FPLAs)

Added complexity may be obtained by ORing together some of the AND gate outputs to form two-level logic functions. There is a major difference between IFL and PAL® devices in this respect; PALs® feed the AND outputs into fixed OR gates, while the OR gates used in IFL devices are fully programmable like the AND gates, as can be seen in fig. 2.22. If any of the transistors with an intact fuse in the emitter has its base pulled high by an 'ON' AND gate, the line connecting the emitters will also be taken high so this line will contain the OR function of all the AND gates connected to it. The structure of AND gates followed by OR gates which can contain any of the AND terms is called a field programmable logic array (FPLA).

Additional flexibility is achieved in both IFL and PAL® devices by connecting some pins to both outputs and inputs. By suitable programming of the output enable control terms, the pins can be defined as input, output, or both, allowing feedback or bidirectional operation. In this way a single device may be programmed not only to customise the logic function internally, but also to allow choice in the allocation of input and output pins.

The most complex field programmable devices contain flip-flops in addition to the features already described. These allow synchronous logic systems to be realised in a single integrated circuit. While masked gate arrays may be adapted to replace discrete logic devices in an existing design directly, the more rigid structure of field programmable logic makes it less amenable to this method of logic replacement.

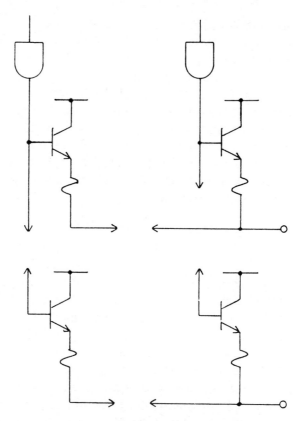

Fig. 2.22 Programmable OR-gate structure

2.3.2.5 Using field programmable logic

Better results are usually achieved by designing a logic system directly into programmable logic and to this end various software aids have been made available to assist this process. These generally work on the basis of first defining the logic in terms of Boolean algebra or state diagrams, the program converts this information into a map of the fuses which need to be blown in the device. This information is fed into a programmer which enables circuitry inside the device to convert the fuses from a logic matrix into a memory matrix. The programmer is then able to blow the fuses as if the device were a PROM. The conversion from device to memory device is achieved by applying a 'super-high' voltage to one pin; this enables the memory addressing circuitry via a Zener diode, which keeps it disabled during normal operation. Care has to be taken to avoid voltage spikes reaching the device during normal operation otherwise additional undesired programming could take place. Programming is the one aspect of a device which cannot be tested before it is supplied, so a small proportion of devices will not be successfully programmed by the user. This is a normal feature of all field programmable devices and most manufacturers will replace rejects free of charge. Of more concern is that most programmers check functionality by testing for the presence or absence of a fuse in memory mode. Faults in the actual logic circuitry may not be detected in this way so the latest programmers include functional testing with pseudorandom inputs; manufacturers supplying preprogrammed devices may use logic simulation to create functional tests for the proprietary test equipment commonly used for device testing.

2.3.2.6 Performance of field programmable logic

Performance of field programmable logic is harder to define than either standard logic families or other semi-custom techniques because of the difficulty in assessing gate count. Particularly in the case of feedback devices, such as registered IFL and PALs® most of the gates can have more than twenty active inputs, a structure which is not usual in any other logic approach, so a new criterion needs to be established for comparison purposes. The amount of logic contained in a system may be defined as the number of gate inputs used in implementing the logic. A typical FPLA application might have twelve inputs and six outputs using twenty-four AND gates with an average of eight inputs per gate and six inputs per OR gate, giving 240 gate inputs if twelve inputs are allowed for the true/complement option at the inputs. A typical semi-custom gate array will probably have an average of three inputs per gate so the FPLA contains the equivalent of eighty logic gates. Power dissipation depends on the number of AND gates being used and will be approximately 600 mW for the case described above, yielding an average of 7.5 mW per gate. Propagation delay per gate is also undefined; delay through an FPLA is 30 ns for the current devices available, but represents five gates in depth compared with other semi-custom devices, input and output buffers, AND and OR gates plus option of true/complement on both input and output. The gate delay is thus 6 ns giving a speed–power product of 45 pJ.

Although the performance is comparable to discrete logic families it is inferior to other bipolar semi-custom approaches, partly because the input and output buffers are included in the assessment of programmable logic. The benefits of programmable logic are to be found in the way in which it is used; development is virtually free and instantaneous, no minimum quantity commitments are required and in most cases the parts are multi-sourced components in volume production.

2.4 Selecting the right approach

2.4.1 Defining the criteria

2.4.1.1 The important parameters

Having examined the technologies available and the possible techniques of using the technologies, we can pursue the most difficult part of any semi-custom design which is choosing which approach to follow. The designer or project leader will probably start by listing all the performance requirements of his circuit and then doing a market survey to estimate which of the many available circuits or methods can meet the required performance. Assuming that more than one is acceptable, the final choice will have to be made on more commercial grounds, cost including development fee, ease of design, track record and second source, are the obvious ones. This final decision is not purely technical, however, and of more immediate interest is how to judge whether a particular circuit can meet the requirements. The usual criteria for determining performance are:

> speed or propagation delay;
> power supply voltage and current;
> number of equivalent gates contained in the logic;
> input logic levels and loading;
> output logic levels and drive;
> number of inputs and outputs;
> operating temperature range.

Some of these paramenters are interrelated as we have already seen, but nevertheless it is worth discussing all the factors which can affect them in a practical design.

2.4.1.2 How to judge AC performance

Speed and propagation delay, although related, are not necessarily the same thing. Propagation delay is the easier to define in a circuit for it may be found merely by adding together the delays of the various stages through which a signal passcs. However, if a manufacturer is offering a circuit with 5 ns gate delay it does not follow that a signal passing through four stages of gating will suffer a delay of 20 ns. Even if the 5 ns is a maximum figure it will be affected by supply voltage tolerance, junction temperature, internal fan-out, track capacitance, delays in input and output buffers, fan-in and fan-out restraints and the possibility of wire-ORing and series gating techniques. Even if the dependence of propagation delay on these factors is not defined in the data sheet, some guidance on the likely effect of these has been given earlier. Unless the circuits are operating internally at the same logic levels as the external interface, buffering or level translation will be required at both input and output, and this will increase propagation delay. If fan-in of the internal gates is low then 'wide' gating can only be accomplished by increasing the number of gating stages. Similarly high fan-outs can often be achieved only by using extra gating stages as buffers; this is particularly a problem for signals such as clocks and common resets.

Clock speed, as we have noted, is related to propagation delay but great care needs to be taken with the way in which it is defined. It may be possible to design a very fast D-type flip-flop but found to be quite impossible to operate a synchronous counter at the same speed. Also a high frequency square wave may be propagated with severe distortion or even lost altogether if leading and trailing edges are subject to very different delays. It is therefore necessary to question very carefully the meanings of maximum delays and operating frequencies, and establish exactly the conditions under which they apply.

2.4.1.3 Power dissipation under DC conditions

Power supply conditions are usually easier to establish than speed criteria since they are usually given as maximum figures in data sheets for both the internal gates and interface buffers. Some difficulty may arise with macrocell circuits where the supply current for a cell may depend on the exact configuration to which it is designed. Care has to be taken that the supplies required will be available on the printed circuit board where it is proposed to use the circuit. It will clearly add cost if extra supplies have to be provided because the circuit has different supply requirements from the rest of the system. The total supply current may be constrained by the total system design; this may rule out bipolar technology completely or at least limit the choice to one of the low power varieties of bipolar. The other major constraint on the power dissipation is junction temperature. Integrated circuits fabricated in the silicon planar process are not usually specified above 150°C junction temperature in a plastic package or

175°C in a ceramic package. Above these temperatures catastrophic failure will occur very quickly; below them failure rate is still dependent on temperature, for example the failure rate at 150°C is about thirty times the failure rate at 85°C. The amount by which the junction temperature exceeds the ambient temperature is equal to the product of power dissipation and thermal impedance, so it may be cost effective to integrate as much as possible using a sophisticated package or additional heat sinking rather than settle for two or three cheaper but overall less reliable circuits.

2.4.1.4 Power dissipation under AC conditions

One other important factor in determining power dissipation is the charging of internal capacitance during high speed operation. When an internal node is taken from LOW to HIGH, charge flows from the supply to the node capacitance, when it goes LOW again this charge is transferred to the negative side of the supply. This represents a current flow giving rise to a power dissipation, $P = CfV_S (V_H - V_L)$. The magnitude of this at various frequencies and logic swings may be seen in fig. 2.23 and illustrates another reason for choosing a circuit

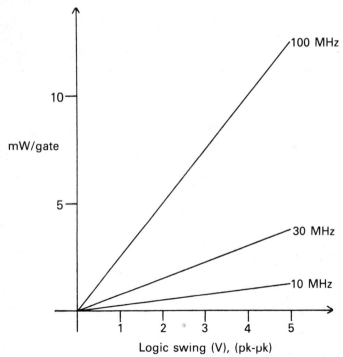

Fig. 2.23 Effect of logic swing on high frequency power dissipation assuming: i) node capacitance = 5 pF; and ii) operating voltage = 5V

with low internal logic swing, since high speed and low logic swing tend to go hand in hand anyway.

2.4.1.5 True gate utilisation

The number of gates which can be integrated in a semi-custom circuit seems at first sight a straightforward parameter which is defined on the data sheet of a gate array or cell array. Here again though there are traps for the unwary since in practice not all gates will be routable, and hand layout tends to be more efficient even though autorouters are quicker and usually cheaper. Layout does, of course, have an impact on speed particularly in low power arrays and if propagation delay is critical it may be beneficial, and even quicker in the long run, to lay out at least part of a circuit by hand. There have been two philosophies adopted in designing semi-custom arrays; one approach is to provide enough routing area on the basic layout to allow close to 100% of the gates or cells to be connected, the second is to pack the cells as closely as possible and deliberately 'waste' cells by using some of the active area for tracking.

The second approach does offer the possibility of keeping interconnections very short in critical areas causing little or no additional delays due to track capacitance, but utilisation may be 80% or less. While utilisation may approach 100% with the first type of design, it is difficult to minimise track lengths for more than a small proportion of the interconnections. Final die size tends to be similar for the two approaches; an 800 gate array with routing channels will be about the same size as a 1000 gate array in the same technology without routing channels, even though it is only possible to use 800 gates.

The situation with cell arrays is slightly different as logic functions are described at a higher level of complexity than single gates. The cells are usually laid down with routing area around them in much the same way as discrete logic packages on a printed circuit board. Gate count is harder to define as the number of gates in a particular cell depends on the function being implemented in that cell, but usually all the cells are capable of being interconnected. Because the internal cell connections are predefined, routing tends to be easier with cell arrays and lends itself more readily to autorouting.

2.4.1.6 I/O considerations

The other factor which can govern the choice of an array is the number of connections which needs to be made to the circuit. Because the design rules for manufacturing integrated circuits define a minimum size for bonding areas and a minimum spacing between bonds, the number of connections will define a minimum perimeter. The aspect ratio of integrated circuits is also controlled by the design rules, so the number of interconnections also defines a minimum area. Thus doubling the requirement for inputs and outputs for a design could lead to a quadrupling in area, so it is probably best to partition systems to minimise the external interconnections rather than the gate count. This gives the added benefit of needing smaller and cheaper packages, reducing the size and complexity of the printed circuit board on which the circuits are mounted and reducing the propagation delays due to external wiring load.

2.4.1.7 Temperature effects

The effect of temperature on device performance is sometimes overlooked, particularly in commercial designs. The reliability of integrated circuits at high temperatures has already been discussed but electrical operating parameters will also be affected at extremes of temperature. The most obvious effects of temperature on transistor parameters are the increase in leakage current and reduction in forward diode voltage as temperature increases, while direct current gain and diffused resistors exhibit a small positive temperature coefficient, the size depending on the process. These factors, plus other basic properties of silicon, have a calculable and measurable effect on propagation delay and logic levels and loading, so it is essential that when a semi-custom circuit is being designed full allowance is made for the extremes of junction temperature which the circuit may experience.

2.4.2 Design example

2.4.2.1 Defining the example

Because there are so many ways of specifying the various parameters of the different semi-custom solutions, the best way to compare them is to design the same circuit in each and compare its performance. A full design of several hundred gates does of course take weeks to complete, but it should be adequate to examine a simple circuit using a mixture of combinational and sequential logic and compare the relevant parameters with a number of approaches. A recent application note shows how a registered programmable logic device may be used as either a counter or shift register in the same application, the actual function being selected with just three inputs,

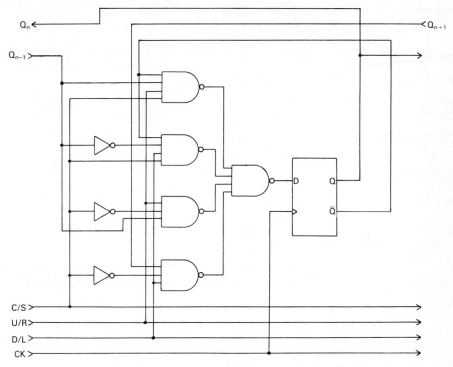

Fig. 2.24 One stage of composite counter/shift register

count/$\overline{\text{shift}}$, up/right and down/left. The device was a 4-bit machine, but a single stage could be implemented with a D-type flip-flop and some gating as shown in fig. 2.24. The logic functions for the D input for each of the four possible modes are:

count up	–	$D_n =$	count.up.$\overline{Q}_n.Q_{n-1}$
count down	–	$D_n =$	count.down.$\overline{Q}_n.\overline{Q_{n-1}}$
shift right	–	$D_n =$	$\overline{\text{shift}}$.up.Q_{n-1}
shift left	–	$D_n =$	$\overline{\text{shift}}$.down.Q_{n+1}

These four functions must be ORed together at the D input; the most convenient way would be to use NAND gates for both stages of gating, although the ECL implementation could be done by ORing the complements of each function and wire-ORing at the D input. The maximum clock frequency may be estimated by making the clock period equal to the total delay plus set up time for the flip-flop, including allowance for fan-out. To compare the programmable solution, power dissipation for four stages plus output buffers has been calculated.

Table 2.5 Comparison of different solutions to the counter/register circuit

	Maximum clock frequency (MHz)	Clock to output delay (ns)
74LS discrete logic	11	40
Programmable logic	20	30
ISL gate array	19	50
LS gate array	25	46
CML/TTL cell array	71	20
CML/ECL cell array	220	5

* Based on estimated gate equivalent of one cell.

2.4.2.2 Comparison of the different approaches

The results of the comparison are summarised in table 2.5, where it can be seen that the integrated gate array and cell array solutions give superior performance as defined by the figure of merit calculated for each. The CML/ECL cell array gives the best result because it is the only solution using an oxide isolated process; it is to be expected that other approaches will equal or better this performance when they are converted to oxide isolation. Another interesting point arising from the comparison is that discrete solutions have a relatively good performance on pure propagation delay because the design of the internal logic is similar for both discrete and integrated logic circuits. The reduction of performance is more noticeable when assessing the maximum operating frequency of the design. In the discrete logic solution the feedback signals have to be taken on to a printed circuit board via an output buffer at each stage causing additional delay; the integrated logic does not suffer from this problem as the feedback signal remains within a single package.

2.4.3 *How to make the choice*

2.4.3.1 Summary of the important parameters

This final section is not intended to be a promotion for a particular manufacturer or technology, but rather a summary of the factors

Maximum power dissipation (mW)	Performance figure of merits (MHz/W)	Array utilisation
195	56	14 packages
500	40	0.5 package
75	253	68 gates
185	135	68 gates
375	190	143 gates*
535	410	133 gates*

which need to be considered before a choice of semi-custom approach is made. The performance criteria have already been defined in section 2.4.1 so I will summarise the salient points.

Speed, or propagation delay, should include intrinsic gate delay, fan-out derating, wiring capacitance derating, delay of input and output buffers, allowance for variation of temperature and supply voltage. Power dissipation should be calculated for maximum supply voltage, should include input and output buffers, an allowance for high frequency operation and in the proposed package should not cause the device to exceed its rated junction temperature in the highest ambient temperature. The size of the array should be sufficient to accept the proposed circuit comfortably. It may be necessary to modify the logic design as simulation proceeds or provide more buffering to reduce fan-out in critical paths. At the layout stage it will be easier to minimise wiring capacitance of critical paths if there is some freedom in placement and routing, indeed in a very 'full' design the last few interconnections may be so tortuous that they suddenly become critical. Another influence on size is number of inputs and outputs and again it is best not to choose an array which has exactly the required number; testing is covered elsewhere, but it is usually advisable to cater for two or three test pins for setting the circuit to a known state and accessing difficult internal nodes. The final point on performance is the interface. It defeats the object of integrating logic systems if they need to be surrounded by level translators or bus drivers in order to interface with others parts of the whole design.

2.4.3.2 Factors influencing cost

The most important factor in choosing a particular approach will probably be the cost. Unfortunately improved performance can usually only be achieved by increasing cost. Process enhancements such as Schottky clamping and oxide isolation normally require extra process steps in wafer fabrication, which increase the cost of the wafer and decrease the yield of good units from each wafer. More basic steps such as reducing geometries may increase the number of units on a wafer, but can usually only be achieved using higher precision equipment or techniques which add to the cost of the wafer; on top of this rejects may be caused by smaller defects than in a large geometry device, so yields will again be lower.

The same is true of the development and design process itself. Sophisticated software can take much of the pain away from designing semi-custom circuits and will normally lead to a better performance both in absolute terms and in terms of providing a component which is identical to the actual requirement. These sophisticated systems do require a high investment in equipment and in human resources and are therefore usually available only at a higher cost than more basic systems. The investment is usually worthwhile, however, in terms of higher confidence in the final result.

2.4.3.3 Why consider bipolar arrays?

This chapter is entitled 'Bipolar and high speed arrays' and has demonstrated that for the highest speed at a given processing level (e.g. oxide isolation, 3μm feature size, etc.) bipolar is the best solution. Also, it has demonstrated that integrated logic will generally give a superior performance to that of a discrete logic equivalent. It should show, in addition, that there is a definite role for bipolar arrays to play even where absolute speed is not the prime requirement, and that this approach should be considered along with any other possibility.

2.5 References

2.1 Ghandi, S.K. (1968) *The Theory and Practice of Microelectronics.* 1st ed. John Wiley: New York.

2.2 Grove, A.S. (1967) *Physics and Technology of Semiconductor Devices*. 1st ed. John Wiley: New York.

2.3 Lau, S.Y. (1979) 'High performance 1200 gate ISL array.' *WESCON Professional Program Session 13*.

2.4 Lohstroh, J. (1979) 'ISL, a fast and dense low-power logic, made in a standard Schottky process.' *IEEE J. Solid-State Circuits* **SC-14**, No. 3 pp 585–90.

2.5 Meyer, C.S., Lynn, D.K. and Hamilton, D.J. *eds*. (1968) *Analysis and Design of Integrated Circuits*. 1st ed. McGraw-Hill: New York.

2.6 Noach, K.A.H. (1982) 'New developments in integrated fuse logic.' *Philips E.C.A.* **4**, No. 2.

2.7 O'Neil, W.D. (1979) 'Combined analog/digital LSI design using I²L gate arrays.' *WESCON Professional Program Session 13*.

2.8 Slater, S.P. and Cox, A.M. (1979) 'A bipolar gate array family with a wide application–performance coverage.' *WESCON Professional Program Session 13*.

Date Sheets etc. as listed:
   Texas Instruments – 74 series TTL
   Philips/Signetics – Composite Cell Logic
   Texas Instruments – TAL series Gate Arrays
   Fairchild – FAST Logic Family
   National Semiconductor – MCA/ALS Gate Arrays
   Ferranti Semiconductors – ULA R series
   AMCC – Q700 series Gate Arrays
   Plessey Semiconductors – Microgate E Family
   Philips/Signetics – 10K/100K ECL
   Motorola – MCA/ECL Gate Arrays
   NEC – uPB 61/63 series Gate Arrays
   Philips/Signetics – ACE Family
   Philips/Signetics – 8A1200 Gate Array
   Texas Instruments – TAT series Gate Arrays
   Monolithic Memories – PAL Handbook
   Philips/Signetics – IFL Handbook

Chapter 3

MOS and CMOS Arrays

BILL ALEXANDER

National Semiconductor (UK) Ltd

3.1 MOS technology overview

3.1.1 P-channel process

As integrated circuit (IC) technology evolved from small-scale integration (SSI) and medium-scale integration (MSI) to large-scale integration (LSI), there was a need for a process that was simpler and gave a higher yield than the original bipolar processes. A process that did lower the manufacturing costs for digital LSI products was the P-channel metal oxide semiconductor (PMOS) process. This was the first in a long series of metal oxide semiconductor (MOS) processes and was used for the early LSI digital products including memories, microprocessors and the original calculator chips.

PMOS involved fewer processing steps than were needed to fabricate bipolar ICs. It required only five masks. Just a single boron diffusion was needed to create the P^+ sources and drains of the MOS transistor. The first mask defined these P^+ regions in the lightly doped N-type substrate wafer. A second mask defined the transistor gate areas and diffusion contact areas prior to the growth of the thin gate oxide. The third mask was used to reopen the contact holes prior to metallisation and the fourth mask defined the gate electrodes and metal interconnects. The fifth mask was for the contact holes to the bond pads through the protective vapox layer.

Figure 3.1 shows the PMOS transistor. The metal gate was purposely extended over the source and drain regions to ensure that the channel would be electrically active even with maximum allowable manufacturing tolerances on mask misalignment. These overlaps of the metal gates and the diffusions increased the input capacitance and slowed down the circuit response times because of

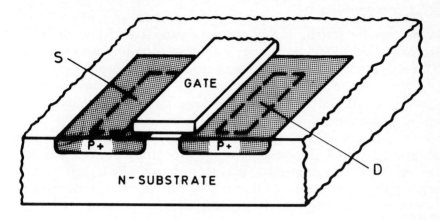

Fig. 3.1 PMOS cross-section

the Miller Effect. The metal gate was electrically insulated from the substrate by a silicon-dioxide layer about 1000 to 1500 Å thick.

There were two general categories of P-channel metal-gate processes. These were high-threshold and low-threshold voltage processes which defined the voltage, V_t, required to turn on a transistor. The high V_t was typically -3 to -5 V and the low V_t, -1.5 to -2.5V.

Originally, the difference in threshold voltages was achieved by using substrate wafers of different crystalline orientation. The high V_t process used <111> silicon, and the low V_t process used <100> silicon. The main advantage of the low V_t process was the ability to interface the device with transistor-transistor logic (TTL) bipolar circuitry. However, the use of <100> silicon carried with it a distinct disadvantage. Just as the surface layer under the gates could be inverted to cause conduction between the source and drain at a low V_t, so it could be inverted at other locations through thick oxide layers by the larger voltages that may appear in the metal interconnections between circuit components. These parasitic transistors are undesirable as they interfere with circuit operation. This field-oxide threshold voltage, V_{tf}, generally limits the overall operating voltage. It was about -17 V for the low V_t process and -28 V for the high V_t process.

The lower operating voltage also produced circuits with lower operating speed but made interfacing with other circuits easier. It consumed less power which was an advantage for battery operated circuits and clocked circuits but it had a low noise-immunity.

3.1.2 Ion implantation

A process for forcing highly energetic doping ions into the silicon lattice, called ion-implantation, was developed in the early 1970's. This was used with the same geometrical structure and materials as the high V_t PMOS process. Boron ions were implanted into the substrate in the area under the gate electrode – the channel. By changing the doping concentration of the substrate under the gate, it was possible to lower the threshold voltage of the transistor without influencing any of the other substrate properties. All other areas of the substrate were protected from the ion beam by a thick oxide or other masking materials so that the N-type ion concentration of the substrate was unaffected, maintaining a high V_{tf}.

If the channel area was exposed to the ion beam for long enough, the N-type substrate in that area could be overcompensated and turned into P-type silicon. This technique was used for making depletion-mode devices. Depletion-mode transistors have a conduction channel between source and drain with no bias voltage on the gate electrode. The most commonly used MOS transistors which have no conduction channel for zero gate-source voltage and require a bias voltage V_t to turn on the channel are called enhancement-mode transistors. In any circuit, some transistors can be enhancement mode while others are depletion mode. The availability of both types of transistors in the same process is extremely useful for circuit design.

Ion implantation certainly increases the number of processing steps involved and so the cost of the process also increases. However, its usefulness in controlling doping concentrations and doping profiles makes it a technique that is used extensively in modern semiconductor processes.

3.1.3 The silicon gate breakthrough

Another major innovation in MOS processing was the use of a polysilicon layer to form the gate of the transistors. The technique is to deposit a thin layer of polysilicon (now simply called poly) to form the gate electrodes. This poly gate is used as the diffusion mask, defining the edges of the source and drain and hence the channel length of the transistor. This is known as a self-aligning technique and greatly reduces the overlap of the gate with the source and drain diffusions down to the amount of lateral diffusion of the source and drain dopant. Figure 3.2 shows the polysilicon gate PMOS transistor.

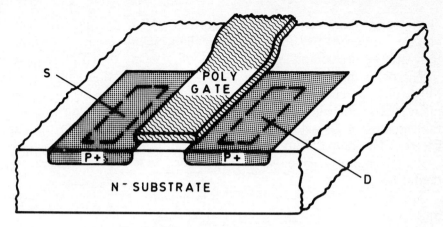

Fig. 3.2 Silicon-gate PMOS cross-section

The smaller overlap significantly reduces the Miller capacitance of the transistors, improving the operational speed and power consumption of the circuits.

The poly gate is heavily doped so that it can be used as a buried layer of interconnections in addition to the normal aluminium interconnections on the surface of the chip. This gives the circuit designer more latitude in layout and allows a reduction in the total size of a chip.

Polysilicon as a material has a different work function to that of metal. So when it is used as a gate and interconnections, changes in other parts of the process such as gate oxide thickness and doping concentrations have to be made to maintain a useful V_t and V_{tf} for interfacing to other electronic circuits.

3.1.4 N-channel process

Historically, the N-channel process and its advantages were well known at the time when the first P-channel devices were being manufactured. N-channel devices were, however, much more difficult to manufacture than P-channel devices. It took improvements in the control of contamination and surface states when growing gate oxides to make N-channel circuits practical.

The N-channel process became workable only after the P-channel process, ion-implantation and silicon-gate techniques were already well developed. Conduction in the N-channel MOS transistor is by electrons, which have a mobility three times greater than holes which are the current carriers in a P-channel MOS transistor. In addition, the increased mobility allows more current flow in a channel of any given size so that N-channel transistors can be made smaller, for a given gain, than can P-channel devices. Also, the positive gate voltage required to turn on an enhancement mode N-channel transistor allows completely compatible interfacing with TTL circuits.

The N-channel process went into volume production with the 4K (4096 bit) Dynamic Random Access Memory (DRAM) and 8-bit microprocessors, both of which required speeds and packing densities that could not be achieved with PMOS. The combination of high speed, TTL compatibility, low power requirements and compactness of design rapidly made NMOS the most widely used process for digital LSI.

The most widely available NMOS technology using depletion-mode pull-ups and a polysilicon gate is a six mask process. To separate one active transistor from another, a thick field-oxide is used. This field oxide is grown into the surface of the silicon wafer to isolate one active region from another. It allows a higher packing density than the guard-ring diffusion techniques employed in earlier processes.

Double- and even triple-level polysilicon NMOS processes have been developed but of course, these use more masking levels. The greater complexity of the process is warranted in that the products will occupy a smaller chip area, increasing yields to levels that more than pay for the increase in wafer process costs.

Mask making improvements and tighter process controls have allowed scaling of the device sizes to smaller dimensions. The semiconductor industry has moved from features measured in thousandths of an inch (mils) to microns (10^{-6} m). Sophisticated N-channel silicon gate processes routinely run in production with feature sizes of 3 microns.

Very Large Scale Integrated (VLSI) circuits have appeared using scaled NMOS processes such as XMOS. These large, very dense VLSI chips often have power density problems and the dissipation of the heat generated in the circuit has become a limit to VLSI circuits in NMOS technology.

3.1.5 Complementary MOS process

The basic complementary metal oxide semiconductor (CMOS) circuit is an inverter which consists of two enhancement-mode transistors; one an N-channel and the other a P-channel device. Both transistor types are fabricated on the same base substrate which can be either N- or P- type.

The 4000 series CMOS family is fabricated on an N-type substrate wafer, into which a P 'tub' is diffused to form the well in which the N- channel transistor is built. Metal gates are used and all other steps to fabricate the circuits are much the same as for the other MOS processes. These circuits can be operated from a single supply voltage which can vary from 3 to 18 V, the higher voltage giving more speed and higher noise-immunity.

The main advantage of CMOS is its extremely low power consumption. Any DC power consumption is only the leakage current of reverse-biased PN junctions. AC power is consumed in the charging and discharging of circuit capacitances and during the short time intervals the input voltage passes between logic switching levels, shorting the power supply. Low threshold voltage CMOS processes have been specifically developed to operate from small batteries such as in watches or credit card-sized calculators.

Silicon gate CMOS is high speed, approaching the speeds of bipolar TTL circuits. However, the use of two transistors in every function with associated wells and guard rings makes CMOS slightly more complex and expensive than NMOS requiring a larger chip size for an equivalent circuit. But, with process improvements and tighter design rules many CMOS LSI/VLSI circuits including microprocessors and memories are now being manufactured.

The lower power-consumption benefit makes CMOS the first choice for VLSI products. CMOS memories, for instance, only draw current when their inputs and outputs switch. So, 16K NMOS RAMs can be replaced by 32K or 64K CMOS RAMs with no significant increase in power consumption!

With smaller geometries the cost penalties for CMOS fabrication over NMOS have significantly reduced. To some extent this has come about by a small reduction in the complexity of CMOS processing and numbers of masks required. More significantly, the complexity of advanced NMOS processes has increased to the level where the differences between CMOS and NMOS costs are more easily offset by the advantages of lower power consumption.

Processes with multiple conducting layers have now been developed which have allowed the integration of sophisticated analogue functions such as switched-capacitor filters along with digital circuitry.

A process that is capable of performing both linear and digital functions on the same chip is the double-level polysilicon CMOS (P^2CMOS) process shown in fig. 3.3. This is a silicon gate process which uses a second poly layer to form capacitors and both poly layers can be used for interconnections. All junctions are formed by

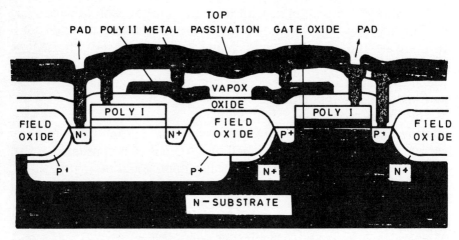

Fig. 3.3 P²CMOS cross-section

ion-implantation. Projection printing of the images on the wafers and dry etching techniques are used to obtain 3.5 micron feature sizes. Short channel lengths and gate oxide thicknesses of 600 Å provide high transconductance in the transistors. Low stray capacitances using field-oxide isolation and tighter design rules allow high speed performance while retaining the advantages of standard CMOS.

The polysilicon layers used in P²CMOS have a sheet resistivity of about 30 ohms/square even though heavily doped. This can be lowered by the addition of special metals, to form a polysilicide, to about 2 ohms/square. For very large chips, the interconnect resistance is high enough to cause excessive propagation delays in high speed digital circuits. This limitation has been overcome by a two-layer metal process, M²CMOS. The sheet resistivity of the metal interconnect is 0.03 ohms/square, 1000 times less than the doped polysilicon layer. This double-level metal CMOS process also uses an N-well to form P-channel transistors. The starting wafer is P-type, making the process compatible with the XMOS process which is used extensively in the production of very high volume components. All the processing experience gained from the XMOS process can thus be directly transferred to this new M²CMOS process.

The operational voltage limit on such scaled modern processes is approximately 6 V and is due to punch-through of the transistors rather than the V_{tf} of the technology. The circuits work very reliably at 5 V which makes TTL interfacing extremely easy. This M²CMOS technology also matches LSTTL in speed performance with a 5 V supply. With further scaling to smaller dimensions, Schottky TTL speeds will be achieved.

3.1.6 Comparison of metal-gate and silicon-gate CMOS

MOS transistors offer advantages over bipolar devices of higher input impedance, lower power consumption, greater circuit simplicity and higher packing density. However, there is one disadvantage which is a slower circuit speed than is achievable with bipolar transistors.

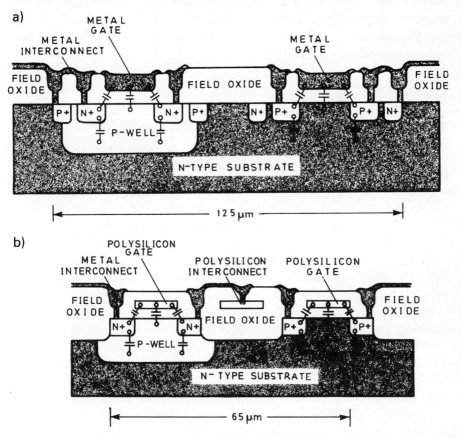

Fig. 3.4 a) Metal-gate CMOS cross-section; b) silicon-gate CMOS cross-section

Some of the modern processing techniques that have reduced this disadvantage are shown in diagrams (a) and (b) in fig. 3.4. The metal-gate CMOS process uses diffusion layers and metal as conducting levels. The polysilicon process can use the poly level as well, increasing design flexibility. The striking factor is, however, the reduction in linear dimensions for the inverter structures shown when going from the old metal-gate technology to modern silicon-gate technology. Since the linear dimensions are halved, the chip area could in theory be reduced by 75% to a quarter of the original size.

Requirements for bond pads and scribe channels, among other factors, limit the overall reduction achievable.

The field-oxide isolation performs the channel stop in the polysilicon process and reduces the parasitic capacitances by a factor of two. Also, since the gate is self-aligned to the source and drain, a shorter gate length, thinner oxide and lower threshold voltage are all used to increase the transistor gain by a factor of four. A full comparison of all the parasitic capacitances associated with this inverter structure is given in fig. 3.5.

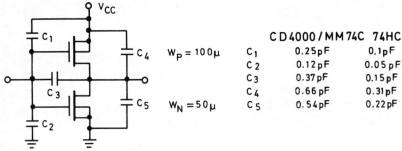

	CD4000/MM74C	74HC
C_1	0.25pF	0.1pF
C_2	0.12pF	0.05pF
C_3	0.37pF	0.15pF
C_4	0.66pF	0.31pF
C_5	0.54pF	0.22pF

Fig. 3.5 Parasitic capacitance comparison

The polysilicon-gate 74HC process is an order of magnitude faster than the metal-gate CD4000/MM74C process when interconnection capacitances are accounted for in LSI designs.

Although the same transistor structures are used to build up a logic function in CMOS, the polysilicon-gate process is far simpler to layout in chip designs. Three conducting mediums can be used, although polysilicon can only be used as an interconnect over field oxide and not over diffusion layers. Contact cuts are made to allow the metal to connect to both the polysilicon and diffusion layers.

Figure 3.6 shows a possible two-input NAND gate construction in metal-gate CMOS. Only the most important geometrical mask levels are shown to convey an understanding of the electrical connectivity. Power is brought into this array of four transistors by a heavily doped diffusion layer that forms the guard bands, and contacts to the power supplies can be accessed between the two types of transistors from both ends as shown. If an N-type wafer is used, the N-channel transistors sit in a P-well which is not shown. The P^+ V_{ss} contact acts as the bias to the P-well and as the access point for the negative rail to bias the N-channel devices.

The P-channel devices will be biased by the V_{dd} contact that is brought in on an N^+ diffusion, connected to the power supply at a point nearby. The diffusions to form the transistors need a specific

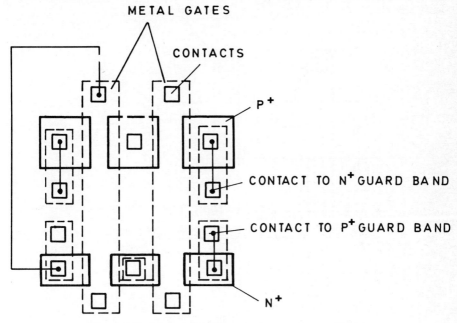

METAL GATES

CONTACTS

P^+

CONTACT TO N^+ GUARD BAND

CONTACT TO P^+ GUARD BAND

N^+

Fig. 3.6 Two-input NAND gate in metal-gate CMOS

mask for the source and drain and this four transistor array has a central common node. For the two-input NAND gate, the central N^+ diffusion acts as the source of one transistor and the drain of the other hence forming a serial connection of two N-channel transistors. The central P^+ diffusion acts as the common drain of both of the P-channel transistors, resulting in two parallel P-channel devices.

Figure 3.7 shows the major geometric mask levels for a two-input NAND gate using a silicon-gate technology. Although there is no necessity for guard bands, it is assumed that power is brought into the cell through diffusion layers to maintain similarity with the metal gate example. The silicon gates are common between the P- and N-channel transistors and only two separate shapes are required to differentiate the N- and P-type diffusion masks as it is a self-aligned process. Metal is used to power up the appropriate transistors and the connection that forms the output of the NAND gate can be made internally as the metal can cross polysilicon layers. This keeps the design compact and contained, allowing access to all gates and all diffusion layers.

3.1.7 Latch-up

The fundamental configuration used for circuit designs in CMOS

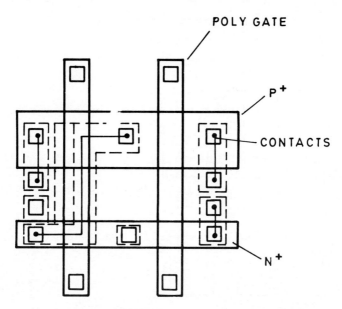

Fig. 3.7 Two-input NAND gate in silicon-gate CMOS

integrated circuits gives rise to parasitic four-layer PNPN structures
that can potentially switch on and destroy a device by a phenomenon
known as latch-up. This four-layer structure is effectively a silicon-
controlled rectifier (SCR) or thyristor which can be represented by
two bipolar transistors; an NPN and a PNP connected so that the
collector of each transistor is directly coupled to the base of the
other, which provides a positive feedback loop.

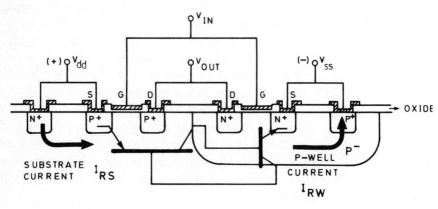

Fig. 3.8 Latch-up thyristor in CMOS inverter

Figure 3.8 shows such a complementary transistor feedback pair superimposed on a CMOS cross-section. A small change in base current of the NPN transistor causes a larger change in its collector current which is the base current of the PNP transistor. The collector current of the PNP transistor also contributes to the base current of the NPN transistor. So, an initial small change in the base current, becomes amplified into a large change because of the positive feedback.

For latch-up to occur three conditions must be satisfied. First, both parasitic bipolar transistors must be biased into the active state by forward-biasing their emitter-base junctions so that appreciable minority-carrier injection occurs. Secondly, the product of the parasitic bipolar transistor current gains (βNPN $\times$ βPNP) must be sufficient to allow regeneration. And thirdly, the power supplies or networks connected to the external terminals participating in latch-up must be capable of sourcing or sinking a current greater than the holding current associated with the PNPN path.

Any mechanism that increases the current gain product to greater than unity will cause latch-up to occur. Leakage currents in a silicon PN junction double for every 8°C rise in temperature so that latch-up can occur due to leakage currents at high junction temperatures. It is, however, relatively easy to design structures to prevent latch-up at high temperatures but it is more difficult to prevent it from occurring because of the voltage across the four-layer diode, the rate of voltage change and in the presence of ionising radiation.

The greatest of care has to be taken in the design and layout of peripheral I/O circuitry to prevent latch-up. Here the input protection circuitry is laid out in close proximity to large output driver transistors which have wide metal tracks to ensure good sink and source capability. It is at this chip interface that there is every possibility that voltages well outside the power supply range can occur due to other circuits and ringing outputs. The two main factors are voltage transients, more positive than V_{dd} and more negative than V_{ss}, and sustained overvoltage stress which exceeds the avalanche breakdown of the P-well to N-substrate junction. A combination of thoughtful layout and optimised processing techniques have resulted in extremely robust circuitry that is almost latch-up proof in modern CMOS processes.

Systems engineers should always ensure that all inputs are at good logic levels and that they lag behind the establishment of the power supply to the chip. They should limit all voltage excursions on any inputs to be within the specification for the technology and ensure balanced, matched impedance lines on all outputs to prevent ringing and oscillations. Finally, the environment of the device is also important. Exposure to radiation such as X-rays or gamma-rays can cause photocurrents which generate electron-hole pairs that will initiate latch-up if the radiation lasts longer than the minority-carrier lifetime and is intense enough to cause a current large enough to trigger the thrysistor. Processing techniques such as gold doping can be used to shorten minority-carrier lifetimes and make CMOS processes very radiation hard but they are not normally used since they result in degradation of other circuit parameters.

3.1.8 Linear functions in CMOS

MOS processes have been used to achieve analog and linear functions but the CMOS process is the closest to the familiar bipolar processes used by linear IC designers. We have seen that besides the complementary P- and N-transistors, there are NPN and PNP parasitic and diodes, specifically Zener diodes, in the CMOS process.

Any basic CMOS inverter can be biased into a linear operation mode with a feedback resistor. The inverter is biased for operation about the midpoint in the linear segment on the steep transition of the voltage transfer curve. The shape of this voltage transfer curve is relatively constant with temperature and a useful gain can be achieved at a frequency of 10 MHz at a high enough supply voltage.

Cascading inverters can produce a much higher open-loop gain which results in a more accurate closed-loop gain. The basic inverter combined with discrete resistors and capacitors can be used to build a number of different oscillators and even an integrator. Other CMOS gates, such as NANDs and NORs can be parallelled to produce high-output drive currents, and one-shot monostables are commonly used in systems.

For a P-well CMOS process, the NPN parasitic bipolar transistor has a high gain and large currents. This transistor is restricted to emitter-follower applications since the collector is tied directly to the positive supply voltage, V_{dd}. The low output impedance of this emitter-follower is often used as a bias voltage reference within an MOS operational amplifier and has been used in NMOS and CMOS processes. The forward voltage drops across these base-emitter junctions are useful voltage references and even bandgap voltage references such as those commonly used in bipolar lincar circuits are possible.

In addition to the above, the component that makes CMOS the

best choice among MOS for implementing linear functions is the excellent analog switch or transmission gate achievable. The challenge in linear IC design is to find new ways of using these switches to build linear circuits.

The same high-performance transmission gates are used in the design of digital-to-analog converters (DACs) and even analog-to-digital converters are being fabricated in CMOS using op amps, DACs and reference voltages on chip.

Switched capacitor filters use the P^2CMOS technology to build capacitors and analog switches, and CMOS operational amplifiers to construct active filters using a sampled data approach. Centre frequency, bandwidth and roll-off are a function of capacitance ratios and the stability of the clock supplied to the device. The characteristic can be varied with the clock frequency. Predictability and repeatability of a filter characteristic are key advantages offered by this technique.

3.1.9 Future MOS technology

MOS technologies have significantly contributed to the wider use of electronic devices in general. They have given rise to a host of portable consumer electronic products – a boom industry – and have altered the way we think, work and live, by placing very cheap electronic equipment at our disposal.

These same technologies are enhancing the capabilities and speeds of response of established systems, and at the same time lowering the prices of products. To achieve the increases in chip complexity and performance and simultaneously reduce per function costs, continuous improvements have to be made in production equipment, methods and control. New tools are continuously needed to enable the design of increasingly sophisticated devices.

Our theoretical understanding of the processes, material science and device physics shows that we are now just over an order of magnitude away from what can ultimately be achieved with MOS technology. The improvements due to scaling to smaller dimensions have made MOS technologies more closely compatible in speeds to bipolar technologies, except emitter-coupled logic (ECL). This compatibility has been reached with lower current densities; another limiting factor in VLSI product design. It is the author's belief that CMOS will become the standard industrial process as it inherently incorporates high speed NMOS devices and some very useful parasitic bipolar structures which will make it generally applicable to whole system solutions.

Silicon-on-Sapphire (SOS) CMOS was hailed as the VLSI technology of the future in the early 70s but the science of growing a well structured silicon epitaxial layer on the costly sapphire substrate has never reached a level where the advantages compete with bulk CMOS in any but military applications. SOS has no parasitic bipolar structures and so is primarily applicable to digital LSI systems. It is of course, latch-up proof in a high radiation environment which makes it highly suitable for use in military and space roles.

The debate on the VLSI technology of the future will continue and it is a dangerous subject on which to speculate as the discoveries and innovations in the semiconductor industry are rapid and revolutionary.

M^{2}CMOS was developed in 1981 using a drawn 3 micron gate length and was to be used specifically for custom and semi-custom designs. Natural extensions of this process will be more metal layers which will give much greater flexibility of interconnections for design. An M^{3}CMOS process will be available in 1984. Research is already under way to scale the drawn gate lengths to 1.25 micron and so reap the advantages of four- to six-times the packing density and improved speed performance. The performance will improve despite a drop in operating voltage to about 3 V necessitated by the physics of such small geometry transistors but the use of such devices in general systems will become more problematical due to interfacing difficulties.

CMOS implemented in a unipolar well are being superseded by a twin-well technology as the characteristics for each device type can be separately adjusted. However, the same advantages can be achieved by using an epitaxial layer on a high resistivity substrate and optimising each device separately in that layer. The use of epitaxial layers on highly doped base substrates also reduces sensitivity to radiation, particularly alpha particles and this is important not only in DRAMs but also in low power, dynamic logic circuitry.

Alternative isolation methods using silicon dioxide such as the utilisation of laser-annealed silicon films on oxidised silicon wafers potentially give the advantages of silicon-on-sapphire without the expensive substrate.

Present bulk CMOS processes are becoming very similar to bipolar structures and the combination of CMOS and bipolar on a single chip offers the potential for single-chip digital and linear functions to be achieved in a remarkably cost effective manner.

3.2 Internal array cells

In order to understand the design and construction of a CMOS gate array we will consider first the details of the internal array cells in this section. Then section 3.3 will examine the peripheral or input/output cells and section 3.4 of this chapter will look at the overall array.

3.2.1 Requirements of the basic cell in a gate array

A cell consists of a number of discrete components with which one can build a set of useful functions in a particular technology. These components enable the functions to be built up to give the best compromise in terms of performance. The basic design will support the use of a number of cells to form a more complex function. A cell includes the active and passive components necessary to build any of the required functions with the greatest flexibility in program-mability.

The layout of these discrete components to give the greatest flexibility is of utmost importance. It will usually be designed symmetrically so that it is easily repeated and mirrored to form a matrix for the size of array required. The layout must ensure that the interconnections to form all required functions are possible. The connections between cells must be designed so that the functional characteristics are optimised and it must be possible to pass unrelated routes through individual cells programmed to particular functions in order to optimise connectivity of the overall array. The cell must be:

* Programmable (intraconnectable)
* Interconnectable
* Permeable
* Repeatable

Cells are generally designed on an open plan basis so that the routing for interconnection of the cells has the maximum flexibility. This becomes the biggest problem once the problem of forming useful functions has been solved.

Today, computers are used to handle this complex intercon-nectivity problem. Hence the cell must be designed such that its characteristics are easily described to the computer so that it can effectively verify the total function that the designer is trying to build. This aspect imposes a further constraint on the design of the cell and its relationship to other cells in terms of the algorithms that are available to solve the problem of obtaining physical routes for all necessary connections in a given design. Cells designed for automatic placement and routing can generally be identified by the simplicity of the routing for interconnections.

3.2.2 Conducting layers

In the technology section we saw that MOS processing falls into two broad categories: metal-gate and silicon-gate. It has also been seen that silicon-gate technology has many advantages over that of metal-gate, one of these being the availability of an extra conductive layer besides the diffusion layers and the metal.

The large gate arrays that are currently available are limited in performance by long interconnections. To keep performance up, silicon-gate processes are the most widely used. The higher packing density allowed by silicon-gate processing has enabled the larger gate arrays to be realised.

The three layers that can be used for interconnections are the diffusion layers the polysilicon layer, and the metal layer. The diffusion layer has a resistance of about 10 ohms/square. The polysilicon layer is variable but has a resistance approximately three times higher, 30 ohms/square. The metal layer has a considerably lower resistivity at about 30 milliohms/square.

All three layers can be used to conduct signals and power but care has to be exercised in design. If polysilicon crosses a diffusion layer, it will form a transistor. Metal can pass over polysilicon and diffusion layers and will only make contact to either if a contact via is cut. Connection between polysilicon and diffusion layers can only be made by metal. So metal is the most versatile of the three layers and is used as much as possible for the interconnections on the chip as it has the least resistance. In particular, metal must be used for the power bussing to avoid the problems associated with resistance in power leads, coupled noise for example.

3.2.3 Specific cell designs

A consideration of layout design rules for MOS processes reveals that, for gate arrays, it is the contacts to the discrete components of a cell that limit the overall size of the cell. The minimum size of the contact via is usually the limiting dimension for that particular process. Due to alignment tolerances, the metal that covers this contact cut must be large enough to overlap the via on all sides.

Contacts are necessary to each discrete component and they are usually placed on a grid arrangement that defines the centre lines of the interconnect tracking. This grid is usually coarser than the minimum that the design rules for the process would allow.

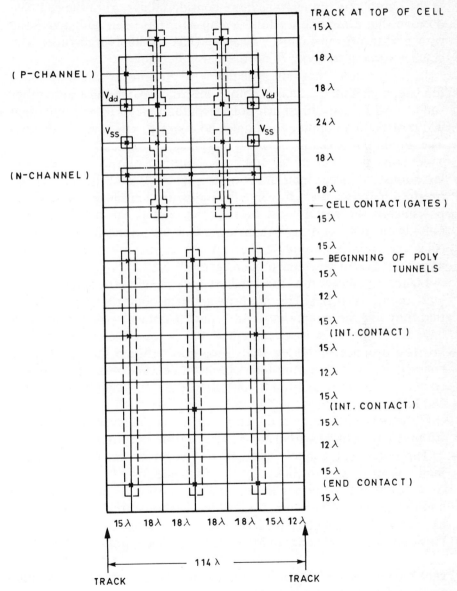

Fig. 3.9 Simple cell showing grid and contact limitation

Let us examine a rather simple cell to understand how this arises. Figure 3.9 shows a four transistor cell where power is brought into the cell by diffusion layers. Contacts need to be made to the diffusion layers for the power, sources, drains and gates of the transistors, and to the polysilicon tunnels which are considered as part of the cell. We observe that a minimum width N-transistor has been designed along with a P-transistor that is twice as wide as the N-transistor. The contact spacing for both is nevertheless the same.

If we assume that all spacings are an integer multiple of a fundamental unit, λ, then we note that the layout rules are rather simple. All layers, diffusions, polysilicon and metal have a minimum width of 6λ. The minimum contact hole size to any layer is also 6λ. The minimum spacing between polysilicon conductors and metal conductors is 6λ. If metal contacts a diffusion layer, the diffusion layer must be larger than the contact hole by 3λ and the metal must overlap the contact via by 3λ on all sides. If metal makes contact to polysilicon, the metal must overlap the contact via by 3λ and the polysilicon must be larger than the metal by 3λ on all sides. These rules are enough to analyse the cell layout but note that any other important layout rules have been ignored.

Figure 3.9 shows that the smallest area of allowed metal to form any contact is $144\lambda^2$. The majority of such contacts are spaced so that they are the minimum of 18λ apart. Contacts would in practice have to be capped with metal and so this is the closest that they can be. The distance of 24λ on the wiring grid between the V_{dd} and V_{ss} contacts is due to the rule for polysilicon overlap of metal around a contact and the minimum distance that unrelated polysilicon conductors can approach. The only points at which a minimum 12λ spacing between metal conductor centres is achieved is on tracks without any contacts, used for general wiring purposes.

The polysilicon tunnels, used for crossover of signals, have been made as wide as 18λ to keep the resistance low. In this case, the capacitance will be larger than if the tunnel was of minimum width and this is yet another compromise that has to be made in the design of such a cell. Enough space is allowed for a vertical metal conductor between the polysilicon tunnels. Having three contacts per polysilicon tunnel is considered to be the optimum for this cell. The centre contacts are staggered on adjacent conductors to maintain the greatest flexibility of wiring for the cell.

An example of wiring this four transistor cell to form a two-input NAND gate has already been discussed in section 3.1.6. Another useful function that can be demonstrated is a pair of transmission

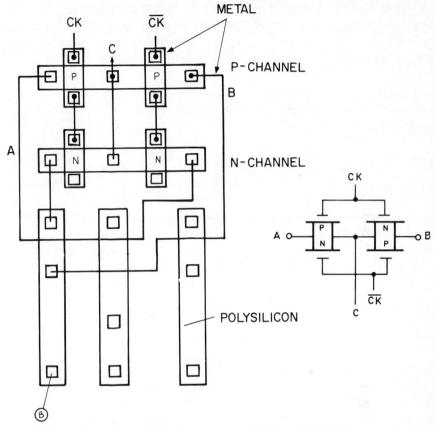

Fig. 3.10 Wiring for a pair of transmission gates

gates as used in the design of a D-type flip-flop. This multiplexer configuration is used as an AND-OR selector and it saves transistors, space, power and time. Figure 3.10 shows the wiring configuration and demonstrates the use of a polysilicon underpass in the cell to form the function.

This particular four transistor cell is probably more complicated than it in fact needs to be. In the majority of cases, the gates for the P- and N-channel transistors are connected vertically. So, the four central polysilicon contacts could be removed and the gates joined by continuous polysilicon conductors. This would reduce the cell size a little but the design rules for the distances between diffusions would have to be observed.

A more significant alteration to the cell would be to join two gates as shown in fig. 3.11 with a 'dog leg' connection. This construction makes the formation of transmission gate pairs easier so that the polysilicon tunnels do not have to be used. The programming for a two-input NAND function is as easy as in the previous layout. The necessary wiring for both functions is shown in fig. 3.12.

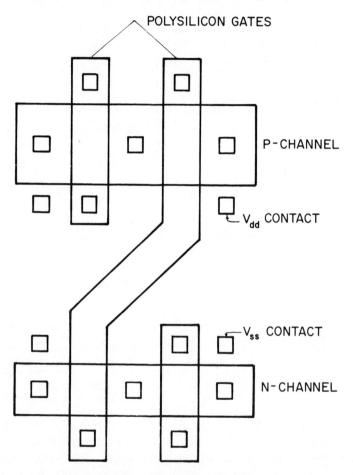

Fig. 3.11 A variation of the four transistor cell

The cell that has been described is made up of a minimum sized N-transistor and a P-transistor that is twice as wide. This gives approximately equal rise and fall times for an inverter structure but unequal transition times for any other gates. This is a feature of any gate array where the gates are constructed from discrete transistors of a particular size. The minimum sized transistors could only be used for small gate arrays of a few hundred gates as the driving capability is not very large and the performance will drop with long interconnections. Further degradation in performance also results from the use of polysilicon tunnels since they have a much larger resistance and capacitance. There is also a contact resistance of

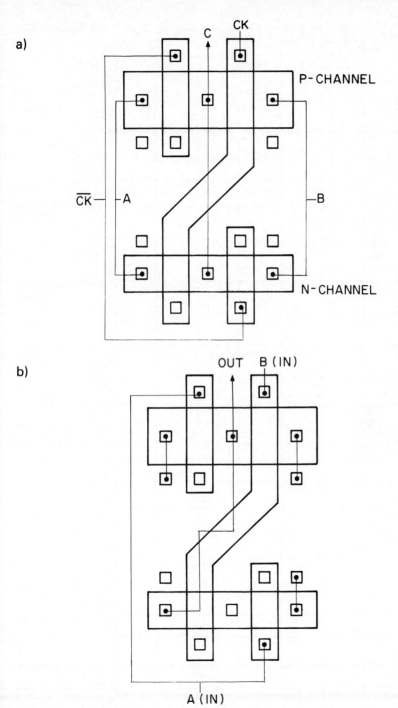

Fig. 3.12 Wiring for: a) transmission gate pair; b) two-input NAND gate

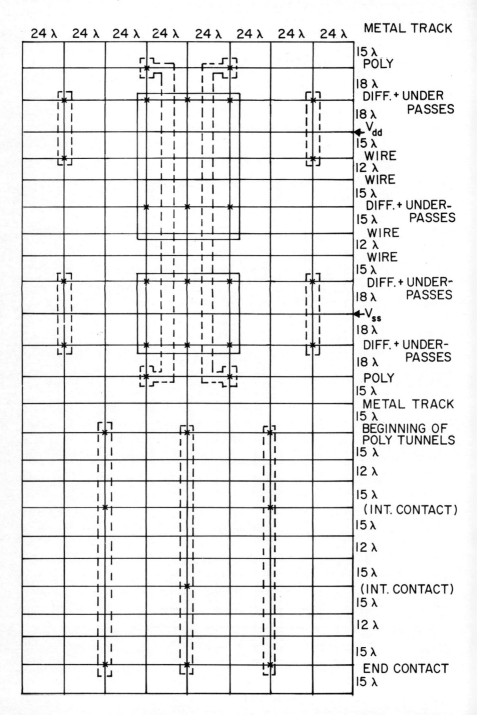

Fig. 3.13 Grid for cell with metal power rails (polysilicon tunnels not shown)

several hundred ohms between the metal and the polysilicon through a minimum sized contact via hole.

So, cell designs with larger sized transistors do have to be used for larger arrays and for higher performance arrays. Distributing the power down to the cells through metal conductors instead of diffusions results in faster transition times for higher performance arrays but does, of course, limit flexibility of wiring quite severely.

When power is brought into the cell on a metal conductor, contacts to the sources and drains need to be available on either side of the power bus. This immediately implies the use of a wider diffusion. A reasonably flexible and workable cell is shown in fig. 3.13. The power is distributed on 9 λ wide tracks and wiring allowances have been made between the V_{dd} and V_{ss} lines so that the interconneciton of the diffusions can be made to form various functions. Figure 3.14 shows how the cell is programmed to a transmission gate and a two-input NOR gate, which is the complement of a two-input NAND gate. Again, a 2:1 ratio of P-width to N-width has been used; this should be adequate for a number of CMOS processes.

So far, a four-transistor CMOS cell has been described to illustrate some important principles. The variations are numerous even for such a cell and it is quite common to have six or more transistor cells to form the basic element of the central portion of a gate array. Sometimes a six-transistor cell and a four-transistor cell will make up the repetitive basic elements. Figure 3.15 shows the layout of a cell with eight discrete transistors, four common gates and two diffusions which are common transistor pair contacts. The layout also shows the underpasses included in the cell and how power is brought in through diffusions. This particular layout is very efficient and a D-type flip-flop with reset, using transmission gate pairs is shown implemented on three adjacent cells in fig. 3.16. Twenty-two of the available twenty-four transistors are used for the function.

All of the cells described are for single layer metal technologies using polysilicon tunnels for wiring flexibility and permeability. With double-layer metal technologies, the polysilicon underpasses can be eliminated and this is desirable from a performance viewpoint.

It is implied in all the cell designs that the active transistor regions have been separated from each other by field oxide isolation. In MOS technologies, there is another way to isolate one active area from another and that is to use gate isolation. This means that an inactive gate of a transistor can be used to isolate active diffusion regions. This technique has given a greater freedom of cell design as layouts do not have to be predetermined to be eight, six, four

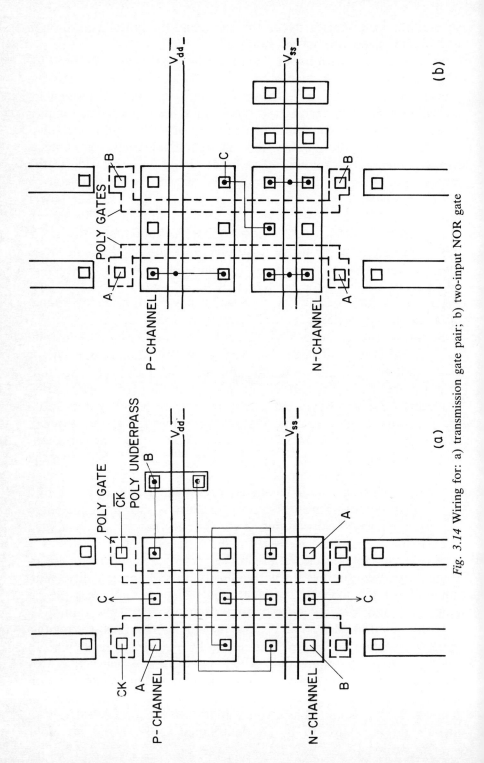

Fig. 3.14 Wiring for: a) transmission gate pair; b) two-input NOR gate

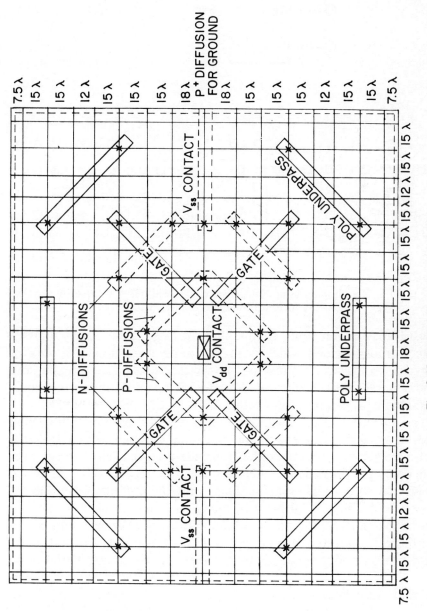

Fig. 3.15 Racal cell layout and grid.
(Courtesy of Racal Microelectronics Systems Ltd)

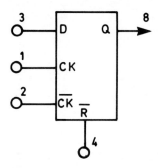

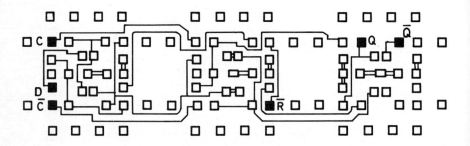

Fig. 3.16 D-type flip-flop using transmission gates with reset in three Racal cells. (Courtesy of Racal Microelectronics Systems Ltd)

transistors, or even some combination of these. Figure 3.17 shows a sixteen-transistor cell which is in fact a small portion of a vertical strip of transistors. This is, however, considered to be the fundamental basic cell unit for describing utilisation and logic functions in a double-layer metal, 3 μm M²CMOS technology.

This proprietary cell has a number of unique features. Only three pairs of transistors have common gates and one pair does a 'dog leg' that makes some structures like transmission gates easier to achieve. The common polysilicon gates are used to enable this cell to be programmed to a logic function using only the first metal layer as far as possible. The second layer of metal can then be used to pick up any connections to the particular logic function. At each end of the cell there is a grid-conversion channel which converts the first metal layer contact points to second metal layer contact points. This is done to minimise the overlap of the two metal layers for tracks running in the same direction.

The grid arrangement used for this cell is shown in fig. 3.18. Effectively, the first metal layer is allowed in orthogonal directions over the cell area. It is on an 18λ pitch in the horizontal direction and a 24λ pitch in the vertical direction. Note that the general

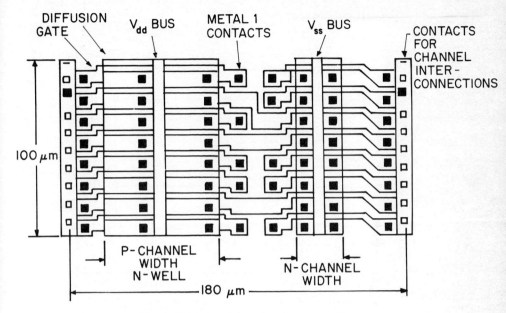

DIFFUSION GATE V$_{dd}$ BUS METAL 1 CONTACTS V$_{ss}$ BUS CONTACTS FOR CHANNEL INTER- CONNECTIONS

100 μm

P-CHANNEL WIDTH N-WELL   N-CHANNEL WIDTH

180 μm

Fig. 3.17 National Semiconductor's cell

design rules described apply roughly to the double-layer metal technology. The minimum width and space for the first metal layer are 8λ and 6λ whereas the minimum respective dimensions on the second metal layer are 10λ and 8λ. This is the reason why integers which are multiples of 3 were previously used to describe the basic rules. In fact, more conservative dimensions are used for both layers so that the second metal layer falls on a 20λ space grid. The whole cell is designed such that a 32λ spacing results between allowed contacts where two cells join. This is enough space for a further metal track of 10λ width on a 8λ spacing. This extra metal track is very useful for isolating diffusions on either side of the end transistor.

In the area around the polysilicon connections and cross-unders, an extra 18λ grid is inserted to give greater wiring flexibility. One of the polysilicon contacts is slightly offset by 6λ to provide enough clearance between the contact itself and the nearest metal tracks. Great care has to be exercised by the designer not to break design rules in this area. Figure 3.19 shows how the tracking for three two-input NAND gates is achieved. This interconnection makes use of the 18λ grid in the centre of the cell that was previously mentioned.

Figur 3.20 shows two cells programmed to a five-input NAND gate. Here, use is made of the extra track at the junction of two cells to bias off the N-transistor gate for isolation of two diffusion regions. To improve the sink current for this element, parallel N-transistors

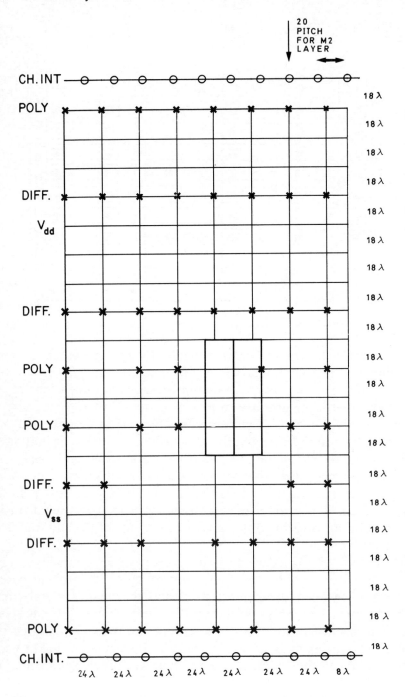

Fig. 3.18 Grid arrangement for National's G.A. cell

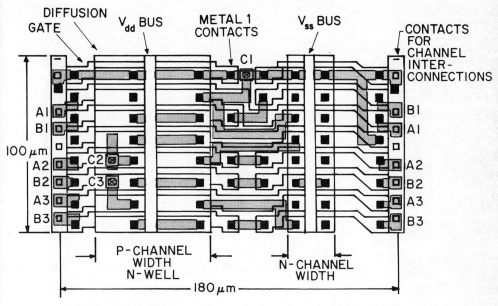

Fig. 3.19 Metal connections for three two-input NAND gates

have been used. The P-transistors have also been paralleled so that wastage is minimised.

Naturally, this cell has routing tracks using the first metal layer either side of the cell. The two metal layers will be orthogonal in the routing areas. With two metal layers, a third mask is designed which defines the interconnection vias between the layers. These contact cuts will occur at the intersection of the two layers in the channel area.

3.2.4 Macro libraries

The last section described how a particular layout of components can be built up into a complete array of cells to form a basic structure on which unique logic designs can be implemented. Despite all the techniques used to make the design implementation as straight-forward as possible, it should be apparent that a complex logic function will still require careful thought to achieve an optimum layout.

To make designing as easy as possible for the user, macro libraries, which consist of a selection of logic gates and functions, are supplied which release the user from the need to interconnect individual component transistors. System engineers can then concentrate on the logic they are designing to create a particular customer-specific circuit.

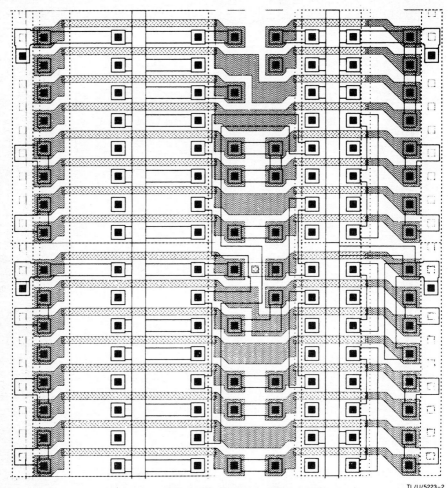

Macro Layout. Note that Pre-Programmed Metal 1 and 2 Patterns are Shown Over Base Diffusion, Poly and Contact 1 Layers.

TL/U/5223–2

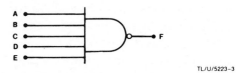

TL/U/5223–3

Note Use of Paralleled Devices to Enhance t$_{PHL}$ Where N-Channels are Stacked.

Fig 3.20 Metal connections for five-input NAND gate on two cells

A particular logic function would have been laid out by a skilled silicon designer who would have made the function as universally applicable as possible ensuring optimum accessibility and interconnectability. He would even have designed some functions, such as an

AND-OR selector in composite gate form, taking full advantage of CMOS and benefitting all users in terms of space and performance. An example of a composite AND-NOR gate is shown in fig. 3.21 which only uses four transistor pairs. The functions would obey all design rules and be thoroughly tested, and a complete performance characterisation can be supplied to the user.

The performance for each hardware macro is given as a base delay, which would be with an imaginary load of zero capacitance, and the delay per unit of capacitance, usually ns/pF. The important factor to the user is not particularly how the macro was designed but to know the exact characteristics and functions of the macro. For example, a

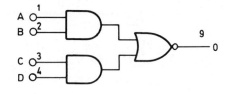

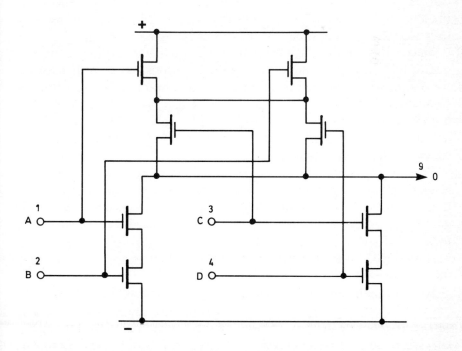

Fig. 3.21 AND-NOR composite gate form

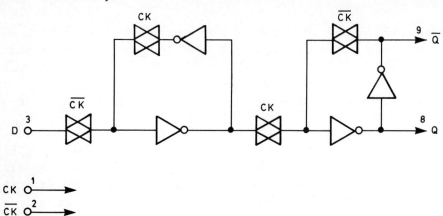

Fig. 3.22 An example of a D-type flip-flop using transmission gates and unbuffered Q and Q̄ outputs

D-type flip-flop is commonly designed as shown in fig. 3.22. It is apparent that a load on either the Q or Q̄ output degrades the performance on the complementary output. The user must understand how the macro performs under different loading conditions in order to be able to implement a good design. He would also need to understand the effects of skew on CK and C̄K̄. This characterisation can be programmed into a computer macro library database to form the basis for logic simulation and software verification of designs. The user would use computed output to verify his complex designs.

Since the layout of each macro is predefined and verified, a simpler description of input and output node positions along with allowed through-tracking can be held in a layout library to assist with the connectivity problem of a large complex gate array. The use of the hardware macro results in a simpler grid of allowable tracking. This eases the task of placing and routing and reduces the amount of checking that is necessary.

From the outset, cell designs are considered in terms of implementing basic logic functions with a scheme for interconnections. Macro libraries contain all of the useful gates and composite gates, and many variations of flip-flops. These hardware macros then form the basis for implementing other functions and the expected performance can be derived from the definition of the macros used, the connectivity and the logic simulator.

Rather than implementing MSI-type functions into a specific hardware format, they may be described as the connectivity of a certain number of macros, producing the desired function, the timing characteristics of which can be obtained from the computer simulations. This then forms a library of software macros for the user to design with. It enables the system to be considered in terms of block functions which is a great help in designing complex systems. Users must understand that the use of these higher level software macros can lead to a large element of redundancy in the design. They should implement their designs at the hardware macro level to maximise the use of the available gates on an array. This method enables the user to gain higher performance, lower redundancy and better testability of the design.

The hardware macro library must be well thought out and provide the user with all functions required to implement present day systems. Their use helps with the complex problem of connectivity on a particular gate array and enables accurate estimates of performance to be made with a computer. Software macros describing MSI functions already have some uses in design of large systems but in the future, specifically desired functions will be synthesised from a basic elemental block and control function to form, for example, large registers and counters. The use of macro libraries has helped control complexity of the design of gate arrays for systems designers.

3.3 Peripheral cells

3.3.1 The general interface compromise

We have seen how the internal matrix of cells can be built up to form many logic functions. The whole core has to be connected to peripheral or Input/Output buffer (I/O) cells so that the connections can be made to, and sensed by, the world outside the chip. This interface has to satisfy physical and electrical requirements that make the gate array as versatile a component as possible.

Probably the area of greatest compromise in gate array design is in the design of the peripheral cells of the array. At the edges of the chip, large bond pads must be placed on a spacing of about 200 μm to achieve compatibility with bonding and packaging technologies. This constraint, the size of chip and the core cell array required restrict the total number of external bond pads to the device. Only a certain number of such bonding pads can be physically located around the edges of a given sized chip. Both input (along with any necessary input protection) and output capability are required at each bond pad with the large output transistors that are required to interface MOS technology to other technologies such as TTL. It is quite difficult to supply both input and output functions in a reasonable amount of space. Sometimes, therefore, pads are preassigned specifically to either inputs or outputs, true transceivers or other I/O functions. This preassignment restricts the applicability of the device in terms of choice and placing of numbers of inputs and outputs for a particular package due to bonding constraints.

Power supplies and ground connections have also to be made for the chip to function and a sensible method of assignment must be devised. Early gate arrays used a flexible arrangement to program a peripheral cell to V_{dd} or V_{ss} as desired but more modern designs have dedicated pads which can only be used for power supplies so the pins for power and ground on a given package are pre-defined.

The number and size of the active components in the peripheral I/O cell must be carefully considered to achieve compatibility with the core array transistors and the overall interface requirements. Inputs probably need to be TTL compatible with pull-up or pull-down resistors. They also need to withstand slowly rising or falling transitions with, perhaps, a lot of external noise coupled into the signal as they act as a buffer between the harsh external environment and the array components. The output transistors need to be large enough to supply 4 mA of sink current at a potential difference of 0.4 V for TTL compatibility, but the load to an internal array transistor must not be too large to compromise performance. Usually a selection of different sized transistors are included in the peripheral cell to buffer the driving signals from the array and provide an optimum speed to drive realistic external loads of 50 pF or more. There also have to be extra transistors of graded sizes to form tristate outputs.

Satisfying, and optimising, all the above requirements is not easy and may be achieved in different ways for different gate arrays.

3.3.2 Choice of peripheral functions

All MOS inputs must have some form of input protection using diodes to prevent the rupture by static electricity of the delicate gate oxides used in the transistors. These gate oxides can be as thin as 400 Å. Provided that input protection is incorporated at the periphery, the conductor carrying the input signal can go directly to the input of a gate in the array. If this is done with an input, the signal on the pin must swing over the full voltage range to ensure that the gate which it drives will switch satisfactorily. This signal should also be free of any noise as there is no certainty about which path it will occupy in the array and, therefore, to what other signal paths it might couple; this could cause circuit problems. This method would normally be satisfactory for, say, a complete CMOS system. With the mixtures of technologies that make up most system designs, it is better to buffer the external pin signal at the periphery before it drives any logic functions in the array. The input buffer can then be designed to give the best interface required by the system. With CMOS, the choice of CMOS- or TTL- compatible input buffers with pull-ups or pull-downs is usually sufficient. It is occasionally nice to be able to specify inverting or non-inverting buffers but other logic functions are not really necessary.

To maintain the noise immunity advantage of CMOS, the input logic levels are designed to be $0.7\ V_{dd}$ and $0.2\ V_{dd}$ for the input high voltage, V_{ih}, and the input low voltage, V_{il}, respectively. This gives about 250 mV of hysteresis to the CMOS input at a 5 V supply.

To implement a TTL compatible input buffer in CMOS with a V_{ih} = 2.0 V and a V_{il} = 0.8 V, the sink current of the buffer has to be greater than the source current to achieve an appropriate shift in the transfer characteristic to a lower voltage of 2.0 V or less. This can be easily achieved by paralleling N-type transistors and putting P-type transistors in series. More transistors are required to achieve TTL compatibility and some small aspect-ratio transistors are usually used for pull-ups and pull-downs. There could quite easily be about eight components at the periphery to achieve this interface compatibility. The drive capability of the input buffer need not be any larger than the average capability of the array components.

For signals that rise and fall very slowly, Schmitt input buffers are very desirable. This is really a linear function but successful logic implementations have been used giving a hysteresis of 0.5 V. A circuit for the Schmitt trigger is given in fig. 3.23 which uses the shifted threshold voltages of the NAND and NOR gates.

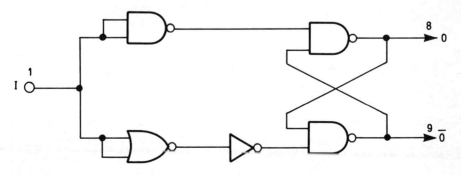

Fig 3.23 Schmitt-trigger implementation

It has already been mentioned that output drivers should be TTL compatible since TTL is the most widely used logic family for building systems. As the transistors needed are very large, a buffered output chain is required to give an appropriate drive speed for loads of 50 pF. Intermediate sized transistors must therefore be included at the periphery unless parallel driver buffers are supplied by the macro library specifically for this purpose. Tristate outputs are also used extensively and a suitable output circuit is shown in fig. 3.24. The ten transistors required for the logic gates are designed at an intermediate size in order not to cause an excessive load on any array output. Each intermediate logic gate only sees the load of one component of the output inverter. The B signal controls whether the buffer is in a tristate condition and A produces the logic state when not in tristate.

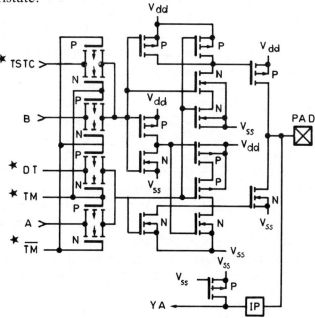

★ ON CHIP TEST CIRCUIT NOT
USER ACCESSABLE

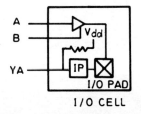

Fig. 3.24 Tristate output circuit

It is usually best to have all of these components at the peripheral cell site rather than using array components to implement these specific output and input requirements. It may even be preferable to use some parasitic bipolar transistors for very high current sinking applications. Certainly, very large open drain N-transistors have been offered with current sinking capabilities of 30 mA or more.

The demands at the interface are very likely to increase in the future. One common requirement is for a crystal oscillator. This is quite easily achieved with an output inverter which provides enough gain to maintain the oscillation. Parallel resonant circuits are the most often used configurations.

For synchronous system designs, a minimum skew clock driver circuit is a desirable function which allows programming at a peripheral cell. This implies that the intermediate and output driver transistor can be used to drive clocked circuits within the array. Alternatively, this could be a completely separate peripheral function and, if so, it must be positioned such that the pad is accessible to a pin in every package that is used for that particular gate array.

3.3.3 Peripheral cell organisation

It is readily apparent that the various requirements for the interface would need twenty or more components for the peripheral cell. This makes its layout and organisation more complicated than that of the array cell since a vast range in size and specification of transistors is needed.

For further discussion we will use a simpler peripheral cell organisation which consists of three N-channel and two P-channel transistors from which a variety of input and output buffers can be constructed. Note that the layout is open enough to allow easy access to and from the array cells so that they can be used for any necessary buffering.

Figure 3.25 shows the layout of this peripheral cell. It consists of two P-transistors at the bottom with separate gates and a common diffusion contact. At the top are three N-transistors. All three have separate gates and two of them share a common diffusion as in the P-transistor pair. The lower metal track is the V_{dd} power bus which has five polysilicon tunnels and two gates traversing it. The metal track that goes round the right and through the left part of the transistors is the V_{ss} power bus. One of the polysilicon tunnels that underpasses the V_{dd} bus also crosses the V_{ss} bus between the input protection diodes. The U-shaped structure is the distributed PN diode to V_{dd}

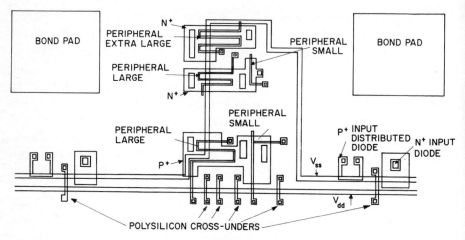

Fig. 3.25 Peripheral cell layout

and the contact to the right of the polysilicon tunnel is the NP diode to V_{ss}.

The smallest P- and N-transistors have about nine-times the current capability of an array transistor pair. The larger P- and N-transistor pair, that share a common diffusion contact with the smallest P- and N-transistor pair, have about three times the current handling capability of the smallest pair or twenty-seven times that of an array pair. Figure 3.26 shows the inverting and non-inverting CMOS output buffers that could be used. Three paralleled array transistors are used to create a buffered chain with a load factor of three at each stage. This factor is the optimum to minimise the delay of the output buffer.

The extra large N-transistor at the top of the cell is about twice as large as the intermediate sized N-transistor or the large peripheral N-transistor. It is used in parallel with the N-transistor of the peripheral large output buffer to ensure a 4 mA sink capability over the whole temperature range for TTL compatibility. Of course, the large P-transistor will source more than 400 μA over the whole operating temperature range which is all the current required to meet the specification. This TTL output buffer will give a skewed waveform for a capacitive load and will have a different speed response to the normal CMOS output.

The output diffusion contacts to the large and extra-large peripheral transistors are to the left of the V_{ss} but so that they can be directly connected to the bond pad if used. The bond pad also has direct access to the input protection circuitry beneath it. Figure 3.27 shows two peripheral cells connected up to form a clock driver circuit

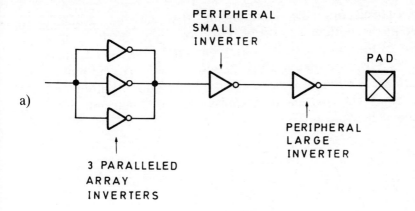

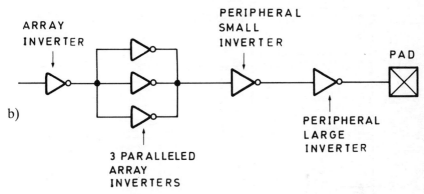

Fig. 3.26 Optimum CMOS output buffer: a) inverting; b) non-inverting

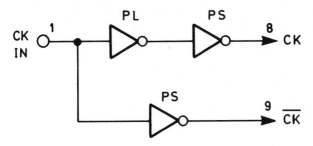

Fig. 3.27 A clock generator driver for internal array

capable of driving about 30 D-type elements in the array. The input pad connects to the gates of the large and small peripheral inverters and the large peripheral output connects to another small peripheral inverter to produce the CK signal. The first small peripheral output produces $\overline{CK}$.

TTL input buffers may be built using the components in the peripheral cell or the array transistors as required. The user has the choice of selecting the components that he has available to implement the buffer. The array transistors used should be in a cell adjacent to the peripheral cell. Suitable configurations are shown in Fig. 3.28. Array transistors can be used for pull-ups and pull-downs and to produce suitable logic to form tristate output buffers and I/O transceivers. The particular organisation, although not ideal, is flexible and it works.

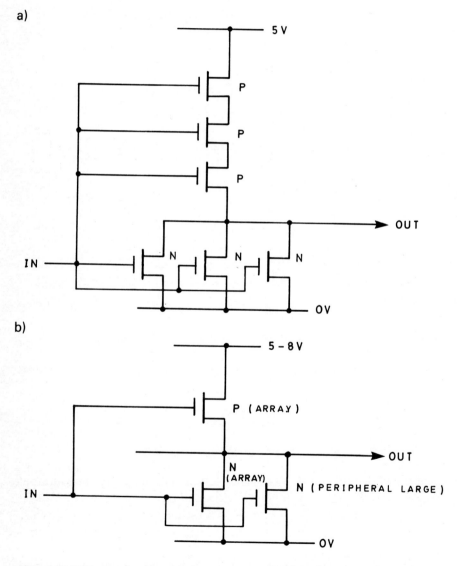

Fig. 3.28 TTL-compatible input buffers: a) using array transistors; b) using peripheral and array transistors

For user convenience, and automation of designs, hardware macros are provided to inform the user of the various possibilities and to ensure proven tested layout of the interface functions.

3.3.4 Power distribution

Modern MOS logic generally requires two supplies for power to enable the chip circuitry to function. For NMOS it is 5 V and ground but for CMOS it is a variable supply. These two potentials have to be supplied from package pins to bond pads and then to all active components. For any gate array, flexibility of location for these power supply pads is required to enable them to be sited where the power demands are greatest.

Naturally all peripheral and array components have to be supplied with power and hence, a good power distribution scheme must be designed in order that all components 'see' a low supply impedance. Metal is the best conducting medium to use for power distribution and the aluminium metallisation layer is used to distribute power to the peripheral cells which have the largest output transistors and demand the highest currents. It would only take 25 heavily loaded TTL output buffers to draw 100 mA of sink current. This current in 5 Ω would cause a 0.5 V drop in supply! Thus, it is important to ensure that the metal widths used can reliably handle the current densities and that the supplies are positioned closest to the maximum number of simultaneously switching outputs. Instantaneous current demands require analysis of impedances in the distribution of power supplies on the chip to ensure that inductances from the pin to the point of requirement on the chip are low enough for satisfactory operation. DC and AC current requirements often result in more than one pair of power supplies being used.

Power distribution to the central array area is just as important but the active components are much smaller, requiring far lower current levels. In CMOS, power is directly proportional to the load capacitance so that a gate driving 0.5 pF load will use more than 12.5 µW or demand just over 2.5 µA with a 5 V power supply and a 1 MHz toggle rate. This level of current demand can be met quite easily by minimum sized metal tracks and even a grid of heavily doped diffusion. In single-level metal technologies, power is often distributed through a grid of P^+ diffusions and the N-type substrate. This distribution scheme should nevertheless be capable of supplying about 50 mA DC current for a 2000 gate array which is the current limit on a single power supply pair on the chip.

In single-level metal processes, two concentric rings of metal carry the power to the peripheral cells and distribution to the array can be supplied through diffusions contacted by the concentric rings. If power is supplied to the array by metal, inter-digitated techniques are used. Figure 3.29 shows a particular scheme for a single-layer metal distribution. As many pads as required can be used at appropriate positions and make easy connection to the buses. In double-level metal processes, the same basic ideas are used but the distribution is very much simpler. One drawback is that thinner metal layers are used in double-level technologies than in single-level and so the buses must be wider to ensure that the critical current density of about 1 to 2 mA per square µm of cross-section of aluminium is not reached.

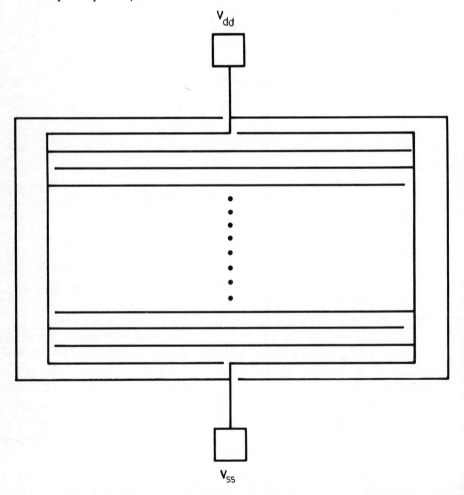

Fig. 3.29 Power distribution scheme with one metal layer

3.4 Example of a complete CMOS gate array

3.4.1 Architecture

A gate array family has been designed using a 3 μm M²CMOS technology to achieve high performance circuit applications. The family consists of a basic cell, multiples of which form the transistor array. Two peripheral cells are used which are an input function only and a true I/O function. Dedicated power supply pads are distributed around the chip with all routing achieved by the two metal layers. A test aid function is also included within the design of the gate array family.

Figure 3.30 shows the architecture of the SCX6324 array. This is a 2.4K gate array, the size being denoted by the last two figures in the manufacturer's code number. The number 3, just before the gate number, denotes the 3 μm technology. The basic cell element is the 16 transistor cell described in section 3.2. The core is configured in

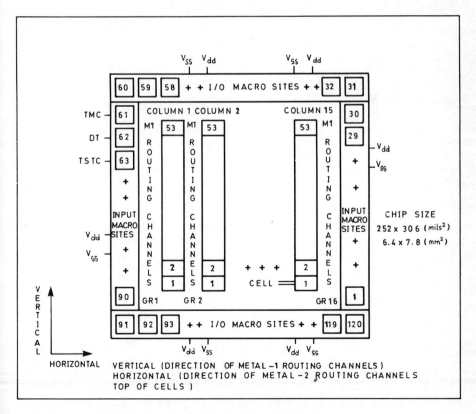

Fig. 3.30 SCX6324 architecture

vertical columns consisting of 53 cells. There are 15 columns of transistors separated by metal 1 routing channels. The number of metal 1 routes is given in table 3.1 which shows that more routes are allowed in the centre of the chip where the connectivity problem is greatest. There are a total number of 284 vertical metal 1 routing channels allowed on a 9 μm pitch with 5 μm wide metal tracks on a 4 μm spacing. Metal 1 is used as far as possible to program the cells to specific logic functions and so metal 2 can pass over the entire array area in the horizontal direction. Metal 2 tracks, 6 μm wide, are used with a 4 μm spacing. Fourteen tracks are allowed at the top and bottom of the transistor columns and ten tracks for each cell. This gives a total of 558 possible metal 2 tracks in the routing area. There are almost twice as many horizontal metal 2 routing resources than metal 1 resources. The routing grid allows adjacent vias in the channel regions for connection of metal 1 to metal 2 ensuring routability of locally congested interconnections.

Table 3.1 Metal-1 channel routes for SCX6324

Metal-1
Wire channels lie vertically between, and outside, the columns of
  internal cells.
Wire width = 4 μm, placed on 9 μm centres.

Channel Group No.	1	2	3	4	5	6	7	8	9	10	11	12	13	14	15	16
Channel Qty.		15	16	16	17	18	19	20	21	21	20	19	18	17	16	16	15

There are a total of 284 vertical channels.

For the SCX 6324 array, input-only peripheral cells are placed on the left and right hand side of the chip. True I/O peripheral cells are placed at the top and bottom of the chip. There are a total of 56 input buffers but one is used for a special test input allowing 55 user inputs. All 56 I/O buffers are available to the user to configure as desired.

Power is distributed around the periphery of the chip on the two metal layers. There are six dedicated pairs of power pads which directly connect to the power buses. Two pairs of power connections are placed on each I/O side to ensure close proximity to the large output transistors. One pair of power pads is placed on the left and right of the chip to give a better power distribution across the entire array. Connections from the power buses pass between the bonding pads to the peripheral cells. The columns of transistors in the array receive power from metal 1 tracks which are derived from the connections to the I/O peripheral cells at the top and bottom of the chip. Two connections are made in each column to metal 2 tracks running from the power pairs on the left and right of the chip. This entire power network is designed to support a 300 mA current consumption which far exceeds the requirements for most designs.

The family consists of 1.2K and 4.8K arrays in addition to the 2.4K array just described. All consist of columns of transistors comprising the basic 16-transistor cell with routing channels between. The different members vary only in terms of peripheral cell layout, positioning and number of power supply pads, height of transistor columns and number of allowed routing channels.

3.4.2 Macro libraries

Since the entire SCX63XX family of arrays is based on the same structure, all the logic functions on any member of the family can be implemented using one general macro library. The input and I/O

Table 3.2 Library of input cells

Input cell	Macro type
Input buffer, non-inverting, TTL IN with pull-up resistor	I1
Input buffer, non-inverting, TTL IN without pull-up resistor	I2
Input buffer, inverting, CMOS IN with pull-up resistor	I3
Input buffer, inverting, CMOS IN without pull-up resistor	I4
Input buffer, short circuit with pull-up resistor	I5
Input buffer, short circuit without pull-up resistor	I6

peripheral cells are also the same for each array, and the different options are supported with macro libraries.

Six input hardware macros are presently offered and the alternatives are given in table 3.2. If the CMOS input buffer is chosen, the signal is inverted. It is faster than the non-inverting TTL input macro because it has one less invertor. Optional pull-ups are included for all types including the short circuit input buffer the use of which has to

Table 3.3 Library of I/O cells

I/O cell	Macro type
I/O buffer, tristate output TTL input with pull-up resistor	IO 12
I/O buffer, tristate output, TTL input without pull-up resistor	IO 1
I/O buffer, tristate output, CMOS input with pull-up resistor	IO 13
I/O buffer, tristate output, CMOS input without pull-up resistor	IO 2
I/O buffer, tristate output, short circuit input with pull-up resistor	IO 14
I/O buffer, tristate output, short circuit input without pull-up resistor	IO 3
Output buffer, non-inverting, CMOS output	IO 4
Input buffer, non-inverting, TTL input with pull-up resistor	IO 6
Input buffer, non-inverting, TTL input without pull-up resistor	IO 7
Input buffer, inverting, CMOS input with pull-up resistor	IO 8
Input buffer, inverting, CMOS input without pull-up resistor	IO 9
Short circuit input with pull-up resistor	IO 10
Short circuit input without pull-up resistor	IO 11

be very carefully examined.

Table 3.3 gives the hardware macros that can be programmed on the peripheral I/O cells. Of the thirteen listed, I/O 6 to I/O 11 inclusive are exactly the same as the input macro library. They have to be offered again since they are part of the I/O peripheral even though the component layout for the input circuitry is the same in both peripheral cells. I/O 4 is the only macro offered that does not use the input components at all and is not tri-state. The six other macros are tristate outputs with the choice of TTL or CMOS compatible inputs or a short circuit input, all three options with or

Table 3.4 Hardware macro library

		Macro type	Quantity of elements/ cell(s)
NAND,	Triple 2-input	S1	3/1
NAND,	Dual 2-input plus complement	S3	2/1
NAND,	Dual 3-input	S2	2/1
NAND,	Triple 3-input plus complement	D3	3/2
NAND,	Triple 4-input	D1	3/2
NAND,	5-input	D2	1/2
NOR,	Triple2-input	S4	3/1
NOR,	Dual 2-input plus complement	S6	2/1
NOR,	Dual 3-input	S5	2/1
NOR,	Triple 3-input plus complement	D6	3/2
NOR,	Triple 4-input	D4	3/2
NOR,	5-input	D5	1/2
XOR,	2-input	S11	1/1
AND-NOR,	2-2 with complement	S15	1/1
OR-NAND,	2-2 with complement	S14	1/1
Latch,	2-input NAND R-S with 2-I NAND	S12	1/1
Latch,	2-input NOR R-S with 2-I NOR	S13	1/1
D-flip-flop		D9	1/2
D-flip-flop	with set & reset	T1	1/3
Invertor,	Quad	S8	4/1
Buffer,	Clock, triple	S7	3/1
Buffer,	Dual tristate inverting	S9	2/1
Buffer,	Tristate non-inverting	S10	1/1
MUX,	2-I	S16	1/1

without a pull-up resistor. The pull-up resistor is the same in all cases and has a value of about 500 kΩ.

The original hardware macro library is given in table 3.4. It consists of 24 basic functions which have been successful in the design of many customer-specific options. The nomenclature of the macro type is based on the number of cells used to form the macro. S stands for single cell, D for double cell and T for triple cell macros. All the basic gates, up to five inputs are included. There are EXCLUSIVE-OR, AND-NOR and OR-NAND selectors, two types of RS latches and two D-type flip-flops, one of which can be set and reset. There is a clock buffer and a 2 to 1 multiplexer. Finally, note the tristate inverting or non-inverting buffers that can be used to form bus structures within the array. Since no internal pull-up or pull-downs are provided, the designer must ensure that one, and only one, of the internal bus drivers is active at all times.

Note also that 6 macros have an inverter included to complement the output. Judicious use of this small macro library can lead to extremely efficient use of the cells in the gate array design. The hardware macro library is being expanded to include about 80 macros in the library.

All of the macros are fully characterised and specified for the user. The worst case delay times for 0 pF and 1 pF are given with each macro, since propagation delay times are proportional to load, to enable the user to assess design types and attain a performance goal. Worst case is considered to be at a junction temperature of 100°C and a 4.5 V supply for a commercial product which is specified for use over a temperature range of −40°C to +85°C. The specification allows for an actual device-operating temperature 15°C higher than the upper limit of 85°C due to internal power dissipation and the thermal resistance of the package. Derating figures are also provided for temperature decrease and power supply increase. As the operating temperature decreases, the propagation delays will shorten by 0.3% per °C. If the power supply could be controlled to better than 5 V ±10%, the propagation delays would decrease by 0.035% per mV. Armed with this information, the worst case performance for any logic design can be calculated.

Figure 3.31 shows the specification for an S1 macro, with three, two-input NAND gates in a single cell. In addition to the logic diagram, component circuit connectivity, functional block diagram and propagation delay with load, the input load factor at each input is also specified where 1 load factor equals 0.155 pF. Also given is the NDL (National Design Language) format specifying the expected

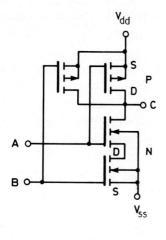

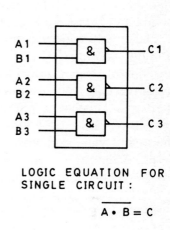

LOGIC EQUATION FOR
SINGLE CIRCUIT :

$$A \cdot B = C$$

DESCRIPTION :

    SIZE : 1 CELL

    PROPAGATION DELAY :

t_{phl}	t_{plh}	c_{LOAD}
1.5 ns	1.3 ns	Ø pF
4.7 ns	4.5 ns	1 pF

    LOAD FACTOR = 1

Fig. 3.31 Macro type S1 – triple two-input NAND

order of inputs and output for the macro in a particular circuit configuration. All the necessary information is provided to the user.

3.4.3 Layout and routing

Utilisation of these arrays should be counted in cells; macros are a discrete number of cells. It should be noted that double and triple cells are composed of adjacent cells in a column of transistors. Also, all macros are designed such that one may be stacked next to any other without violating any conditions. So the placement procedure is relatively simple. An S macro can be placed at any cell location, a D macro at any two adjacent cells and a T macro at any three adjacent cells in any column of transistors.

On the SCX6324, the two power buses that run across the cells in metal 2 to give better power distribution prevent the traversed cell locations from being used. In any column, there will be 17 usable cells below the lower power bus, 16 between the power buses and another 16 above the top bus. This restricts how many of what type and what mixture of each can be located in each third of any column.

All spare cell locations are denoted as empty cells. Empty cells allow all metal 2 tracks to traverse while used cells will have specific contact points and barriers to metal 2.

The architecture of these arrays and the optimised placing and routing software allows the designer to completely specify the pad assignment if so desired. Some critical paths may also be specified using certain cell locations in conjunction with peripheral cell locations. This user input and some other placement algorithms then seed the placer program to form a distribution of macros. This placement can be assessed very quickly to highlight the congested areas. A figure of merit for congestion arises for each channel and a decision is made to try and improve this or not. Improvements can be made by cell swapping or completely reseeding the placer. When swapping macros, particular cell sizes can only be exchanged with macros of the same size. Once an achievable figure of merit for channel congestion has been reached, the routing algorithms go to work. A number of different routing algorithms are used in a specific order (e.g. the stub router, the channel router and the maze router) until success is achieved or the programmed limit has expired. If a number of unroutes exist, the engineer can reconfigure the placement and run the routing software again or interactively modify the routes on a graphics workstation to complete the option.

For an option using 80% of the cells, the software will almost certainly complete the routing. It is quite apparent that utilisation of cells is only a guide to the problem as placement and routing is affected by the type of design and the types of macros used. The numbers of connections, or from-tos, in a random logic design can be exceedingly high and cause some routing congestion problems. Also, use of a large number of macros with a high contact density in the design can exacerbate the problem. Different assessments can be made to analyse the completion problem and a number of designs exceeding 85% utilisation and using 120 pins have been done.

Since this double layer technology was intended to apply to high performance solutions, the routing software is given one less degree of freedom in its task. Every macro has equipotential contact points to an input node on either side of the cell. The software analyses which is the best node to use and then only uses that node. The routing does not allow the use of equipotential nodes as that could put a polysilicon track in a critical signal path which could degrade performance considerably, especially if it happened many times in a particular path. This stringent condition does make the problem more difficult but leads to a higher performance product.

3.4.4 *Important aspects of design*

Before embarking on the design of a gate array the user should establish some quite fundamental points. A functional block diagram and a description of the component to be designed must be established together with a complete interface specification showing the number and type of I/O pins, logic level compatibility, loading and desired driving currents. The number of simultaneously switching outputs should be determined. A logic diagram, drawn in the available macros, forms the master schematic from which the netlist for the customisation can be derived and checked. Each macro type should be uniquely identified for easy interpretation and identification. This gives the utilisation figure rather simply. If possible, some preverification work should be carried out. Creating a breadboard of the function is a common approach but is often implemented in a different way to the gate array design and will have a different timing to the final part. Alternatively, a CAD simulation of the component would provide an even better approach; this is discussed in chapter 5 of this book.

Along with the system and design understanding, a complete test pattern specification is needed. This should be devised to provide adequate fault coverage of the design and functional verification of the part with, perhaps, some diagnostic capability for design faults (see chapter 7). Ideally the length of the test pattern will be known and minimised by including appropriate test circuitry in the design. Minimising the length of the test pattern is extremely desirable as it reduces the description of the pattern, the simulation time, the amount of output to check and the testing time. These are extremely important in the development and production of a component and the inclusion of up to 20% extra circuitry to give a shorter test could probably be very beneficial. The functional test pattern should be supplied along with a timing specification of the customisation highlighting the critical paths and the maximum delay time that can be tolerated for those paths by the system. The time delay on some or all of these paths might have to be measured at final package test to ensure that the part meets the specification. Naturally, the logic design that gives the greatest amount of latitude for the critical paths is the one that should be implemented.

The package and any specifically required pin-out must be reviewed and defined from the outset. This ensures that enough power pins have been allocated and that the required signal pins can be accommodated for that design in that package. The environmental specification, which should also be established, affects the choice of package but the satisfaction of the electrical and AC performance of the device is very package dependent. Physical details of the package must be defined showing maximum limits and tolerances for sizes and pin lengths. Type of coating material on the pin is sometimes important and any other relevant details should also be defined.

The environmental specification should give the operating temperature range, storage temperature range and specify the quality-control screening that the vendor should have carried out on the device given its particular application. The semiconductor manufacturer will have an internal procedure to supply devices to a particular commercial specification and in a variety of packages. For standardisation purposes it is best to keep the choices as small as possible. The semicustom business is service orientated and special requirements have to be entertained but both parties must understand the commercial impact when varying the requirements from the standard procedures. Military and space/satellite component specifications are very expensive but well within the capabilities of CMOS technologies.

3.4.5 Design system

A means to allow the user to design with any array in the family of products has been established in a computer-aided design (CAD) system. It is based entirely on macros, an appropriate description being given for any particular function that needs to be checked and verified.

Commercially available software is used in the design system. At present LOGCAP is used for the circuit simulation and MARTYN is used for the physical layout. The customisation of these rules for a particular design comes through the macros used and the architecture of a particular array in the physical files. There are two entirely different software packages to perform quite different functions using very different databases. The trick has been to merge both sets of rules into a design system that produces a correct physical representation of a logic function.

The simulation environment is highly interactive and consists of two separate macro descriptions: a unit delay library for logical simulation and fault grading and an AC library for timing verification. The latter simulations are more CPU intensive and are performed using statistical interconnect loadings with macro performance based on fans-outs and loads. In other words, even though a macro library is used, the timing performance of a macro in a specific connectivity arrangement will be individually calculated for each instance. The only inaccuracy is in the calculation of the interconnection lengths but correlation between estimates and actual lengths is very good indeed. The continual update of the statistical interconnect data is shown in fig. 3.32. Its incorporation into the design system is done in exactly the same way as the true performance verification would be done from the actual placed and routed design.

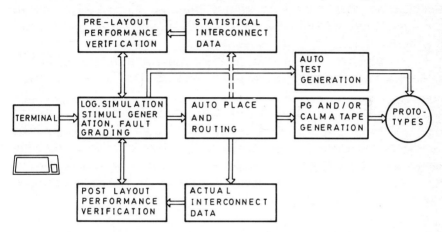

Fig. 3.32 Gate array design automation system

The master file in the system is the connectivity description of the hardware macros that comprise the specific design. The file is termed a 'netlist' and has specific format rules which allow it to be used for simulation, timing verification, fault grading and physical layout. The user has to achieve three important objectives before releasing the design for placing and routing. These are logic verification, pre-layout performance verification and at least an 85% fault coverage of the circuit design. Other information such as package pin-out and macro layout for critical path optimisation is also supplied for the next step that uses the MARTYN software.

The placing and routing is directed by the customer but is done by the semiconductor company's in-house engineers. A chip design file database is built up for the particular array being designed and the physical details of the macros used. Various placements are tried and analysed until a satisfactory figure of merit for channel congestion is achieved. A number of different routers are run for varying lengths of time until the design is complete.

Optimising the use of the various routing algorithms is achieved through a study of the different types of designs that have been implemented for each type of gate array. The success that can be achieved automatically today is a compliment to the teams who have performed fine tuning of the software package. 80% utilisation is guaranteed to be placed and routed but 95% and higher utilisation has certainly been achieved automatically.

When automatic routing is not achieved by the system, an interactive wiring completion facility is available on a graphics workstation. This system is driven by the original chip-design file database so that only wire routes may be altered. The macro placements and wire-ends are fixed and the possibility of human error is eliminated.

The completed design can now be turned into a CALMA™ database. This will have design rule checkers (DRCs) and electrical connectivity checkers (ECCs) run on it to ensure a consistent and correct database. A new network description is also generated for logic and timing verification. Here the physical metal lengths are used for the actual loading at each node. Provided the logical function agrees with the original user specification, a post-layout performance verification is done for the user to evaluate. If that is satisfactory, masks are generated for the fabrication process.

3.4.6 Testing

While the user is simulating the design to ensure it is functional, checks are also made for single stuck-at fault coverage. It is quite normal for users to achieve fault coverage figures much greater than 85% which is National's minimum. Because defects will normally cover a number of stuck-at faults, it is estimated that a level of 99% confidence in functionality will be achieved. The techniques used to achieve the fault coverage include methods for enabling greater controllability and observability of the design. Test control circuitry is included, long counters are broken into a number of shorter counting stages, presettability is designed in wherever possible and extra pins for test access are added whenever needed and possible. At the design stage, the requirements for achieving a satisfactory level of testing must be taken into account.

The simulation pattern that gives the required fault coverage is used as the functional test for the device. The CAD environment is arranged to automatically generate a SENTRY™ VIII test program from the LOGCAP output. The entire test program is built up from a shell program that will perform both DC and AC parametric tests and functional tests.

The DC parametric tests are aided by an on-chip test facility that uses one dedicated test pin and two user pins. The test mode control pin (TMC) is dedicated and when it is pulled low it puts the array into a test state. There is a user pin that is multiplexed with a tristate test control (TSTC) pin. If this is active, all outputs of the chip will be in a tristate condition. If this pin is non-active, a second multiplexer user pin data test (DT) will control the state of all the output buffers. It is fairly simple to check the sink and source currents of all the output buffers with this test facility. The entire DC parametric checking can be carried out independently of the particular user-customisation of the device, except for pin-out.

The logical function of the device is checked from the translation of the simulation vectors. AC parametric tests are done on critical paths that adhere to a particular timing in the system. All of these tests are built up by the shell program from files generated by the user.

Other tests carried out are continuity tests, interpin shorts, noise immunity tests, input and output stress tests, and temperature correlation tests. The test program is comprehensive and sophisticated to ensure that the component functions in the way the customer defined and that the part will work when in a system.

3.4.7 Packaging

To give the greatest flexibility of the gate arrays, a wide range of packages is offered. Table 3.5 shows the range of packages. This includes plastic and ceramic dual-in-line (DIP), plastic and ceramic chip carriers (CC), and pin grid arrays (PGA).

The DIP packages are the most familiar to users because they are generally able to deal with these packages on production assemblies. These packages occupy a large amount of board space and it is generally accepted that using chip carriers is preferable as they give a better pin to area ratio; chip carriers are the new generation. The area saving on printed circuit boards can be a major cost saving. Techniques for mounting these leaded chip carriers are radically different to DIPs but are definitely worth looking at. The PGAs give the best pin-to-area ratio but are expensive packages. They are excellent for high reliability systems and military applications when large accelerations are encountered but field repair is very difficult as removing such a package from a PCB is very difficult.

Every package that is supported for a family of gate arrays requires a particular assembly line for that package. This is a move away from the standardisation which arrays are supposed to introduce. Table

Table 3.5 Standard packages

Package type	Pins	CMOS SXC series				
		6306	6312 6212	6324 6224	6325 6225	6348 6248
Plastic DIP, N	28	×	×			
	40	×	×	×	×	
	48		×	×	×	
Ceramic DIP, (side braze), D	28	×	×			
	40	×	×	×	×	
	48		×	×	×	
Ceramic DIP, (CerDIP), J	28	×	×			
	40	×	×	×	×	
Plastic leaded chip carrier, PCC	28	×	×			
	44	×	×	×	×	
	68		×	×	×	×
	84			×	×	×
	124			×	×	×
Ceramic leaded chip carrier, LDCC	124			×	×	
Ceramic leadless chip carrier, LCC	28	×	×			
	44	×	×	×	×	
	68		×	×	×	×
	84			×	×	×
	124			×	×	×
Ceramic pin grid array, PGA	68		×	×	×	×
	84			×	×	×
	120/124			×	×	×
	149					
	172					×

3.5 shows which devices will fit into which types of package; physical size is the restriction considered here. It should be noted that the ceramic and plastic packages offered are footprint compatible. Generally, prototypes are supplied in ceramic packages. Sockets are available for all types of package but the sockets for ceramic chip carriers are usually different to those for the plastic chip carriers.

The packages chosen to support a given array are fundamental not only to the number of active pins that will be available but also to the performance of the particular design. Table 3.6 shows more details for the 1.2K gate array in the various possible packages. Even with four pairs of power supplies, the DIP limits the design to 20 simultaneous switching outputs (SSO) whereas the device is designed to be able to support 24 SSOs. The limitation arises from the lead inductances which are greater on the DIPs than on the chip carriers. The maintenance of device performance when packaged is an area of great research and development. Particular attention has to be paid to the large pin-out packages and the best performance is usually achieved with PGAs. The problems are certainly not simple and the design and layout of the lead-frames for such multi-layer packages are critical to maintaining desired performance.

Table 3.6   6312/6212 package options

Number of pins	Package	Package type	Number of power pairs	Number of Is*	Number of I/Os	Max. number of SSOs
28	Ceramic DIP	D28-2	2	3	21	10
28	Plastic DIP	N28-2	2	3	21	10
28	Ceramic DIP	D28-4	4	3	17	20†
28	Plastic DIP	N28-4	4	3	17	20†
40	Ceramic DIP	D40-2	2	3	33	10
40	Plastic DIP	N40-2	2	3	33	10
40	Ceramic DIP	D40-2	4	3	29	20†
40	Plastic DIP	N40-4	4	3	29	20†
44	Ceramic leadless	E44-2	2	5	35	10
44	Plastic leaded	V44-2	2	5	35	10
44	Ceramic leadless	E44-4	4	3	33	24
44	Plastic leaded	V44-4	4	3	33	24
48	Ceramic DIP	D48-2	2	8	36	10
48	Plastic DIP	N48-2	2	8	36	10
48	Ceramic DIP	D48-4	4	4	36	20†
48	Plastic DIP	N48-4	4	4	36	20†
68	Ceramic leadless	E68-4	4	18	42	24
68	Plastic leaded	V68-4	4	18	42	24
68	Ceramic pin grid	U68-4	4	18	42	24

* including TMC-input buffer (not available as an input)
† no. of SSOs limited by the package

3.5 Market analysis

3.5.1 Why Gate Arrays?

Gate arrays have become more popular because of software advances that have enabled the reliable development an an array in a time suitable for system developments. A complex gate array can now be designed and developed, and prototype samples produced in the same time as it takes to design and develop the PCBs for an equivalent system.

The advantages of integrating a system instead of building a discrete version are lower cost, space saving, higher performance, confidentiality of design and greater reliability. These are great advantages to the equipment manufacturer who will also make considerable savings in production by having lower inventory and assembly costs.

The manufacturers of gate arrays also see advantages in the product as it is essentially a standard product. In the M^2CMOS process only three custom masks are required in a total of thirteen masks. The custom masks are at the back-end of the process which is technically and administratively relatively easy to control. The manufacturers also make use of the skilled designers in the system companies to design silicon chips for their own needs allowing the skilled semiconductor designers, who are few and far between, to concentrate on other, high volume, commercial designs.

Gate arrays also open up areas in which to apply silicon devices and pass the responsibility of device definition from the manufacturer to the user. This solves an enormous problem for the silicon manufacturer who needs to develop very complex devices to take advantage of the technologies he can produce and to satisfy the demands of the market place. The design investment in a new VLSI device is measured in tens of man-years and millions of dollars. The advantages to both manufacturer and user are set against the lower functional density of the chip and hence a higher price for the device than for a full custom design if this were economically feasible.

The design of the component must be firm before release to the manufacturer and must be kept to a strictly agreed schedule to meet overall time scales. The disciplined design procedure required to ensure success is new to many system engineers but the tools to help with this are becoming more easily available and will increase the demand for arrays and other semi-custom products.

3.5.2 What is available?

There are three technologies that we can classify into array sizes. The highest performance applications requiring 0.5 nS gate delays are supported by ECL up to a complexity of 2500 gates. Bipolar or TTL equivalent technologies have been traditionally used by medium performance applications (about 5 nS gate delays) up to a complexity of about 5000 gates while the lowest performance applications used CMOS technologies which, theoretically, can go to almost any array size. A 10 000 gate array is about the largest conceived so far in CMOS.

The scaled CMOS technologies now available enable the application of these arrays to areas with performances such as 1 nS gate delay. This is undoubtedly the area for TTL interfacing and it is very interesting to observe that all suppliers have products with a TTL equivalent interface. Even ECL array suppliers like National Semiconductor offer TTL interfaces on such parts. Array sizes range from fifty gates up to the 10 000 gate level. Out of about 40 sources, the majority of suppliers offer CMOS arrays of which about 60% are silicon gate technologies. The average size of array supplied by these manufacturers is below 1000 gates. This is obviously where there has been the greatest market demand. This is also the level of complexity that could be handled without CAD in a reasonable time-scale. Now, with CAD support, the demand for larger arrays is increasing and the average size required has shifted to about 1500 gates and is still rising. There are only a few companies that can support 2000 gates array designs and even fewer who can go beyond that array size. This highlights the poor availability of a modern process to achieve the packing density for large arrays on a die size with a respectable yield. At the sophisticated end of the market there is not a lot of choice.

3.5.3 Important aspects to consider

When a user goes out to the array manufacturers with a tender, he will highlight and concentrate on some technical aspects of his design. These are such things as:

* Operating voltage
* Power consumption
* Maximum clock frequency
* Critical path delay times
* Operating temperature range
* Number of gates

* I/O drive and voltage level requirements
* Pin-out and packaging
* Screening specification
* Time-scales

A number of these points are design dependent and gate utilisation is vendor dependent. The emphasis on the technicalities is debatable and other factors should be looked at. One of the main items a user should consider is support. Development of semi-custom circuits is never black-and-white and it is important to enter into a mutually beneficial partnership, where co-operation and understanding will form the most fruitful relationship.

The software aids or CAD support for the design system should be critically reviewed as this will give a strong insight into the commitments made by the vendor. Proof should be requested of the technology capabilities and the specific parts that are being designed. Control over the procurement of the devices should be investigated and questioned to ensure availability on time. The liabilities during the entire development phase should be reviewed and understood so that both parties are quite clear about their responsibilities in the whole program.

It is also worth considering the future products that will be developed and it is worth investing engineering expertise in design systems that will contribute positively to further developments.

3.5.4 Quality and Reliability

One of the factors that drives systems designers to higher levels of integration is increased reliability of the end product. Crudely calculated, reliability is a function of the number of pins and connections in a system. It is easy to see that integrating a board with 100 ICs and an average of 14 pins each into a gate array with about 140 pins will increase the reliability by a factor of 10. This is an astounding figure and can be remarkable when a complete system integration is implemented.

Semiconductor manufacturers run reliability tests and analyse failure modes to gain much better understanding of the failure mechanisms and to improve their products thereby achieving much greater reliability. The efforts put into these quality programs and quality circles should be investigated by the users. The end results of such programs run by the manufacturer should give the user a product with added value that could potentially save him vast amounts of money in field repairs.

The quality of a device is important to the user at all levels starting with the design of the component. An in-depth understanding of the design should lead to questions concerning current densities; these should be much less than 1 or 2 mA per μm^2 of metal to avoid metal migration. The instantaneous demand for current on the power supplies created by simultaneously switching outputs is an example of design guidance that should be supplied by a vendor to build in reliability. Quality of the software used for designs and control of data plus the number of checks made during development are extremely important. The amount and methods of testing the components, as well as the screening specifications that a vendor can support, are all indicators to the capability of the vendor and the final integrity of the device.

The methods and terminology used in qualifying devices are complex and are based on Arrhenius models. The user wants to know the reliability in terms of FITS (failures in 10^9 hours) or percentage, or he may want to know the probability of failure in a 20-year lifetime for a component. Whatever the requirement, the vendor should be forced to expose his programs and expertise and to give an answer on quality and reliability that is satisfactory.

3.5.5 Second Sourcing

As more and more semi-custom integrated components are introduced into systems, the need to obtain products from more than one source (multisourcing) becomes greater. This means that the equipment manufacturer is not dependent on one component supplier.

The important factor is to be able to truly 'second source' a semi-custom component. Some gate array vendors actually source their products from a number of silicon foundries. This would only be a true second source if the specification of the performance of the macros was the worst of all the suppliers. It is very important to understand this point to prevent problems that could occur during the production of parts if material had to be sourced from a different foundry. Second sourcing should of course mean that exactly the same device architectures and design rules are used. It need not mean exact processes; only that they produce equivalent performances.

As device dimensions are reduced, the ability to stock wafers and use them at a different processing plant becomes more and more difficult due to the masking tolerances required. With 2 μm feature sizes the accuracy of registration can only be achieved by a single aligner. This is an extremely important point that will change the business to a large extent as more sophisticated processes are used. The efforts necessary to ensure equivalent performances from different manufacturers are large and if a second source is available, it should lead to a higher level of confidence in that technology and component.

3.6 The future

3.6.1 Cell based designs

The next logical step for semi-custom components after gate arrays is standard cell arrays. Here, cells are designed with a fixed height but a variable width. Characterisation is done as on the macros for gate arrays but the performance could be very much higher for equivalent functions due to more optimised cell designs. The cells butt together in rows, allowing routing in channels in between, almost exactly equivalent to gate arrays. Naturally, cells need not butt together if routing access is required between cell blocks.

The greater routing flexibility and variable architecture lead to better packing densities and a smaller overall chip. This gives quite considerable savings in component production costs at the expense of somewhat higher initial development costs. Complexities of twenty-to thirty-thousand gates are achievable. The simulation software used today is quite applicable to standard-cell arrays but software for placing and routing will have to be smarter to cope with flexible architectures and to obtain good compaction of all the cells.

Products like this already exist in the market place but none are supported by a sophisticated software suite. Comprehensively supported products should be available during 1984 and anybody with a vested interest in the semi-custom marketplace will bring out products in this area.

As all masks have to be fabricated to produce the device, the turn round time will be longer but only by a few weeks. The design time should be equivalent to that required for gate arrays.

The next stage on from standard cells can be classified as functional block arrays. Here the functional blocks are more complicated and include CPUs and memories. Here the software has to deal with shapes that have different aspect ratios and this implies an improvement in software requirements for compaction and optimisation of area.

To a large extent, functional blocks could have dedicated sizes. This makes the characterisation of performance simple but does not lead to an optimum layout. Memory blocks should certainly be capable of having different shapes as all kinds of sizes and word lengths could well be used on-chip. The software problem with such complexity must not be underestimated and may well be insoluble in the short term. One way round the problem could be to have a number of different shapes for a given macro function and allow the software to choose the most appropriate shape to obtain the best chip size.

Functional block arrays apply to true systems on a chip which are composed of pre-designed and complex functions. The building blocks used will in many cases be taken from existing standard designs and tools must be developed to put these blocks together and accurately simulate the system. Functional level simulators have to be used and such simulators are already appearing.

3.6.2 Silicon compilers

The previous section described a practical approach to the problem of designing and coping with complexity. The true approach to the problem of designing complex systems on a chip is through a silicon compiler. This is an expert system that will understand the physics of the devices and all design rules of a technology so that the detailed geometrical mask shapes can be built up from a high-level description of the required system. The system has to be hierarchical and be able to examine problems at all levels to emulate a super silicon designer and cope with the complexity.

The approaches and research work into silicon compilers are varied and attack different aspects of the problems. However, some of the best brains in the world are involved in this work and advances in hardware and software should help form such a system in the future, probably within a decade. Industrial support for such research at academic institutions is presently at a high level and government initiatives in Japan, the U.S., the EEC and the U.K. are already funded.

3.6.3 Linear Functions

When systems on a chip are being discussed, linear functions cannot be ignored as we live in an analog world. It has been pointed out that CMOS is quite ideal for linear applications and there is a vast spectrum of linear products developed in CMOS available in today's marketplace.

Linear arrays and a mixture of linear and digital functional arrays are already available and support an extremely important need for total integration of systems. Linear functions will be introduced at the standard cell array level and their use and application will expand in time.

The difficulty in implementing linear functions is predictability. Simulators that can deal with such functions cannot deal with large complexities and are very CPU intensive. The development of easy-to-use simulators is key to the mixture of linear and digital functions on-chip.

Even digital simulators require at least four states to give any real information about the operation. There are many simulators now available which do a better job of emulating a digital function by using as many as thirteen states. To incorporate linear functions would require a simulator with an infinite number of states. However, in practice we may well be able to cope with a tool that only approximates to reality.

3.6.4 Computing methods and improvements

This section has highlighted the importance of software tools to the future of semi-custom and full custom designs. The software always runs on a computer and the hardware configuration limits the structure and performance of the particular task. Hardware tools are changing quite rapidly and becoming more easily available and more powerful. Radically different techniques like parallel processing are being investigated and a vast amount of work on fifth generation computers is going on worldwide.

As software algorithms become established in performing a specific. function in the semi-custom or custom area, it will most likely be implemented in a hardware form to increase the efficiency and throughput. Different types of machines will emerge which are geared up to perform very specific tasks and to do them very efficiently. Many machines of different types will be networked together so that the design of very complex components such as VLSI chips will be done quite simply by system designers who have very little knowledge of the details of chip design and manufacture.

This will be quite an evolutionary process that will undoubtedly be impacted by the significant advances made in specific areas of hierarchical system simulators, mosaic placers, routing algorithms, programming languages and hardware advances. There is no doubt that the semiconductor industry will continue to contribute to its own growth, keeping costs down and time-scales to commercially acceptable levels by being one of the most advanced users of its own products.

3.7 References

3.1 Alexander, W.T. et al (1979) 'High density uncomitted arrays using an advanced CMOS technology'. Fifth European Solid State Circuits Conference, *IEEE Conference Publication 178*, pp. 76–8

3.2 Burne, J.R. (1969) 'Switching response of complementary symetry MOS transistor logic circuits'. *RCA Review*, No. 25 pp. 627–61.

3.3 Eidsmore, Douglas (1983) 'Designers guide to gate arrays'. *Digital Design*, May 83 pp. 60–66

3.4 Kanuma, Akira (1983) 'CMOS circuit optimisation'. *Solid State Electronics*, Vol. 26 No. 1 pp. 47–59

3.5 Kash, Richard (1981) 'Building quality analog circuits with CMOS logic arrays'. *Electronics*, Aug 81 pp. 109–112

3.6 Oldham, H.E. and Partridge, S.L. (1982) 'A comparative study of CMOS processes for VLSI applications'. *IEEE Transactions on Electron Devices*, Vol. ED-29 No. 10, Oct 82 pp. 1593–8

3.7 *National Semiconductor Application Notes*, Nos. 317, 320, 321, 322, 331, 332, 333 and 339

3.8 Alexander, D.R., Autinone, R.J. and Brown, G.W. *SPICE 2 MOS Modelling Handbook*. (Alexander and Autinone, BDM Corporation: Brown, Saudia Laboratories.)

Chapter 4

Analog/Linear Master Slices

DEREK BRAY

Interdesign Inc.

4.1 Introduction

The words 'analog' or 'linear' are often used synonymously when referring to circuits which contain non-digital functions. Typical examples of such analog/linear circuits include: amplifiers, comparators, voltage references and regulators, current sources, sample and hold circuits, phase locked loops, mixers, automatic gain control circuits, A–D and D–A circuits, filters, waveform generators, transducer interface circuits, power control circuits, oscillators, modulators, multipliers, limiters, function generators, etc. There are many possible circuit configurations in each of these categories with implementation in a wide range of applications. Generalised applications include such areas as: consumer, military, telecommunications, industrial, medical, automotive, audio, radio, T.V., video games and home electronics.

The implementation of specific circuits, for a given application and to satisfy a defined set of performance characteristics, can be influenced by many factors including such variables as: designer's experience, available technology, design aids, circuit simulation tools, circuit complexity, circuit specifications, testing requirements, price/volume tradeoffs, etc. Given all these variables it comes as no surprise that two circuits designed by different engineers to the same set of specifications will look entirely different from each other and still meet the overall objectives of the specifications. With this in mind, the concept of semi-custom, master slice, integrated circuit products has been found to provide a flexible solution to the designer. He is able to customise a circuit to his own special functions.

The 'analog/linear master slice' concept has been available since

1970 when Interdesign, under the direction of its founder Hans Camenzind, introduced the first of a complete family of *Monochip*™ integrated circuits using a standard bipolar process available at that time. The original master slice concept consisted of a standardised chip design providing a fixed array of components which could be interconnected to give configurations by customisation of the metallisation pattern on the array. This original idea has been expanded into a wide range of chip sizes and a variety of technologies such as: standard bipolar, bipolar with a sinker diffusion, high voltage bipolar, ion implantation, NMOS, metal gate CMOS, silicon gate CMOS, dielectric isolation and collector diffusion isolation (CDI). Many of these technologies are also used in digital gate arrays allowing combinations of linear and digital functions to be implemented at the same time. New master slices are being designed which include both analog and digital oriented component sets on the same chip.

An understanding of the fundamental components and parameters, and how these can be used to advantage by the designer, can best be illustrated by considering specific technologies. How the linear/analog master slice concept has evolved and how it can be used by the designer will hopefully become clear as this chapter progresses.

4.2 Linear bipolar technologies

It is very rare that linear system requirements have identical functions. Most standard linear integrated circuits, such as operational amplifiers, comparators, voltage regulators and timers, are building blocks used to implement the many functions necessary in a wide variety of applications. In special areas such as telecommunications, consumer electronics, automotive and military applications, more complex circuits have been developed aimed at satisfying more complex functions. In addition, special custom circuits have been designed to meet a specific customer's needs. However, it is only the *master slice* or *semi-custom* approach that allows optimisation of circuit configurations required over a broad range of applications. Since there is no universal solution to the problems these present, it has been necessary to develop a family of products with a complete range of chip sizes. This family, based on a twenty volt breakdown bipolar process, is shown in fig. 4.1. Its historical development provides some insight into the need for and rationale behind such a family.

COMPONENT LIST FOR A BIPOLAR LINEAR ARRAY FAMILY														
	MOA	MOB	MOC	MOD	MOE	MOF	MOG	MOH	MOJ	MOL	MOM	MON	MOP	MOQ
NPN Transistor, small	57	69	22	50	48	92	58	70	36	76	137	170	71	55
NPN Transistor, 100mA								2	2	2	8	4	4	2
NPN Transistor, 200mA	2				4	2				2	4	4		
NPN Transistor, low noise											4			
PNP Transistor, single	18	12	8											
PNP Transistor, dual				16	15	36	18	22	12	22	44	64	54	21
PNP Transistor, quad										4	8			
PNP Transistor, vertical											4	6		
Schottky Diodes	15	16	6											
15Ω N+ Resistors								4		8	15	12	8	3
Base Resistors														
200Ω	16	27	8	15	8	18	19	29	8	23	60	68	21	18
450Ω	43	44	18	30	32	88	68	82	34	103	188	244	140	68
900Ω	43	45	20	28	28	68	65	75	30	77	140	226	142	57
1.8kΩ	29	39	13	29	25	61	44	54	24	53	104	161	96	40
3.6kΩ	28	36	12	24	26	61	27	36	20	36	84	111	64	26
Total Base Resistance	214kΩ	265kΩ	94kΩ	180kΩ	180kΩ	433kΩ	269kΩ	337kΩ	159kΩ	345kΩ	712kΩ	1014kΩ	597kΩ	250kΩ
Pinch Resistors														
30kΩ B/E	4	6	2		5	9								
100kΩ B/E	4	6												
2×60kΩ B/E							4	4	2	5	8	12	12	4
60kΩ Bulk				2										
Pads	16	24	14	16	18	24	18	18	18	24	28	40	24	18
Size (mils)	71×81	81×81	51×56	80×80	70×70	91×110	75×78	77×88	61×65	81×100	101×151	123×157	92×119	72×74

Fig. 4.1 Linear Monochip product family

4.2.1 Historical development

1970:   Introduction of the MOA chip utilising a standard 20 V bipolar process with low current Schottky diode capability.

1971:   Addition of MOB chip to provide higher component count and pin-out capability.

1972:   Addition of MOC chip to satisfy market needs for a small, cost effective solution.

1974:   Addition of MOD utilising a higher voltage process for special high voltage applications.

1977:   Addition of MOE and MOF chips to take advantage of new device geometries and improved layout techniques as well as going to a larger chip size (MOF).

1978:   Introduciton of the MOG as a more cost effective replacement for the MOA with improved layout capability.

1979/80: Addition of three chips to satisfy various complexities of circuits:
   (a) MOH – replacement for MOB
   (b) MOJ – more cost effective small chip
   (c) MOL – medium size chip as 'fill in' to the product range.

1981:   Addition of the MOM as a larger (101 × 151 mils) chip for more complex applications.

1983:   Addition of a larger MON chip to provide even more system complexity.

1983:   Addition of MOP to provide a medium size chip with a larger percentage of PNP transistors making it more suitable for designs requiring either low voltage or low current operation.

1983: Addition of MOQ to provide smaller geometry transistors and more efficient/economic use of silicon area.

4.2.2 The bipolar technology

Bipolar technology is probably the 'oldest' technology being used in the production of ICs. It is also ideally suited to the area of linear circuits. The process chosen for the linear semi-custom array family has stood the test of time and has proved itself applicable in many different areas. The specific bipolar process which provides these features can be defined by the following:

Starting material	P type, <111>, 15 mils, 7–21 ohm-cm
Buried layer	N type, 14–23 ohms/square
Epitaxial layer	N type, 11 μm, 1.5 ohm-cm
Isolation	P type, 2–5 ohms/square
Base	P type, 2.5 μm, 135 ohms/square
Emitter	N type, 3.5 ohms/square
Metallisation	Aluminium, 17 000 Å

This particular process flow results in components having the following parameters:

Small geometry PNP transistor

h_{FE}	10–80	$I_C = 50$ μA, $V_{CE} = 5$ V
LV_{CEO}	>20 V	$I_C = 100$ μA
I_{CBO}	<0.1 μA	$V_{CB} = 20$ V

Small geometry NPN transistor

h_{FE}	80–350	$I_C = 100$ μA, $V_{CE} = 5$ V
LV_{CEO}	>20 V	$I_C = 100$ μA
$V_{CE\,SAT}$	<0.2 V	$I_C = 1$ mA, $I_c = 0.1$ mA
V_{BE}	0.61–0.73	$I_E = 100$ μA
BV_{EBO}	6.1–7.1 V	$I_E = 10$ μA
BV_{CS}	>20 V	$I_C = 100$ μA

Base diffused resistors

Absolute tolerance   + or − 25%

4.2.3 Linear array organisation

The design of a monolithic component array intended to produce many semi-custom ICs is somewhat different from that of a fully dedicated chip aimed at one specific circuit. The overriding concern in the semi-custom chip is the metal interconnect. The device geometries and component positioning must be optimised for ease and flexibility in interconnecting the components in virtually any conceivable way.

The devices designed for a *linear array* have multiple contacts in some diffused areas to facilitate easy interconnection. For example, the placement of two or more contacts in the epi collector of an NPN is very common. This allows connections to the high impedance collector without having to cross base and emitter traces.

Another consideration in the design of a linear array is the type and number of components to be on the chip. It is best to have as few different structures as possible and to make all the components as general purpose as possible. Specialised devices reduce flexibility because many circuit configurations may not be able to use them; and unless they are sprinkled throughout the chip they will not be where needed. Thus, all NPNs are typically the same, all PNPs are identical, and there are only four or five values of resistors.

Since the components must be general purpose to be used in as wide a variety of circuits as possible, some parameters may be a compromise in specific applications. For instance, medium large NPN devices can offer better VBE matching, low $V_{CE\,SAT}$ and low noise, whereas small areas geometries use less area, provide higher speed and better low current operation. Therefore, a device size is chosen to achieve the best compromise between these parameters.

The proper mix of components is also very important if the component array is to find wide usage. Experience has shown that a good ratio of NPNs to lateral PNPs for the linear arrays is anywhere between 2.5 and 3.5 and the absolute useful minimum is 2.7K of base resistance per active device; however, 3.5K per device is quite adequate in the majority of applications. Because there can never be too many base diffused resistors, chip area is usually the limiting factor.

For ease of interconnection, all small NPN devices have four collector contacts with the facility for passing a metal track between adjacent contacts. This is illustrated in fig. 4.2. The lateral PNPs have two separate collectors so that one PNP can perform the function of two in current source or current mirror applications. Again, there is

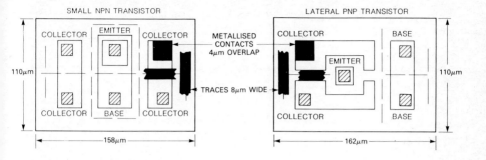

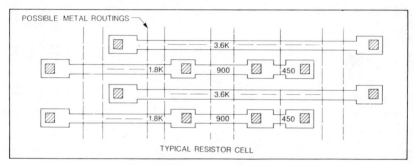

Fig. 4.2 Linear array components

room for one trace between adjacent base or collector contacts.

All resistors are arranged in cells containing two 3.6K resistors and two 3.15K resistors. Each 3.15K resistor is actually composed of a 450 ohm resistor, a 900 ohm resistor, and a 1.8K ohm resistor connected end-to-end. The resistor values are in exact ratios of 1:2:4:8 since integrated circuit design relies on component matching and ratios rather than absolute values. Note that this cell is designed with resistor contacts staggered to allow easy access from all directions. In addition, there is room for two traces between contacts in the crosswise direction and room for one trace between contacts in the lengthwise direction.

The overall component arrangement on the latest chips in the family is such that most of the active devices are placed in groups of eight or ten with no more than two transistors abreast. These groupings are generally surrounded by the resistor cells providing every transistor in the grouping with easy interconnect and direct access to the resistors. Devices are best orientated in the same direction to provide good matching, even between devices that are on opposite sides of the chip. See fig. 4.3 for a typical chip layout.

A wide metal trace runs completely around the periphery of each chip and is connected to the substrate. Hence, this trace serves as

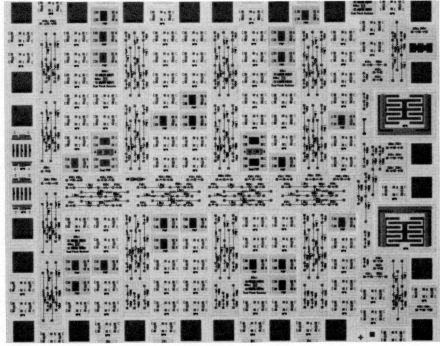

Fig. 4.3 Typical chip layout sheet

either the ground or negative supply rail, so that the positive supply traces usually snake throughout the middle of a chip. For this reason, most NPNs line the periphery of the chip and most PNPs are in the middle.

By far the most important aspect of the component layout is the silicon area devoted to metal traces. There is room for at least two traces between adjacent transistors and between transistor and resistor cells. There is also enough space to run two traces in addition to the negative supply behind the bonding pads. All these considerations contribute to making complex linear circuits relatively easy to interconnect on the chip.

4.2.4 Historical yield improvements

Due to the longevity of the bipolar linear semi-custom array product line, it is possible to reconstruct many factors which have contributed to overall yield improvements over a ten year period. Factors involved include:

* Photolithographic and mask improvements resulting in better mask alignment and fewer mask defects.

* Improvements in process control and monitoring resulting in tighter parametric distributions on devices.
* Improvement in process manufacturing areas and equipment resulting in lower defect densities on wafers.
* Improvements in equipment, etc., allowing for larger wafers to be processed.
* Continued updating of device characterisation and design information resulting in more predictable circuit performance.
* Availability of improved test systems allowing more comprehensive testing and resulting in the ability to meet tighter product requirements.
* Gradual upgrading of engineering expertise at both end users and suppliers resulting in better design which are more representative of the array capabilities.
* Wider range of product availability with improved layout capability resulting in better engineered final products.
* Availability of circuit analysis programs which aid the engineer during the initial design phase.
* Better Q.A. and operator control to avoid human errors in production.
* Improved assembly and packaging capability resulting in high final test yields.
* Better engineering interface between supplier and end user with applications information provided by design ideas.

Many of these factors are 'intangible' from the point of view of being able to put a specific number on their contribution to yield improvement. However, the important criteria today is how cost effective can a specific die/package/specification combination be in relation to the desired application.

4.2.5 Die sort yields

One of the major concerns in overall yields is the basic die sort yields on wafers. This again is dependent on many factors such as:

* defect densities
* parameters
* test limits.

However, parametric problems and testing limitations can be overcome by suitable engineering and Q.A. expertise leaving basic process defect densities as a critical factor.

Experience has shown that the yield on a wafer can be expressed by the formula:

$$Y = \exp\left[\frac{1}{C} N_{\text{eff}} \frac{A_c}{R^2}\right]$$

where C = constant slightly less than pi
R = the useful radius of a wafer
A_c = the active area on a chip
N_{eff} = the effective number of defects on a wafer.

R is related to the wafer diameter by:

$$R = R_W - P$$

where P is the width of the peripheral annulus where the yield is very low. Generally P is approximately 0.25 inch.

Using the yield data available, it has been possible to see how N_{eff} has improved with time. This is represented by fig. 4.4.

On a given size chip the greater than 3:1 improvement in N_{eff} has had the result of reducing the loss due to random defects by over 2:1 and improving yields by a factor of almost 2:1. The effect of wafer size on net good die which can be obtained for a given N_{eff} is shown in fig. 4.5 for various die sizes. Conclusions to be drawn from these curves are:

(a) An MOF size chip only became reasonably cost effective with 3 inch wafers.
(b) MON size chips are marginally cost effective with 3 inch wafers but will be satisfactory with 4 inch wafers.
(c) Larger die sizes will have to rely on both larger wafers sizes and lower values of N_{eff}.

4.3 Bipolar collector diffusion isolation technology (CDI)

When a combination of linear and digital functions is needed on the same chip, the bipolar technology can still be used. The CDI process, developed by Ferranti, is a simplified five-step process which has been utilised in many digital uncommitted logic arrays and also in a family of 'Digilin' arrays. These Digilin arrays are organised to provide basically digital implementation in the central matrix core of the chip and either linear or digital in the peripheral area of the chip.

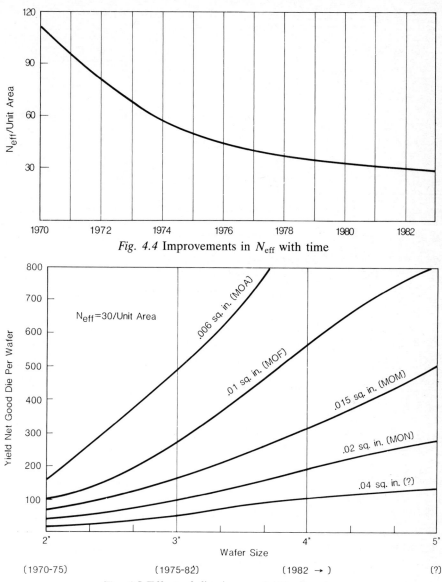

Fig. 4.4 Improvements in N_{eff} with time

Fig. 4.5 Effect of die size on yield/wafer size

The components and layout of a matrix cell are illustrated in fig. 4.6. Each cell consists of four NPN transistors, one dual current source, two load resistors, one biasing resistor and three low valued crossunder resistors. The components are laid out to provide optimum interconnection flexibility for single layer metal customisation.

MATRIX CELL   MATRIX CELL LAYOUT

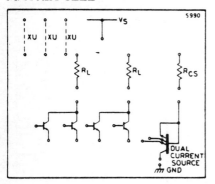
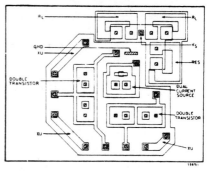

Fig. 4.6 Digilin matrix cell components and layout

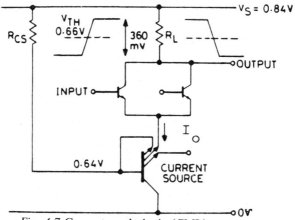

Fig. 4.7 Current mode logic (CML) gate structure

All arrays use a P-type epitaxy grown on top of a P-type substrate. The transistor pairs, current source and crossunders (denoted by XU) of the matrix cell lie on an epitaxial island completely surrounded by an N^+ diffusion. In addition, each individual transistor within this island is itself surrounded by a thin N^+ diffusion to isolate it from its neighbours and to facilitate contact to its collector. The three pinch resistors R_L, R_L, and R_{CS} are then produced from sections of epitaxial land into which N^+ has not been diffused and, being pinch resistors, they are overlaid with an emitter diffusion. All contacts are denoted by the cross-hatched areas of the layout diagram with emitters being identifiable because of the emitter diffusion surrounding the emitter contact. Crossunders are produced from N^+ diffusion. A positive voltage supply V_S ($= 0.89$ V) obtained from the on-chip regulator is distributed throughout the matrix of cells by the N^+ diffusion. The ground return current is then carried by the chip

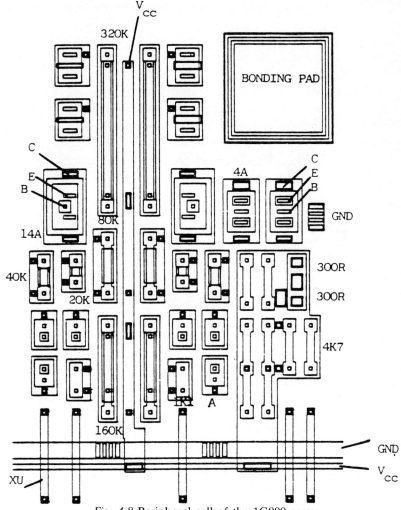

Fig. 4.8 Peripheral cell of the 1G000 array

substrate which is connected to each cell by the GND contact.

The components of each matrix cell were designed primarily for interconnection as two 2-input NOR gates using the 'Current Mode Logic' (CML) gate structure as shown in fig. 4.7.

The peripheral cells are primarily designed to provide a wide range of linear functions but can also be used for producing standard interfaces between matrix cell logic functions, and external circuitry. A typical peripheral cell is shown in fig. 4.8 and contains matched pairs of NPN transistors and matched pairs of different valued resistors. In addition to the repetitive peripheral cells, the arrays may also contain several larger geometry NPN devices and, in some cases, dedicated components which can be used in bandgap regulator configurations.

The table in fig. 4.9 shows the component breakdown of a family of such 'Digilin' arrays. Note that these specific chips make extensive use of high valued pinch resistors as well as nominal base resistors thereby enhancing the designer's ability to implement low power circuits for battery operation. CDI technology is also ideally suited to high frequency operation due to the inherently high f_T of the process. Therefore, it is feasible to consider other arrays with a dominance of lower valued base resistors for high frequency operation.

COMPONENT LIST FOR DIGILIN ARRAYS

	1G000	1U000	2U000	3U000
Matrix Cells				
NPN Transistor Pairs (collectors connected together)	98	286	512	578
NPN dual collector current source	49	143	256	289
Pinch Resistors 90 kohm / 150 kohm	147	429	768	867
Total Resistance	22 Mohm	38.6 Mohm	69.1 Mohm	78.0 Mohm
Peripheral Cells				
NPN Transistor 1A size	96			
NPN Transistor 4A size	32	104	240	128
NPN Transistor 14A size	32			16
NPN Transistor 100mA	2	–	–	–
Capacitor 35pF at 5 volts	2	–	–	–
Bandgap voltage reference	2	1	1	1
Base Resistors				
300 ohm	32	52	–	72
600 ohm	–	–	40	–
1.1 kohm	32	–	–	–
1.2 kohm	–	26	–	36
4.7 kohm	128	–	–	–
Pinch Resistors				
10 kohm	–	26	40	36
20 kohm	32	–	–	–
40 kohm	32	52	40	72
80 kohm	32	52	64	72
160 kohm	32	52	64	72
320 kohm	32	–	–	–
500 kohm	–	26	80	72
Total Resistance	20.6 Mohm	27.9 Mohm	57.4 Mohm	56.6 Mohm
Bond Pads	25	30	40	40
Chip Size (mils)	104 x 104	120 x 134	154 x 154	156 x 156

Fig. 4.9 Component list for Digilin arrays

4.4 CMOS technology

CMOS technology also has the ability to provide both linear and digital functions on the same chip. Standard analog products have been developed using CMOS processing and these circuit concepts can be easily adapted to semi-custom array implementations.

Presently two CMOS processes are being used in combination analog/digital arrays – metal gate and silicon gate.

4.4.1 Metal gate CMOS

Utilisation of metal gate CMOS in semi-custom arrays with analog content has taken two distinct phases: (a) implementation of analog circuitry on arrays designed for purely digital functions, and (b) the design of specific arrays incorporating device geometries and components more ideally suited to analog circuits. The component availability of the latter can best be illustrated by reference to the die photograph shown in fig. 4.10. The areas designated contain the following components:

A. A digital array cell containing five inverters with both P- and N-channel MOSFETs.
B. 6.5 Zender diodes for low power reference circuits.
C. 1.7 pF MOS capacitors for amplifier frequency compensation and switched capacitor circuits.
D. Input/output buffer transistors for digital I/O applications or medium resistance analog switches.

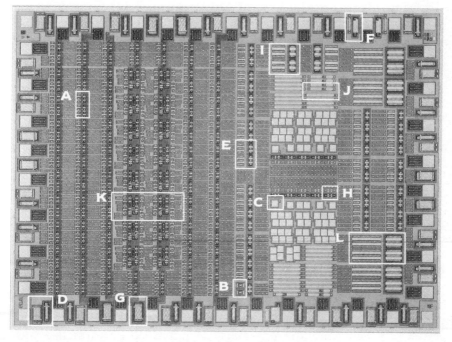

Fig. *4.10* Metal gate analog/digital array

E. MOS transistors for medium performance analog circuits requiring improved matching characteristics.
F. High impedance MOS transistors for low current inverters and analog start-up circuits.
G. Large NMOS 'power' transistors for digital I/O or low impedance analog switches.
H. Minimum geometry transistors suitable for analog switches for switched capacitor circuits.
I.   Matched pairs of P-channel and N-channel transistors suitable for active loads or differential input stage.
J. Large value P resistors for bias circuits and low power amplifier loads.
K. Dedicated flip-flops for logic implementation.
L. Large analog transistors for high performance analog circuits such as differential input stages with minimum noise and offset voltage.

In addition, any N-channel MOSFET can be used as an NPN bipolar transistor with its collector connected to V^+. P^+ crossunder resistors which can be used as matched resistors (typically 900 Ω each), and, in the peripheral cell areas, low valued N^+ resistors which can be used as low impedance crossunders (50–100 Ω) are available throughout the chip. Typical electrical parameters for a selection of these components are shown in fig. 4.11.

4.4.2 Silicon gate CMOS

A silicon gate CMOS combination analog/digital array bears many similarities to the metal gate array both in terms of component availability and chip layout. The technology itself provides some advantages over metal gate in such areas as:

smaller geometries
improved logic speed
reduced logic gate delay
better matching of transistors
lower noise
reduced gate capacitance
polysilicon crossunders (lower capacitance).

Circuit design techniques are equally applicable to both metal gate and silicon gate with the possibility of improved performance with silicon gate.

Active Components

MOSFETs

PARAMETER	NMOS	PMOS	UNITS	CONDITIONS
V_T	0.7 to 1.3	– 0.7 to – 1.3	V	$V_{GS} = V_{DS}$, $I_{DS} = 1\mu A$
Beta	18 to 32	5.9 to 10.2	$\mu A/V^2$	
Beta/L_{eff}	3.0 to 5.7	0.9 to 1.7	$\mu A/V^2 - u$	
V_{TF}	6.5 (min.)	– 6.5 (min.)	V	$V_{GS} = V_{DS}$, $I_{DS} = 1\mu A$
BV_{DSS}	20 (min.)	20 (min.)	V	$V_{GS} = 0$, $I_{DS} = 1\mu A$
BV_{N-P-}	22 (min.)		V	$I_{N-} = 1\mu A$
V_T T.C.	– 2.7 (typ)	– 2.1 (typ)	mV/°C	
Beta T.C.	– 0.4 (typ)	– 0.4 (typ)	%/°C	

NPNs

PARAMETER	MEASURED VALUE	CONDITIONS
d.c. current gain, h_{FE} temperature coef.	80 (typ) 0.2 %/°C	$I_E = 1mA$
LV_{CEO}	20V (min.)	$I_E = 1mA$
V_{BE} (Driver NMOS)	635mV (typ)	$I_E = 1mA$

Passive Components

ZENER

PARAMETER	MEASURED VALUE	CONDITIONS
BV	6.6V	$I_D = 10\mu A$
T.C.	2.1 %/°C	$I_D = 10\mu A$

RESISTORS

TYPE	SHEET RESISTANCE	T.C.	VOLT COEF.
P +	50 to 100 ohms/☐	.07 %/°C	
P –	1.5K to 4K ohms/☐	.40 %/°C	2 %/volt
N +	5 to 20 ohms/☐		

MOS CAPACITOR

SIZE	VOLT COEF.	MATCHING ACCURACY
1.7pF/Unit	.002 %/volt	.04 %

Fig. 4.11 Metal gate CMOS component parameters

4.5 Engineering, costs and applications

Knowing what technologies and products are available is the first step. Being able to utilise these products to satisfy specific needs requires consideration of several major factors such as engineering interface, development and device costs, and guidance in the types of applications which can be addressed.

4.5.1 Engineering interface

Developing a new semi-custom IC is a joint effort combining the user's circuit design efforts with the vendor's circuit integration, testing and production capabilities. The starting point is generally a design manual which provides all the data necessary to implement a design meeting specific applications requirements. Design manuals generally provide such information as: component parameters, circuit ideas, breadboarding and kit part data, layout guidelines, circuit analysis data, test plan information, etc., so that the end user design engineer can fully understand and specify how the final integrated circuit should be manufactured and tested in a production environment.

The major steps covered during a typical design program are shown in fig. 4.12, with estimates of the average times involved in the various stages.

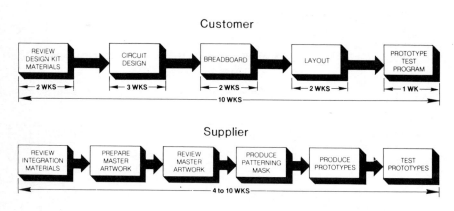

Fig. 4.12 Engineering design activities

4.5.2 Cost considerations

The cost accounting methods used in most companies fail to disclose the real difference between a product designed with standard ICs/discrete components and one designed with a custom IC. This is especially true for semi-custom linear approaches which have brought down the tooling charges of a full custom design, making its use economically feasible in a wide range of applications.

All of the factors outlined below have to be considered in order to make a realistic appraisal of the complete costs:

CIRCUIT DESIGN AND BREADBOARDING: A custom IC design incorporates new technology and, therefore, normally increases circuit design and breadboarding costs. However, with a semi-custom approach, the difference is relatively small.

An IC design must accommodate a broad range of transistor and resistor parameters. These tolerances are usually specified in a design kit. Extra design time will be required to accommodate the unusual tolerances. On the other hand, an IC provides excellent matching of parameters which often allows for a less complex circuit.

IC LAYOUT: After breadboarding the design, the next step is laying out the metallisation to interconnect the various components into the desired circuit configuration. The number of hours required to complete a layout depends largely on the percentage of utilisation of the available chip components.

IC TOOLING FEE: The cost of converting a layout to a metallisation mask pattern and subsequent wafer processing, testing and packaging is in the range of $2000 to $10 000 for semi-custom linear ICs.

PC BOARD LAYOUT: A PC board layout with a custom IC takes less time because of the reduced number of interconnections.

RELIABILITY TESTING: The cost is about the same as that for standard reliability testing of a custom or discrete design. The intrinsic quality level of a custom IC design, however, will always be superior due to the reduced number of components and interconnections.

SPECIAL PACKAGE DEVELOPMENT: Often PC board space is a critical factor, and a discrete design is not usable without creating a more efficient or larger system package. In addition to the cost of this special packaging effort, a larger system size could make a product less marketable.

DOCUMENTATION: Normally the following items require documentation:

* assembly procedures
* testing procedures
* PC board debugging procedures
* components and vendor listing
* inventory control procedures.

A semi-custom IC will reduce documentation costs related to component count.

OVERHEAD: Development overhead costs must include supervisory personnel, facilities costs, indirect supplies, power, etc.

COMPONENTS: Semi-custom pricing is closely tied to manufacturing yields, the chip type used, the package type and the production quantity.

SUPPLIES: The cost of supplies associated with production is about the same with either design approach.

PC BOARD: PC board costs and quality vary from vendor to vendor. As a general guideline on pricing in 1000 quantity levels, vendors usually charge as follows:

* set-up charge: $100–200
* single-sided boards: $0.037–0.045 per square inch
* double-sided boards: $0.065–0.75 per square inch
* cost per hole drilled: $0.0025–0.0035

The reduced number of components in a semi-custom IC design allows for a smaller PC board, perhaps a one-sided board.

DIRECT LABOUR:
1. Incoming inspection: ·
   Since a custom IC reduces the component count, incoming inspection costs are proportionately lower.
2. Assembly:
   As a cost guideline, PC board assembly usually works out to be about 2 cents per component inserted.
3. Test:
   Product testing costs should be the same for either design approach.
4. Rework cost:
   Rework costs are significantly reduced with a custom IC.

OVERHEAD:

1. Supervision:
    On the average, production supervisory costs consist of the
    following:

    * one line supervisor per four hourly employees
    * one section leader per three line supervisors
    * one general manager per four section leaders
    * one corporate officer per three managers.

    Salaries as a percentage of the hourly salary rate were:

    * line supervisor   175%
    * section leader   300%
    * general manager   400%
    * corporate officer   500%

    This results in a total supervisory overhead of 80%.

2. Purchasing and stocking:
    Purchasing costs are dependent on the number of vendors dealt
    with and, to a limited extent, volume. Stocking costs relate
    directly to the number of piece parts.

3. Inventory:
    A minimum stocking inventory is required of each component in
    order to sustain production. The cost of maintaining an inventory
    tends to be proportional to the component cost and delivery
    uncertainty. A significant advantage of a semi-custom approach
    is the reduced turnaround time since only the last step is custom
    and the wafers are pre-processed up to this point and held in
    inventory. Turnaround time for large quantities is eight weeks;
    for small quantities, five weeks.

4. Quality assurance:
    Quality assurance steps such as visual inspection of components
    are less time consuming with a custom IC design.

5. Field service:
    Field service costs will always be less for a PC board which uses a
    custom IC. This is due to the reduced component and
    interconnection count, resulting in an inherently more reliable
    product.

In deciding which solution is most cost effective, each particular
situation has to be evaluated. The factors contributing to the overall
cost of producing a piece of equipment should be calculated and used
to define the slope/crossover parts on the graph shown in fig. 4.13.

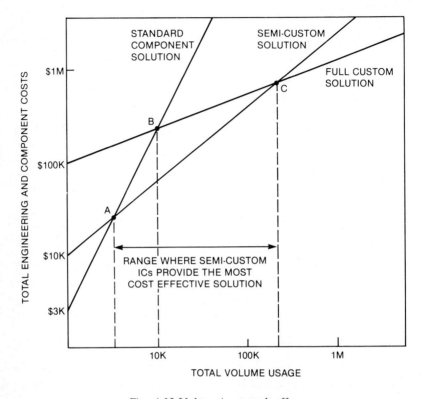

Fig. 4.13 Volume/cost tradeoffs

The scale factors in fig. 4.13 are variables depending on the cost parameters involved. The values shown are fairly typical for many applications. The semi-custom solution is therefore most cost effective in volume usages in the range of 2000 to 200 000 units, although examples exist where the concept has been fully cost effective outside these ranges – actual numbers being one hundred units to three million units.

4.5.3 Design aids and applications

Each technology, when used in linear designs, has its own individual set of components and characteristics. The design information provided by relevant design manuals attempts to present all the necessary information for independent designers to put together a basic design package which can then be used to produce an integrated circuit.

A design manual will contain information such as:

process description
component geometries
device characteristics
layout information
computer circuit analysis guidelines
kit parts
circuit building blocks
breadboarding guidelines
testing information
packaging information
reliability and quality data
application notes
circuit design examples.

The best way to understand how each technology can be used in linear circuit design is to look at some specific circuit configurations. The design techniques used in any technology take advantage of the inherent close matching capability of identical devices on the same chip rather than the wide absolute value tolerances attributable to process variations.

4.6 Standard bipolar circuits

NPN transistors, PNP transistors, base diffused resistors and pinch resistors in various combinations are available with this technology. Many circuits have been designed with these arrays and many ideas are available in the literature. The following circuits are representative of some that have been implemented.

4.6.1 Bandgap voltage regulator

A very common circuit configuration is shown in fig. 4.14. The basic bandgap circuit operates by producing a reference voltage, at the base of Q7, which is the sum of a V_{be} voltage and a voltage equal to 2R3/R2 times the current density difference between Q7 and transistors Q3–Q6 in parallel.

$$V_{ref} = V_{be} + \frac{2R3}{R2} \Delta V;$$

$\Delta V = 36$ mV in this example.

$$V_{ref} = 1.22 \text{ V (T.C.} \approx 0)$$

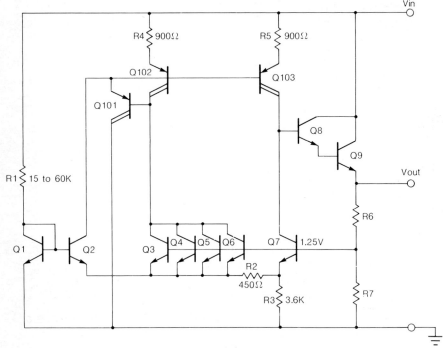

Fig. 4.14 Bipolar bandgap regulator

The currents in Q7 and Q3–Q6 are kept equal by means of the PNP current mirror circuit consisting of Q101–Q103. A negative feedback loop is completed by means of the Darlington emitter–follower stage, Q8 and Q9, and resistors R6 and R7. This allows the output voltage to be set to some multiple of V_{ref}.

$$V_{out} = V_{ref} \frac{R6 + R7}{R7}$$

Additional circuitry in the form of Q7 and Q2 provides a means of starting the circuit. Initially, when voltage is applied, Q1 is forward biased causing Q2 to conduct.

There are many other 'bandgap' configurations which, when combined with many regulator configurations such as positive or negative, series or shunt provide a whole range of regulator circuits to meet almost any possible circuit demand.

4.6.2 *Low voltage precision comparator with hysteresis*

Low voltage operation (1 volt supply) is possible with bipolar circuits provided any series path from V^+ to V^- does not include more than

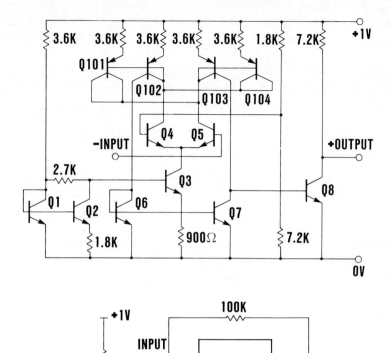

Fig. 4.15 Low voltage comparator with hysteresis

1 V_{be} voltage drop. One such circuit, incorporating several circuit concepts is shown in fig. 4.15. The comparator consists of a current source derived by Q1, Q2 and Q3; and NPN differential input stage, Q4 and Q5; and a cross-coupled active load consisting of Q101–Q104.

Hysteresis is defined by the number of collectors used in cross-coupling back to the opposite base of the active loads. In fig. 4.15 a 2:1 ratio will result in a 36 mV hysteresis at the input. With other ratios, different hysteresis values can be achieved.

No. of collectors	2	4	8	16
Hysteresis (mV)	36	72	108	144

The hysteresis is independent of the bias current provided by Q3. Additional current gain to drive the output load is provided by Q6, Q7, and Q8.

The circuit shown in fig. 4.15 utilises the comparator as a variable duty cycle oscillator. The duty cycle can be varied over the complete range of 0% to 100%. Nominal frequency at 50% duty cycle is 5kHz.

4.6.3 Gain control circuit

Figure 4.16 is a schematic of a simple AGC circuit. The input signal is attenuated by a voltage divider consisting of R_L and the impedance from the base of Q1 to the base of Q2. The low impedance voltage source on the back of Q2 keeps this point at AC ground. The impedance across Q1 and Q2 is the sum of their dynamic emitter resistance, R_E. This varies directly with emitter current. The emitter current of each transistor is half of the current in Q3 because of the current mirror Q101, Q102. The AGC input voltage is converted to a current by Q3 and R_E.

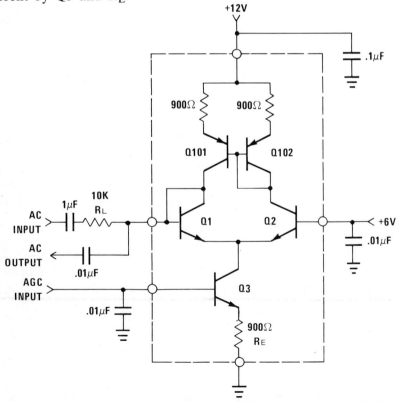

Fig. 4.16 Gain control circuit

The circuit gain as a function of control current I_{C3} is:

$$A_v = \frac{1}{1 + R_L\, I_{C3}/4V_T}$$

$$\text{where } V_T = kT/q$$

4.6.4 Analog switch

Selection of one out of a multiple of analog signals can be achieved by utilisation of an equivalent number of unity gain buffer amplifiers which can be switched on and off by means of controlling the bias current. Figure 4.17 shows a two-input switch in which the channel selection circuit consists of the differential pair Q3 and Q6 which can be switched into either state, Q3 conducting or Q6 conducting. The analog gates, consisting of Q1, Q2, Q101; and Q4, Q5, Q102, act as a unity gain buffer stage when energised or act as high impedance buffers if not energised.

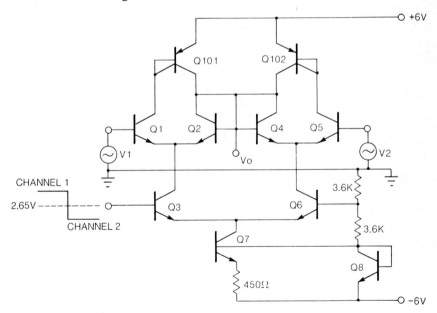

Fig. 4.17 Analog switch

4.6.5 Triac phase control circuit

As an example of a relatively simple circuit combining several circuit blocks into a functional IC, the block diagram of a triac phase control circuit is shown in fig. 4.18. This particular configuration could be used as an incandescent light dimmer. The IC generates its own dc

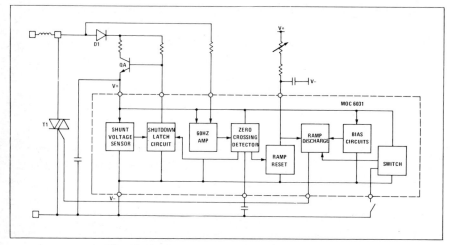

Fig. 4.18 Phase control system block diagram

power supply by means of selectively controlling the conduction of a high voltage transistor QA. Detection of the line frequency, 50 Hz or 60 Hz, is achieved by a current amplifier and zero voltage crossing pulses derived from it. These pulses are used to reset a timing circuit which, in turn, generates trigger pulses for the triac power device at a selected phase angle which can be controlled by a potentiometer.

A photograph of the completed IC is shown in fig. 4.19.

4.7 CDI circuits

The absence of PNP devices requires special design techniques to be able to utilise the CDI technology. However, utilisation of level shifting techniques allows many useful circuits to be implemented.

4.7.1 Bandgap voltage regulator

The circuit shown in fig. 4.20 is another form of bandgap regulator which is provided as a dedicated section in the periphery of Digilin arrays. This circuit generates a reference voltage equal to the sum of the base emitter voltage of Q3 and the voltage drop across R3. A 10:1 area difference between Q2 and Q1 results in a voltage across R2 which is amplified by R3 in the collector of Q2. Suitable ratioing of NPN transistor geometries and resistor ratios generates a zero T.C. bandgap reference at the plus input of the operational amplifier. The regulated output voltage can then be defined by choice of R4 and R5 in the feedback loop.

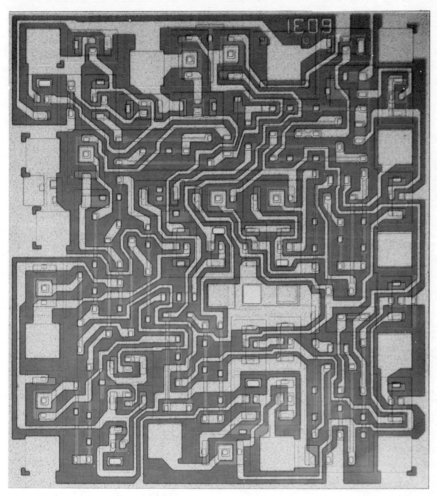

Fig. 4.19 Phase control die photograph

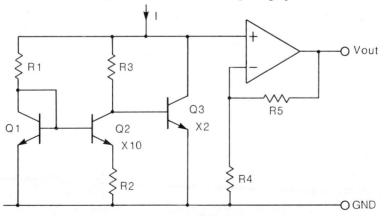

Fig. 4.20 Digilin bandgap regulator

4.7.2 Wideband operational amplifier

The operational amplifier circuit shown in fig. 4.21 uses NPNs exclusively and has inherently high bandwidth. The input stage consists of a differential Darlington configuration Q1, Q2, Q3 and Q4 with current sources Q5, Q6 and Q7 referenced to Q8. The level shifting and conversion to single-ended drive is accomplished by Q9, Q10, Q11, and Q12. The output stage can consist of two transistors in parallel – Q13 and Q14 with their base terminals brought out for frequency compensation. Open loop gain is typically 1000 with an open loop bandwidth of 300 kHz.

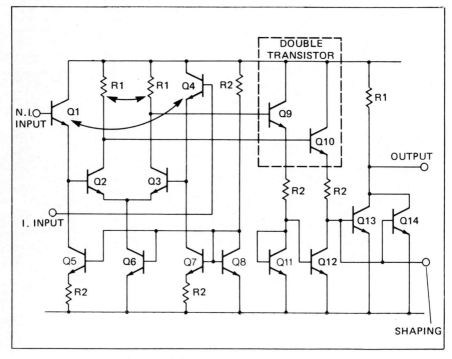

Fig. 4.21 Wideband operational amplifier

4.7.3 Four bit D–A converter

The circuit of fig. 4.22 consists of ratio'd current source Q1, Q2, Q3 and Q4 with ratio'd resistors R, R/2, R/4 and R/8 respectively referenced to a diode-resistor bias chain, Q5, Q6 and R/6. Differential amplifiers: Q7, Q8; Q9, Q10; Q11, Q12; and Q13, Q14; switched by inverters coupled to the logic inputs provide the digital to analog conversion switching required. The operating range of this converter is 0 to 70°C and is accurate to ± ½ LSB.

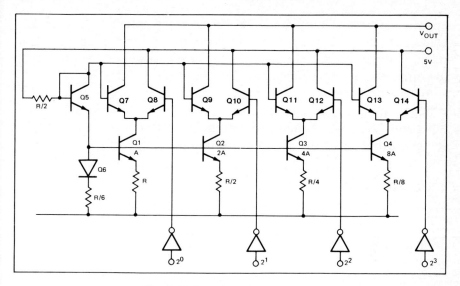

Fig. 4.22 Four-bit D–A converter

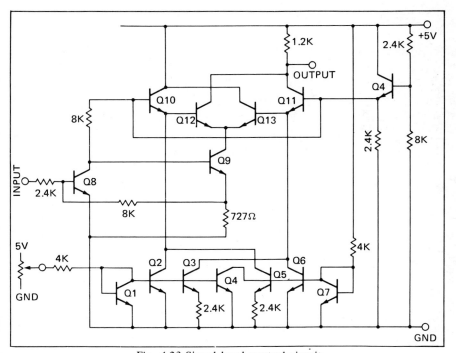

Fig. 4.23 Signal level control circuit

4.7.4 *Signal level control circuit*

The circuit of fig. 4.23 uses a well-known current splitting technique: Q1–Q7 provides differential ground reference variable DC current sources such that the currents in Q2 and Q6 are complementary and also the currents in Q3 and Q5 are complementary but of smaller value. Q8 and Q9 form a feedback amplifier converting the input signal voltage to a signal current at the collector of Q9. Q4 provides a low impedance bias voltage for Q10 and Q11.

When the current in Q10 is high, the current in Q11 is low, Q13 conducts most of the current from Q9 and very little signal current flows into the load. When the current in Q10 is low, almost all the signal current flows in Q12 and maximum current gain is achieved.

4.8 CMOS circuits

The circuit design techniques used in CMOS products do not differ significantly between metal gate or silicon gate technologies. The following circuits were implemented in metal gate but could be equally applicable to silicon gate.

4.8.1 Bandgap voltage regulator

To achieve both a low temperature coefficient and good supply rejection, a bandgap reference such as the one shown in fig. 4.24 is required. A two-stage operational amplifier with inputs Q101 and Q102 maintain equal voltages at the emitter of QN1 and the junction of R2 and R3. QN1 runs at $5R2/R1$ times the current density of QN2. The positive temperature coefficient voltage, V_{be} QN1 $- V_{be}$ QN2, appears across R3, is increased across R2, and is added to the V_{be} of QN2 to produce a temperature stable voltage of 1.25 V at Vo. The 8 kΩ resistor in series with the drain of Q3 ensures start-up of the reference. Stabilisation is achieved internally by tying the unused gates of QN1 and QN2 to the gate of Q3. To achieve a low output voltage temperature coefficient the voltage generated across R3 must be considerably larger than offset voltage of the operational amplifier.

4.8.2 Comparator with input hysteresis

The comparator of fig. 4.25 is useful when positive switching is required in the presence of noise. The magnitude of the hysteresis is independent of the common mode input voltage. The hysteresis is dependent on the bias current and the W/L ratio of Q106 to Q107 and Q108 to Q109 and can be set accurately anywhere between 2 mV and 100 mV. In this design the second-stage load consists of a cross-coupled current mirror arrangement (Q106–Q109) that behaves like a set–reset flip-flop. To insure a snap action, the hysteresis of this load is made much larger than the inherent mismatches of the transistors

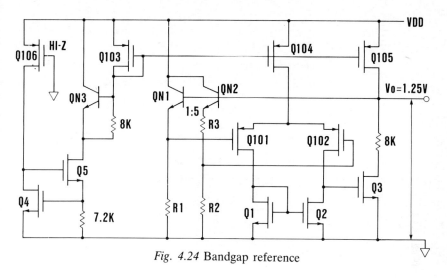

Fig. 4.24 Bandgap reference

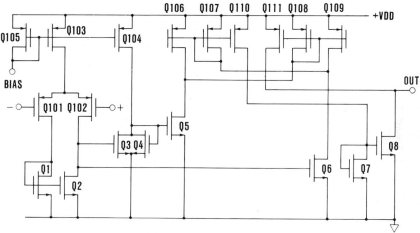

Fig. 4.25 Comparator with input hysteresis

themselves. The large hysteresis is divided by the gain of the first stage and appears as only a small input hysteresis.

4.8.3 Two-stage amplifier

This simple op amp design has proved to be the work horse of many linear/digital semi-custom CMOS designs. Using only digital array transistors with bias = 10 μA, the typical gain is 8000 with 60 dB CMRR and 25 mV of input offset voltage. Medium and high performance transistors are available which can boost the voltage gain as much as twenty-five times while dropping V_{os} below 10 mV and input flicker noise below 100 nV $Hz^{-\frac{1}{2}}$.

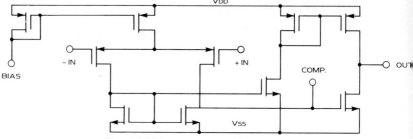

Fig. 4.26 Two-stage amplifier

4.8.4 Low power crystal oscillator

The total power consumption of this micropower crystal oscillator design, shown in fig. 4.27, is controlled by high impedance N-channel MOSFETs which operate at approximately 4 μA drain current when $V_{DD} = 5$ V. Using a 32 kHz quartz crystal the total power dissipation is $\frac{1}{4}$ mW.

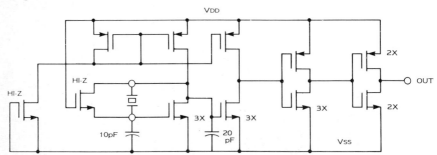

Fig. 4.27 Low power crystal oscillator

4.8.5 Switched capacitor second-order low-pass filter

Two second-order switched capacitor filter sections which use the basic circuit topology can be designed. The schematic in fig. 4.28 represents a Chebychev low-pass filter with a 2 kHz cutoff frequency and 0.3 dB passband ripple. The integrating amplifiers' frequency compensation as well as continuous time anti-alias filtering is available on chip.

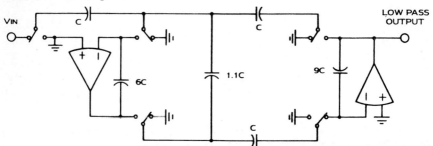

Fig. 4.28 Switched capacitor second-order low-pass filter

4.9 Future trends

There have been many recent developments in the technologies used and in the availability of semi-custom arrays targeted for general purpose and special function applications. While it is too early to determine which of the techniques presented will become successful products, it is of interest to look at these as a means of identifying and stimulating ideas for new products. In addition to the three major technologies discussed in detail, other available alternatives are:

4.9.1 Analog array with on-chip photodetector

An analog array is available from Cherry Semiconductor which contains a large photodetector that exhibits good linearity from 50 pA to 50 μA. It is similar to the MOA chip and can be housed in clear plastic dual-in-line packages.

4.9.2 Analog array with on-chip FETs

By the use of ion implantation and other process improvements, Exar has developed a 36 V array which contains P-channel JFETs, high value ion implant resistors, oxide capacitors and also utilises nitride passivation to improve reliability. This enables the designer to incorporate precision operational amplifiers, BIFET op amps with high slew rate, sample and hold amplifiers, and A–D converters.

4.9.3 Analog array with high current/power capability

This array, available from MCE, combines ion implant technology with 15 A power transistors on a chip which can be housed in a power package with a capability of 30 W. The chip is structured to provide five dedicated op amps two of which utilise zener zapping to trim offset voltage to less than 200 μV.

4.9.4 High frequency analog arrays

Analog arrays utilising low resistivity epi material, shallow base diffusion, and washed emitters will be available to provide higher frequency capability with NPN f_Ts in the 1–2 GHz range. Applications in the areas of read/write channels for floppy and hard disk memories as well as conditioning amplifiers in fibre optic systems can be visualised.

4.9.5 I^2L technology

Combination linear/digital arrays utilising I^2L technology are available from Exar, Cherry and MCE. These chips allow the user to combine general purpose analog designs with medium speed digital capability.

4.9.6 Switched capacitor filters

Both Silicon Systems Inc. and EG&G Reticon have introduced chips which provide components suitable for the implementation of switched capacitor filter circuits. Silicon Systems utilises metal gate CMOS technology with the components arranged in bi-quad blocks. EG&G Reticon utilises a double polysilicon NMOS process with the chip divided into a digital section, operational amplifier section and a switched capacitor array section. Filters can be designed to operate up to 20–30 kHz with passband accuracy of 0.2 dB.

4.9.7 Standard cells

The standard cell concept lies between full custom and semi-custom arrays in that specific circuit configurations are available and can be put together on a single chip which then has to be processed fully through all diffusion steps. The concept reduces design time but still requires fully customised mask sets and diffused wafers. Products available in this area utilise many different technologies:

Zymos – Produces combined analog/digital arrays using a silicon gate CMOS process.

AMI – Has produced a codec chip with μ-law and A-law data converters with 8-bit accuracy from standard building blocks which include bandgap reference, low-pass filter, switched capacitor arrays, sample and hold amplifier, A–D encoder and others.

SGS – In the area of higher performance, a series of arrays offered by SGS, called MTL^3V (merged transistor logic, linear, low voltage), are available in a standard cell format. This technology allows the integration of high performance analog, I^2L, and high speed ECL circuits on the same chip. Typical cells available include 200 MHz binary divider, wide band op amp, bandgap reference, 6-bit D–A converter and 500 mA output capability.

Harris Corporation – Has utilised a silicon gate process to produce mixed function CMOS standard cells designed for subthreshold operation. Typical analog cells include op amps, comparators, bandgap regulators, filters and multiplexers.

NCR – Utilises CMOS to provide analog cells on otherwise all-digital arrays. One such cell is an op amp with 90 dB gain, 2 MHz bandwidth, and 15 mV offset capability.

The boundary between standard cells and semi-custom arrays will eventually become blurred by concepts that will allow fabrication of identical functions on both cells and arrays.

4.9.8 Other technologies

Development work is known to be underway with other technologies such as dielectric isolation, high voltage bipolar, mixed MOS and bipolar, and thin film processing. It is expected that all viable technologies will eventually emerge with some form of analog array capability.

4.9.9 Additional information

For those readers who require more detailed information on semi-custom arrays most companies provide design brochures and manuals covering their specific products. Following is a list of companies who are known to provide some form of analog capability:

Interdesign, Inc., Scotts Valley, California, U.S.A.
Ferranti Electronics Ltd, Oldham, England
Exar Integrated Systems, Sunnyvale, California, U.S.A.
Cherry Semiconductor Corporation, East Greenwich, Rhode Island, U.S.A.
Micro Circuit Engineering, West Palm Beach, Florida, U.S.A.
California Devices Inc., San Jose, California, U.S.A.
Linear Technology Inc., Burlington, Ontario, Canada
Harris Corporation, Melbourne, Florida, U.S.A.
Telmos Inc., Sunnyvale, California, U.S.A.
Silicon Systems Inc., Tustin, California, U.S.A.
EG&G Reticon, Sunnyvale, California, U.S.A.
Holt Integrated Circuits, Irvine, California, U.S.A.
Mitel Corporation, Kanata, Ontario, Canada
NCR Corporation, Fort Collins, Colorado, U.S.A.
American Microsystems Inc., Santa Clara, California, U.S.A.
Siliconix Inc., Santa Clara, California, U.S.A.

SGS-ATES, Milan, Italy
Micro Power Systems Inc., Santa Clara, California, U.S.A.
Zymos Corporation, Sunnyvale, California, U.S.A.
Plessey, Swindon, England
Thomson-CSF, Grenoble, France

Some of the larger semiconductor companies are probably preparing to penetrate the semi-custom analog field with their own offerings although no detailed information is available at this time.

4.10 References

4.1 Interdesign Application Notes, *APN1-35*, (covering many aspects of Semi-Custom IC design).

4.2 Bray, Derek, 'Design and applications using a family of bipolar linear arrays', *Proceedings of the 1st International Conference on Semi-Custom ICs*, November 1981.

4.3 Bray, Derek, 'The advantages of large bipolar semi-custom arrays in linear systems', *Proceedings of the 2nd International Conference on Semi-Custom ICs*, November 1982.

4.4 Bray, Derek, 'The use of bipolar semiconductor junctions in linear circuit design', *Microelectronics Journal*, Vol. 14, No. 3 (Benn Publications Ltd.) 1983.

4.5 'Semi-Custom Analog Capabilities', Papers by: Derek Bray, (Interdesign); James Norrish, (M.C.E.); Alan Buxton, (Ferranti); and Ted Pickerrell, (Interdesign). *Session 14, WESCON*, 1982.

4.6 '201 Analog IC Designs' by Interdesign Engineering Staff, published by Interdesign, 1980.

4.7 'IC Lecture Series' an introduction to integrated circuit design, published by Interdesign, 1978.

4.8 Bray, Derek, 'The impact of semi-custom ICs on automotive applications', *IEEE Chicago Spring Conference on Consumer Electronics*, June 1980.

4.9 Bray, Derek, 'Semi-custom analog bipolar arrays', various EDN Seminars, 1981.

4.10 Bray, Derek, 'Design and applications using a family of bipolar arrays', various EDN Seminars, 1982.

4.11 Bray, Derek, 'Bipolar semi-custom ICs in consumer non-entertainment applications' *IEEE Chicago Fall Conference on Consumer Electronics*, 1980.

4.12 Bray Derek, 'Analog capabilities in gate arrays' *IEEE 1979 Workshop*; Solid State Circuits and Technology Committee.

4.13 'Semi-Custom Linear and Digital IC Arrays', papers by: Alan Cox, (Ferranti); Bill O'Neal, (Exar); Charlie Allen, (Master Logic); and Derek Bray, (Interdesign). *Session 13, WESCON*, 1979.

4.14 'Analog Circuits Using MOS Technology', papers by: David Hodges, (University of California, Berkeley); Bill Nicholson, (A.M.I.); Robert Holm, (Intel); David Bingham, (Intersil); and Rich Kash, (Interdesign). *Session 26, WESCON*, 1980.

4.15 'Semi-Custom Integrated Circuit Design', papers by: Derek Bray, (Interdesign); Jim Feit, (Interdesign); Robert Probst, (I.B.M.); and Ewan MacPherson, (Countermeasures Inc.). *Proceedings of the National Electronics Conference, Session 7,* Vol. 32, 1978.

4.16 Irissou, Pierre, (Atac Diffusion), 'Combining linear and digital functions on single bipolar/CMOS/ULA chips', *Proceedings of the 2nd International Conference on Semi-Custom ICs*, November 1982.

4.17 Brown, Paul, 'Processing sparks improvements of semi-custom linear chips', by Paul Brown, *Electronic Design*, December 1982.

Chapter 5

Computer Aided Design for Logic Arrays

GRAHAM HETHERINGTON

Texas Instruments Ltd, UK

5.1 Introduction

The design of integrated circuits is one of the few 20th century technologies which is always carried out with the aid of computers. The major reason for this is the size and complexity of integrated circuits. Manual design is possible, but it is characterised by a high incidence of human error, together with long schedules; a result of the time-consuming process of manual design verification.

On the other hand, a computer aided system allows designs to be generated in shorter periods of time, and with a high degree of design correctness. The attendant extra costs of computer hardware, and support for a computer aided system, are less than the alternative costs of longer schedules, and greater incidence of committing 'final', but incorrect designs, to silicon.

A computer aided system provides a medium in which designs may be postulated and then verified by simulation and analysis. Once verification is complete, the design is then resident on a computer and generation of the numerical control tapes used for pattern generation is usually a simple task. Such pattern generation tapes are used in the fabrication of the integrated circuit.

Whilst limited by the media of computer hardware and the inventiveness of computer programmers, computer aided design is roughly a replacement for the breadboards, waveform generators, oscilloscopes and logic analysers traditionally used in the process of design. As such, it is all that is needed to perform VLSI design. Careful note, however, must be made of the term 'computer aided design'. The computer is so often seen as an all powerful replacement for the design engineer. Instead of talking about computer aided design, one is tempted to use the term, 'design automation:' whilst it is true that some areas of computer aided design do embody automatic synthesis such areas are few and far between.

The computer is a great practical and economic help to design, but software development is far from the stage of producing a program which takes as input a functional requirement and produces, as output, a complete design! With this in mind, we will next consider the relationship between computer aided design and logic arrays.

5.1.1 Computer aided design for logic arrays

Until recently, the use of computer aided design has been the preserve of elite groups of designers working on the leading edge of integration, producing the standard building blocks used by system and logic designers. The advent of logic arrays has caused the beginning of a revolution in computer aided design. The present population of IC designers numbers in the thousands worldwide, now with the arrival of logic arrays are added the tens of thousands of logic system designers.

In the initial stage of this revolution the computer aided design systems used for in-house, full custom design, were stripped of all unnecessary parts such as circuit design and released to this new population of logic array designers. Such systems were, and still are, big, cumbersome and difficult to use. The result has been a strong movement towards compact, fully integrated, and above all, easy to use computer aided design systems tailored specifically for logic arrays. Such systems have taken advantage of the recent leaps in computer hardware capability combining 32-bit computing power with high resolution graphics to present the traditional functions of computer aided design in a highly usable and ergonomic form.

These functions of computer aided design, and their embodiment in logic array design systems, form the subject of the current chapter.

5.1.2 Organisation of this chapter

This chapter will describe those areas in which a computer can aid the design of logic arrays. Wherever possible design examples will be used to illustrate the various uses of available design functions.

Having described the individual functions, we will consider the important question of their packaging, both software and hardware, into a product recognisable as a logic array design system.

Finally, the future of semi-custom computer aided design is examined. It is recognised that logic arrays fall into a spectrum of customisable products from microcomputers through to logic arrays, standard cell products and full custom integrated circuits. The recognition of this spectrum, together with the thrust to provide more customisable integration which it represents, strongly indicates the future of design products, of which logic array systems are the first.

5.2 The logic array design cycle

Having decided to use logic arrays in a product, there are several recognisable stages in the design process which can be described as follows:

Logic array choice

System design, partitioning and behavioural design

Logic and electrical design

Test generation

Layout

Design verification

These design stages are not always followed for particular logic array products and their relative importance in project schedules will vary. An atypical example might be the conversion of an existing logic function, currently implemented with TTL logic, to logic array form. Here system and functional design have already been executed. A typical logic array product would have the project breakdown shown in fig. 5.1, where the dominance of system and logic design are evident.

There are always at least two parties involved in a product development, the logic array customer and the vendor. This relationship will involve a splitting of the design responsibilities between the two. A novice user would probably leave all stages to the vendor, presenting the vendor with just a product specification. A mature customer could conceivably carry out all stages in the design process providing the vendor with a pattern generator tape. A typical responsibility split is shown in fig. 5.2. Here the customer is responsible for function and logic design and test generation and the vendor carries out layout, pattern generation and fabrication. Notice the feedback paths in this design interface. A vendor will usually

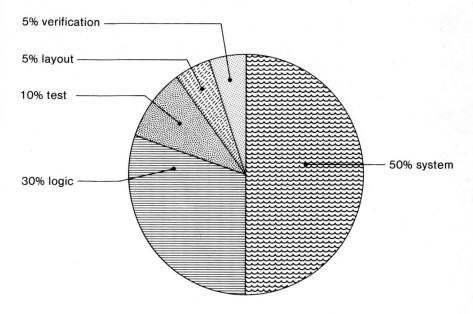

5% verification

5% layout

10% test

30% logic

50% system

Fig. 5.1 Breakdown of logic array design time

provide accurate delay information after layout which can be used for a final design verification prior to fabrication.

5.3 Logic array choice

Choosing a logic array from amongst the burgeoning number on offer is one of the key activities in logic array design, for it is at this stage that array performance and compatibility are decided. The key technical issues are logic function capability, performance and array buffering. The latter determines whether an alien array technology will fit into the requisite product system. Design tradeoffs are made here, concerning speed, cost, power consumption and compatibility.

There are secondary effects of the logic array choice. For example, the actual design process and cycle time will be determined: these being a function of the associated vendor.

At the present time, and for the foreseeable future the whole of this activity must be carried out manually. Eventually, database systems might be set up containing complete product specifications, and these could be used as a basis for answering array choice questions.

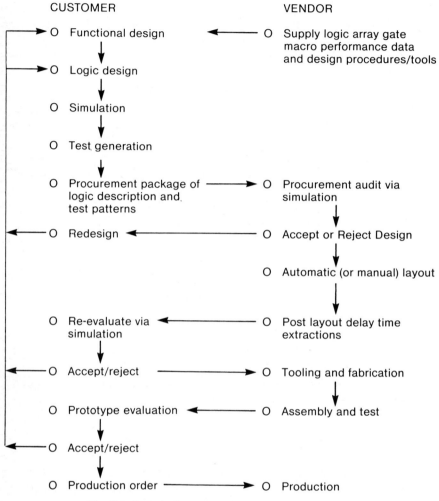

Fig. 5.2 A typical customer/vendor design interface

5.4 System design, partitioning and behavioural design

A logic array will be part of the electronic system such as a computer, a flight control system, a video games machine. Such systems often have specific design tools which aid or automate their design. It is beyond the scope of this work to consider the whole field of specific design tools; as a couple of examples one could site the register transfer level simulators used in computer system design, and the filter function generators used in communications applications.

Whatever the system into which the logic array is placed the functions relegated to the logic array must be partitioned into the array and during system design the array somehow simulated. There are no formal tools to aid in system partitioning, the major questions here are overall logic array utilisation in terms of number of input and output signals, or pins, and percentage use of the actual array of gates. The pinout will be limited by package to anything from twenty to approaching 200, whilst array usage can be anything from 75% for logic arrays which need guaranteed autolayout to 98% for arrays where manual layout completion is feasible.

System level design simulators are available for modelling whole arrays or electronic systems, of which logic arrays form a part. Such simulators allow the input of a design description in terms of a behavioural programming language, they then execute such programs under system conditions providing both confirmation of the design architecture and an environment from which more detailed design partitioning and development can proceed.

A feeling for such behavioural simulation can be obtained by considering an example system, a simplified 8-bit microcomputer. A behavioural program for such a microcomputer is shown in figs 5.3 and 5.4. In crude terms the program specifies how the micro's outputs change with time for a given set of input signals. This description is compiled and then simulated with a behavioural simulator. The simulator is commanded to set the micro input signals to required values, execute the program until all activity within the program has ceased whereupon the resultant output values and their timing can be verified.

For the micro in question the inputs comprise one for integer values, a function selection input, enter and onoff inputs. The outputs are simply an integer output for results and an error condition indicator. After the input and output definitions the program declares several variables which are used during simulation to hold information. Notable amongst these variables are the micro's ROM and RAM represented by arrays of 8-bit words and the ACCUMULATOR and PROGRAM COUNTER registers represented by a single 8-bit word and an integer variable respectively.

The program has three main sections dependent on the values of the micro inputs:

● power-up
● illegal input
● legal computation.

The power-up is activated by setting the onoff input to logic high, whereupon the program counter is 'zeroed', several variables and registers are cleared and the outputs scheduled to reach zero at 10 time units after onoff is set high. Notice the key statements of SCHEDULE and EXIT. A behavioural program, having determined output values must be able to output these values at specific times and cease execution.

The illegal input operation is activated when 'onoff' is low and 'enter'

```
                              Part 1
BLOCK EIGHT_BIT_MICRO DESIGN;
(*                                                                    *)
(*          INPUTS ARE:-     INTEGER 8 BIT NUMBER ENTRY               *)
(*                           INTEGER 8 BIT FUNCTION ENTRY             *)
(*                           ACCEPT INPUT   ('ENTER')                 *)
(*                           ONOFF SWITCH                             *)
(*          OUTPUTS ARE:-    INTEGER 8 BIT NUMBER DISPLAY             *)
(*                           ERROR INDICATOR                          *)
(*                                                                    *)
(*          WORD LENGTH IS 8 BITS.                                    *)
(*          CONTAINS 256 WORDS OF RAM.                                *)
(*          CONTAINS 256 WORDS OF ROM HOLDING STORED PROGRAM.         *)
(*          INSTRUCTION FORMAT IS THE FOLLOWING WORD TRIPLETS         *)
(*          OPERATOR, MEMORY ADDRESS, DATA                            *)
(*                                                                    *)
(*          BASIC COMPUTER INSTRUCTIONS ARE:-                         *)
(*                                                                    *)
(*   ADD    MEM         ADD MEM TO ACCUMULATOR                        *)
(*   SUB    MEM         SUBTRACT MEM FROM ACCUMULATOR                 *)
(*   LOAD   MEM         COPY CONTENTS OF MEM INTO ACCUMULATOR         *)
(*   STORE  MEM         COPY CONTENTS OF ACCUMULATOR INTO MEM         *)
(*   CLEAR              CLEAR ACCUMULATOR                             *)
(*   DEC               DECREMENT ACCUMULATOR                          *)
(*   INC               INCREMENT ACCUMULATOR                          *)
(*   SHFTLL            LOGICAL SHIFT LEFT ON ACCUMULATOR BY N BITS,   *)
(*                     N GIVEN BY CONTENTS OF MEM                     *)
(*   AND               LOGICAL AND OF ACCUMULATOR WITH MEM, ANSWER    *)
(*                     IN ACCUMULATOR                                 *)
(*   COMP   MEM        COMPARE CONTENTS OF MEM WITH ACCUMULATOR       *)
(*                     SETTING FLAGS REGISTER ACCORDINGLY             *)
(*   JUMP   MEM        UNCONDITIONAL JUMP IN PROGRAM CONTROL BY DATA  *)
(*   JUMPC  MEM        CONDITIONAL JUMP IN PROGRAM CONTROL            *)
(*                     BY AMMONT GIVEN IN DATA ACCORDING AS CONTENTS  *)
(*                     OF MEM SAME AS FLAGS REGISTER                  *)
(*   READ   MEM        COPY CONTENTS OF INPUT TO MEM                  *)
(*   READF             MOVE CONTENTS OF FUNCTION INTO MEM             *)
(*   LOADC             LOAD DATA INTO MEM                             *)
(*   WRITE  MEM        COPY CONTENTS OF MEM TO OUTPUT                 *)
(*   WAIT              SUSPEND MICRO OPERATION                        *)

(*                 MICRO INPUTS AND OUTPUTS                           *)

INTEGER_INPUT(7 TO 0)          a   INPUT;
FUNCTION_INPUT(7 TO 0)         a   INPUT;
ENTER                          a   INPUT;
ONOFF                          a   INPUT;
OUTPUT(7 TO 0)                 a   OUTPUT;
ERROR                          a   OUTPUT;

BEHAVIOUR FUNCTIONAL PROGRAM;

(*      DECLARE MEMORY- PROGRAM ROM, RAM,                             *)

BOOLEAN
ROM( 1 TO 256, 7 TO 0 ),
RAM( 1 TO 256, 7 TO 0 ),

(*      DECLARE REGISTERS                                             *)

ACCUMULATOR( 7 TO 0 ),
RAM_ADDRESS_REGISTER( 7 TO 0 ),
RAM_TRANSFER_REGISTER( 7 TO 0 ),
FLAGS(7 TO 0),
INSTRUCTION_REGISTER(1 TO 3, 7 TO 0);

(*      DECLARE LOCAL VARIABLES                                       *)

INTEGER
PROGRAM_COUNTER,
OPERATOR,
MEMORY1,
DATA,
COMPUTING,
DIFFERENCE,
WORD;
```

Fig. 5.3 Behavioural description of a microcomputer

Part 2

```
(*        POWER UP DEVICE, CLEAR DISPLAY AND REGISTERS, INITIALISE        *)
(*        PROGRAM COUNTER                                                  *)

IF ONOFF = B'1' THEN
POWERUP:      BEGIN
              PROGRAM_COUNTER := a-2;
              OUTPUT(7 TO 0) := B'00000000';
              ACCUMULATOR := RAM_ADDRESS_REGISTER := FLAGS :=
              RAM_TRANSFER_REGISTER := B'00000000';
              COMPUTING := 0;
              ERROR := 0;
              SCHEDULE OUTPUT,ERROR AT 10;
              EXIT;
              END;(* OF POWERUP *)

END;(*IF ONOFF HIGH*)

(*        ILLEGAL INPUT, ENTER AND FUNCTION INPUT EQUAL                    *)

IF ( ENTER = 0 #* FUNCTION_INPUT = 0) #+
                        ( ENTER <> 0 #* FUNCTION_INPUT <> 0 )  THEN
                        SCHEDULE ERROR AT 10;
                        EXIT;
END;(* ENTER AND FUNCTION HIT TOGETHER ILLEGALLY *)

(*        LEGAL ENTRY OF INPUT AND FUNCTION OR INPUT AND ENTER            *)

IF FUNCTION_INPUT = 0 THEN
                        DO PROGRAM_EXECUTION;
                        EXIT;
                        ELSE
                        PROGRAM_COUNTER := a-2;
                        OUTPUT(7 TO 0) := B'00000000';
                        SCHEDULE OUTPUT AT 10;
                        DO PROGRAM_EXECUTION;
                        EXIT;
END;(* LEGAL FUNCTION OR ENTER MADE *)

PROGRAM_EXECUTION:
    BEGIN
    WHILE COMPUTING = 0 DO
    PROGRAM_COUNTER := PROGRAM_COUNTER a+ 3;
    FOR WORD := 1 TO 3 DO
    INSTRUCTION_REGISTER(WORD,7 TO 0)
                        := ROM(PROGRAM_COUNTER a+ WORD a- 1, 7 TO 0);
    END;

(*        DECODE INSTRUCTION                                              *)

    OPERATOR := INSTRUCTION_REGISTER(1);
    MEMORY1  := INSTRUCTION_REGISTER(2);
    DATA     := INSTRUCTION_REGISTER(3) a- 127;

(*        FETCH CONTENTS OF MEMORY1                                       *)

    RAM_ADDRESS_REGISTER := MEMORY1;
    RAM_TRANSFER_REGISTER := RAM(RAM_ADDRESS_REGISTER, 7 TO 0) a- 127;

(*        EXECUTE OPERATION                                               *)
    CASE OPERATOR OF
    (*ADD*)   1:   ACCUMULATOR := ACCUMULATOR a+ RAM_TRANSFER_REGISTER;
    (*SUB*)   2:   ACCUMULATOR := ACCUMULATOR a- RAM_TRANSFER_REGISTER;
    (*LOAD*)  3:   ACCUMULATOR := RAM_TRANSFER_REGISTER;
    (*STORE*) 4:   RAM_TRANSFER_REGISTER := ACCUMULATOR;
                   RAM(RAM_ADDRESS_REGISTER,7 TO 0) :=
                                        RAM_TRANSFER_REGISTER a+ 127;
    (*CLEAR*) 5:   ACCUMULATOR := 0;
    (*DEC*)   6:   ACCUMULATOR := ACCUMULATOR a- 1;
    (*INC*)   7:   ACCUMULATOR := ACCUMULATOR a+ 1;
    (*SHFTLL*)8:   ACCUMULATOR := SLL(ACCUMULATOR,RAM_TRANSFER_REGISTER);
    (*AND*)   9:   ACCUMULATOR := AND(ACCUMULATOR,RAM_TRANSFER_REGISTER);
    (*COMP*)  10:  DIFFERENCE := ACCUMULATOR a- RAM_TRANSFER_REGISTER;
                   IF DIFFERENCE  < 0 THEN FLAGS := 1; END;
                   IF DIFFERENCE  = 0 THEN FLAGS := 2; END;
                   IF DIFFERENCE  > 0 THEN FLAGS := 3; END;
    (*JUMP*)  11:  PROGRAM_COUNTER := PROGRAM_COUNTER a+ 3 a* DATA;
    (*JUMPC*) 12:  IF FLAGS = RAM_TRANSFER_REGISTER THEN
                   PROGRAM_COUNTER := PROGRAM_COUNTER a+ 3 a* DATA;
                   FLAGS := 0;  END;
    (*READ*)  13:  RAM(RAM_ADDRESS_REGISTER,7 TO 0) :=INTEGER_INPUT a+ 127;
    (*READF*) 14:  RAM(RAM_ADDRESS_REGISTER,7 TO 0) := FUNCTION_INPUT
                                        a+ 127;
    (*LOADC*) 15:  RAM(RAM_ADDRESS_REGISTER,7 TO 0) := DATA a+ 127;
    (*WRITE*) 16:  OUTPUT := RAM_TRANSFER_REGISTER;
                   SCHEDULE OUTPUT AT 10;
    (*WAIT*)  17:  EXIT;
    END;(* OF OPERATOR CASES *)
    WAIT 20;(* PROGRAM EXECUTION CYCLE TIME *)
    END;(* OF PROGRAM EXECUTION CYCLE *)
    END;(* OF PROGRAM EXECUTION *)
END EIGHT_BIT_MICRO;
```

Fig. 5.4 Behavioural description of a microcomputer

and 'function' are both high or low. This mode simply schedules a high output on ERROR after 10 time units.

The legal computation section has two cases: function low activates the 'program-execution' loop and exits without necessarily scheduling any change in the micro's outputs, function high resets the program counter, schedules zero on the result at 10 time units and activates the 'program-execution' loop. The 'program-execution' loop comprises the operations:

1. get an instruction
2. decode instruction
3. execute instruction

repeated indefinitely at the rate of one instruction per 20 time units. The programming construct:

COMPUTING: = 0;

WHILE COMPUTING = 0 DO

. . . . get instruction

. . . . decode instruction

CASE instruction OF

1. . .

2. . .

etc.

17: EXIT;

END (*CASE*)

WAIT 20

END (*WHILE*)

implements this function. Notice that 'COMPUTING' in this case is a variable used solely as a programming construct. Also simulation proceeds indefinitely until an EXIT instruction is encountered.

The simulation of this behavioural program was accomplished via the simulator commands given in fig. 5.5. The trace statements are instructions to trace the activity of the micro's inputs and outputs and selected behavioural variables, e.g. ACCUMULATOR. The first display instruction is used in conjunction with later display statements

```
(* SIMULATION CONTROL LANGUAGE COMMANDS *)

      (* SET UP SIGNALS TO BE TRACED *)

TRACE  VAR=(INTEGER_INPUT,FUNCTION_INPUT,ENTER,ONOFF,OUTPUT,ERROR),
          OUTFORM=TABLE,FORM=DEC;
TRACE  VAR=(OPERATOR,MEMORY1,DATA,ACCUMULATOR),
          OUTFORM=TABLE,FORM=DEC;
DISPLAY VAR=(INTEGER_INPUT,FUNCTION_INPUT,ENTER,ONOFF,OUTPUT,ERROR)
        ,OUTFORM=TABLE1,FORM=DEC;

      (* LOAD ROM *)
          READ INFORM=SVAL;
      (* SWITCH ON MICRO *)
          SET ENTER  : = 0;
          SET FUNCTION_INPUT  : = 0;
          SET INTEGER_INPUT  : = 0;
          SET ONOFF  : = 1;
          RUN UNTIL STEADY;
          TESTPATTERN;
          DISPLAY OUTFORM=TABLE1;
      (* DO AN ADDITION  10 + 5 *)
          SET ONOFF  : = 0;
          SET INTEGER_INPUT  : = 10;
          SET FUNCTION_INPUT  : = 1;
          SET ENTER  : = 0;
          RUN UNTIL STEADY;
          TESTPATTERN;
          DISPLAY OUTFORM=TABLE1;
          SET FUNCTION_INPUT  : = 0;
          SET INTEGER_INPUT  : = 5;
          SET ENTER  : = 1;
          RUN UNTIL STEADY;
          TESTPATTERN;
          DISPLAY OUTFORM=TABLE1;
      (* DO A SUBTRACTION 100 - 25 *)
          SET ONOFF  : = 0;
          SET INTEGER_INPUT  : = 100;
          SET FUNCTION_INPUT  : = 2;
          SET ENTER  : = 0;
          RUN UNTIL STEADY;
          TESTPATTERN;
          DISPLAY OUTFORM=TABLE1;
          SET FUNCTION_INPUT  : = 0;
          SET INTEGER_INPUT  : = 25;
          SET ENTER  : = 1;
          RUN UNTIL STEADY;
          TESTPATTERN;
          DISPLAY OUTFORM=TABLE1;
      (* DO A MULTIPLICATION 18 *  6 *)
          SET ONOFF  : = 0;
          SET INTEGER_INPUT  : = 18;
          SET FUNCTION_INPUT  : = 3;
          SET ENTER  : = 0;
          RUN UNTIL STEADY;
          TESTPATTERN;
          DISPLAY OUTFORM=TABLE1;
          SET FUNCTION_INPUT  : = 0;
          SET INTEGER_INPUT  : = 6;
          SET ENTER  : = 1;
          RUN UNTIL STEADY;
          TESTPATTERN;
          DISPLAY OUTFORM=TABLE1;
      (* DO A DIVISION  123 / 8 *)
          SET ONOFF  : = 0;
          SET INTEGER_INPUT  : = 123;
          SET FUNCTION_INPUT  : = 4;
          SET ENTER  : = 0;
          RUN UNTIL STEADY;
          TESTPATTERN;
          DISPLAY OUTFORM=TABLE1;
          SET FUNCTION_INPUT  : = 0;
          SET INTEGER_INPUT  : = 8;
          SET ENTER  : = 1;
          RUN UNTIL STEADY;
          TESTPATTERN;
          DISPLAY OUTFORM=TABLE1;
```

Fig. 5.5 Microcomputer simulation instructions

to output a table of the micro inputs and outputs at various key points during the simulation. The READ INFORM statement is the means by which ROM data is loaded into the microcomputer program. Finally, the simulation control statements comprise five sets of commands which contain one or a pair of the following sequence of operations:

* Apply input values; SET commands.
* Simulate the micro for a period of time until program activity ceases; the RUN command.
* Display the resultant output in table form and in test machine language form; the DISPLAY and TESTPATTERN commands.

The simulation performs the simple operations of loading the micro's program, powering it up, then (with the knowledge of what the program does) performing one each of addition, subtraction, multiplication and division. The program is shown in fig. 5.6 and performs addition and subtraction by directly using the micro's operators, multiplication is accomplished by binary long multiplication and division by successive addition of the divisor.

The simulation results are shown in figs 5.7 and 5.8. Figure 5.7 displays the inputs and outputs indicating the correct operation of the four arithmetic functions with execution times of 221, 261, 3301 and 3301 time units respectively. These timings could be further used to develop quicker and thus more efficient micro programs. Figure 5.8 illustrates a useful simulator feature, that of outputting a test program for the device. The program is in a machine independent language, but would more often be in a programming language for a particular test machine. Apart from the initialisation statements it just comprises a set of testpatterns which could be loaded into a tester and used for testing the final fabricated microcomputer. In other words, our high level behavioural simulation has enabled the generation of a testpattern set.

To summarise, behavioural simulation allows system design and functional specification to proceed jointly towards an accurate and complete specification and model of the product. Key features of such behavioural simulation are:

1. A comprehensive hardware programming language comprised of the usual programming language constructs, plus features for supporting such things as operations on signals, scheduling of signals and concurrent processing. A typical programming language such as Pascal, exhibits desirable programming constructs; indeed some behavioural simulators accept an enhanced variant of Pascal as the behavioural programming language.
2. A flexible simulation control whereby simulation activity can be set up easily and quickly. A good feature here is a comprehensive control language containing all the usual programming language constructs. Additional features should be available for tracing

```
(* FUNCTION_INPUT HIGH: -   *)
15        50      127         LOAD   0 INTO ZERO
15        51      128         LOAD   1 INTO ONE
15        52      135         LOAD   8 INTO EIGHT
15        53      255         LOAD   B'10000000'
15        54      129         LOAD   2 INTO TWO
15        55      130         LOAD   3 INTO THREE
15        56      131         LOAD   4 INTO FOUR
13       100      127         READ A
14        98      127         READ FUNCTION
17         1      127         WAIT
(* ENTER INTPUT HIGH; CHECK VALUES OF FUNCTION: - *)
13        99      127
 3        98      127         LOAD FUNCTION INTO ACCUMULATOR
10        51      127         COMPARE ACCUMULATOR WITH ONE
15        40      129         LOAD JUMP CONDITION FOR =
12        40      133         IF FUNCTION IS ONE JUMP FORWARD       6
10        54      127         COMPARE ACCUMULATOR WITH TWO
12        40      136         IF FUNCTION IS TWO JUMP FORWARD       9
10        55      127         COMPARE ACCUMULATOR WITH THREE
12        40      139         IF FUNCTION IS THREE JUMP FORWARD    12
10        56      127         COMPARE ACCUMULATOR WITH FOUR
12        40      163         IF FUNCTION IS FOUR JUMP FORWARD     36
(* ADD *)
 5         1      127
 1       100      127         ADD A
 1        99      127         ADD B
 4        60      127         STORE A + B
11         1      176         JUMP 49 TO END FOR WRITE
(* SUBTRACT *)
 5         1      127         CLEAR ACCUMULATOR
 1       100      127         ADD A
 2        99      127         SUB B FROM A
 4        60      127         STORE A-B
11         1      171         JUMP 44 TO END FOR WRITE
(* MULTIPLY *)
 3        52      127         LOAD EIGHT INTO ACCUMULATOR
 4        42      127         STORE LOOPCOUNT
 5         1      127         CLEAR ACCUMULATOR
 4        60      127         STORE 0 INTO RESULT
 3        42      127         LOAD LOOPCOUNT INTO ACCUMULATOR   <-----
 6         1      127         DECREMENT LOOPCOUNTER                  I
 4        41      127         STORE SHIFTCOUNT                       I
 3       100      127         LOAD A INTO ACCUMULATOR                I
 8        41      127         SHIFTLEFTLOGICAL BY SHIFTCOUNT         I
 9        53      127         AND ACCUMULATOR WITH '10000000'        I
10        50      127         COMPARE ACCUMULATOR WITH ZERO          I
15        40      129         LOAD JUMP CONDITION FOR =              I
12        40      130         IF NSB IS ZERO JUMP FORWARD   3        I
 3        60      127         LOAD RESULT INTO ACCUMULATOR           I
 1        99      127         ADD B TO RESULT                        I
 4        60      127         STORE RESULT                          I
 3        99      127         LOAD B INTO ACCUMULATOR                I
 8        51      127         SHIFTLEFT LOGICAL BY ONE BIT           I
 4        99      127         STORE SHIFTED B                        I
 3        42      127         LOAD LOOPCOUNT INTO ACCUMULATOR        I
 6         1      127         DECREMENT ACCUMULATOR                  I
 4        42      127         STORE LOOPCOUNT                        I
10        50      127         COMPARE LOOPCOUNT WITH ZERO            I
15        40      130         LOAD JUMP CONDITION FOR >              I
12        40      106         JUMP BACK IF LOOPCOUNT > ZERO  --------
11         1      145         JUMP 18 TO END FOR WRITE
(* DIVIDE *)
 5         1      127         CLEAR ACCUMULATOR
 4        60      127         STORE 0 INTO QUOTIENT
 4        70      127         STORE 0 INTO SUM
 3        60      127         LOAD QUOTIENT INTO ACCUMULATOR    <-----
 7         1      127         INCREMENT ACCUMULATOR                  I
 4        60      127         STORE INCREMENTED QUOTIENT             I
 3        70      127         LOAD SUM INTO ACCUMULATOR              I
 1        99      127         ADD DIVISOR TO SUM                     I
 4        70      127         STORE SUM                              I
10       100      127         COMPARE DIVIDEND WITH SUM              I
15        40      128         LOAD JUMP CONDITION FOR <              I
12        40      118         JUMP BACK IF SUM < DIVIDEND   ----------
10       100      127         COMPARE DIVIDEND WITH SUM
15        40      129         LOAD JUMP CONDITION FOR =
12        40      130         JUMP FORWARD IF SUM = DIVIDEND
 3        60      127         LOAD QUOTIENT INTO ACCUMULATOR
 6         1      127         DECREMENT QUOTIENT
 4        60      127         STORE QUOTIENT
(* OUTPUT RESULT *)
16        60      127         WRITE A
17         1      127         WAIT
```

Fig. 5.6 Microcomputer program for addition, subtraction, multiplication and division

```
INTEGER_INPUT7-0   FUNCTION_INPUT7-0   ENTER   ONOFF   OUTPUT7-0   ERROR
```

TIME	INTEGER_INPUT7-0	FUNCTION_INPUT7-0	ENTER	ONOFF	OUTPUT7-0	ERROR
10	0	0	0	1	0	0
191	10	1	0	0	0	0
412	5	0	1	0	15	0
593	100	2	0	0	0	0
854	25	0	1	0	75	0
1035	18	3	0	0	0	0
4336	6	0	1	0	108	0
4517	123	4	0	0	0	0
7818	8	0	1	0	15	0

Fig. 5.7 Output display of microcomputer simulation

```
CONNECT P, VAR = (INTEGER_INPUT(7),INTEGER_INPUT(6),INTEGER_INPUT(5),
INTEGER_INPUT(4),INTEGER_INPUT(3),INTEGER_INPUT(2),INTEGER_INPUT(1),,
INTEGER_INPUT(0),FUNCTION_INPUT(7),FUNCTION_INPUT(6),FUNCTION_INPUT(5),
FUNCTION_INPUT(4),FUNCTION_INPUT(3),FUNCTION_INPUT(2),U
FUNCTION_INPUT(1),FUNCTION_INPUT(0),ENTER,ONOFF,OUTPUT(7),OUTPUT(6),5
OUTPUT(5),OUTPUT(4),OUTPUT(3),OUTPUT(2),OUTPUT(1),OUTPUT(0),ERROR),
DEFPIN=( IN   18, OUT    9);
            SETR P:=T'LLLLLLLLLLLLLLLLLLHO00000000';
            SETR P:=T'LLLLHLHLLLLLLLLLHLL000000000';
            SETR P:=T'LLLLLHLHLLLLLLLLHL000011110';
            SETR P:=T'LHHLLHLLLLLLLLLHLLL000000000';
            SETR P:=T'LLLHHLLHLLLLLLLLHL010010110';
            SETR P:=T'LLLHLLHLLLLLLLLHHLL000000000';
            SETR P:=T'LLLLLHHLLLLLLLLLLHLO11011000';
            SETR P:=T'LHHHHLHHLLLLLHLLLL000000000';
            SETR P:=T'LLLLHLLLLLLLLLLLLHLO00011110';
```

Fig. 5.8 Microcomputer simulation output of testpatterns

variables and signals during simulation, setting up signal values, running simulation and performing operations on signals.

3. A structuring feature within the hardware programming language which allows top down design and as system architecture evolves, structuring of the program in a manner which reflects the intended hardware structuring.
4. Along with design structuring, the ability within the same hardware programming language, to describe the logic structure of parts or all of the design. Then a simulator which can simulate in either or both behavioural and logic mode. This feature allows behavioural design to evolve naturally into logic design whilst ensuring compatibility at all times.

The microcomputer example above can illustrate this structuring and evolution of design. Once the basic behavioural model has been written one has specified and verified the design and such details as the word size and instruction set are defined. Next, the design might be broken into high level functions such as RAM, ROM, ALU, accumulator, instruction decoder, memory transfer register, etc. Each of these can be represented by a behavioural program and simulated together. At this level of description one would have additional detail, such as overall design timing, or clocking. Next, these individual functions would be refined into greater detail. Let us assume that the ROM and RAM will be targeted for standard memory components and the rest to be implemented using logic arrays. Our ROM and RAM models would then be always behavioural but the ALU, accumulator, etc. would evolve from behavioural descriptions to logic descriptions. Design activity would proceed as follows:

1. Simulate microcomputer with single behavioural model.
2. Decompose microcomputer into high level blocks, ROM, RAM, etc., writing behavioural programs for each.
3. Behaviourally simulate these high level blocks stand alone to verify their descriptions.
4. Simulate all high level blocks together behaviourally to check against top level microcomputer model.
5. Continue behavioural decomposition carrying out the dual-level simulation verifications until blocks are suitably sized for logic design.
6. At the logic design level, continue design decomposition but use logic simulation for stand alone verification and either logic or

behavioural, or a mixture for joint simulation with the other blocks in the design.

Clearly, the structuring for logic array implementation would reflect both design functional structure and logic array partitioning. This is illustrated in fig. 5.9 where a single logic array comprising a 4-bit shift register is 'bit sliced' with an identical brother to comprise the memory address register of the microcomputer. During behavioural system simulation this logic array register is modelled with the behavioural program shown in fig. 5.10.

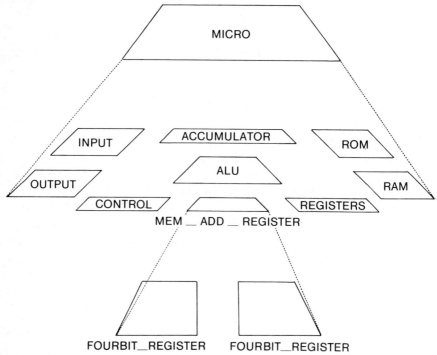

Fig. 5.9 Structural decomposition of a microcomputer bit sliced memory address register

5.5 Logic design

As implied by their name, logic arrays physically comprise an array of devices whose behaviour closely resembles simple logical operations such as the NOT and NAND functions. The target of logic array design is a description of the required system function in terms of these logic operations. Synthesis of such descriptions is mostly a creative manual activity, here and there one can come across logic

```
BLOCK REGISTER @ DESIGN;

PRESET(1 TO 4) @ INPUT;
PRESET_ENABLE   @ INPUT;
SERIAL_IN       @ INPUT;
CLEAR           @ INPUT;
CLOCK           @ INPUT;
Q(1 TO 4)       @ OUTPUT;


BEHAVIOR FUNCTIONAL PROGRAM;


(*          PRESET OPERATION        *)

IF AND( PRESET_ENABLE, NOT(CLOCK), NOT(CLEAR)) THEN

    Q(1) :=   PRESET(1);
    Q(2) :=   PRESET(2);
    Q(3) :=   PRESET(3);
    Q(4) :=   PRESET(4);
    SCHEDULE Q AT 50;
ENDIF;

(*      SERIAL IN PARALLEL OUT OPERATION        *)

IF AND(CLEAR, NOT(PRESET_ENABLE)) THEN
(*  TEST FOR A RISING CLOCK EDGE            *)
    IF AND( VCHANGE(CLOCK), CLOCK ) THEN
        Q(1) := Q(2);
        Q(2) := Q(3);
        Q(3) := Q(4);
        Q(4) := SERIAL_IN;
        SCHEDULE Q AT 100;
```

Fig. 5.10 Behavioural program for memory address register

synthesis programs which take as input such things as a behavioural model, a Boolean equation or a state table and synthesise the logic description. Such tools are often specific to functions and also generate designs which make inefficient use of logic gates. The classic example is the PLA generator. However, few if any logic arrays have built in programmable PLAs. Given that manual synthesis of logic description is the order of the day, what aids are available for supporting this activity? The primary aids are a graphical user interface, logic simulators and timing analysis tools.

5.5.1 *Graphical user interface*

The activity of logic design requires the entry and inevitable editing of logic descriptions into the computer. Computer information entry historically started in the form of punched cards or tapes and developed from there into the modern video display tube terminal with its typewriter keyboard and display tube. This device allows the efficient entry and edit of text. The behavioural programming described above would involve entry and edit of textual programs using a video display tube.

However logic design has traditionally taken advantage of mans' visual thinking skills and used diagrams for the representation of logic and waveform diagrams to represent their activity. We consequently find two classes of interface for computer aided logic design, textual and graphical. Often a textual approach is taken for hardware cost effectiveness and occasionally transportability, however, graphical interfaces are now relatively cheap and much preferred.

Hardware systems for graphical logic design will include a colour or black and white graphics tube, a data pad or light pen for drawing, a typewriter keyboard for text entry and a plotter for hard copies of either text or diagrams. Data pads are the most popular drawing device being the closest emulation of paper and pencil drawing. For logic design, black and white tubes are quite adequate, however, if the hardware doubles as a layout editor then colour is a more costly but better option. Such systems would then be completed with a 16- or 32-bit multiprocessor computer replete with several megabytes of memory, disk space measured in tens or hundreds of megabytes and a tape drive or floppy disk drive for design and software releases.

The central aid within a graphical interface is the editor. It is very hard to describe in words the good features of such tools, however, the principle talents of such an editor will be facilities for the creation of gates to represent such objects as NANDS, registers, etc; and then the creation of logic networks by connection of these gates using interconnect and bus symbols. Gross facilities would include support for structured logic diagrams with tie up of the logic description to behavioural programs where supported. Quite often a block of logic at one level of the design hierarchy will need several sheets for its diagrams. This feature of the pencil and paper days has been carried over to graphical computer systems and is a boon to data management, whilst simultaneously limiting display sizes and therefore placing an upper limit to the speed of display of the system.

Together with these structuring and organisational data divisions would come corresponding management functions such as automatic boundary scrolling from sheet to sheet and the 'pushing' and 'popping' of diagram displays up and down the structural hierarchy.

Actual geometric edit features start from basic line drawing, progress in complexity to line and geometry edits such as delete, move and stretch and usually feature advanced group geometry functions such as two-dimensional arraying and group data edits. The best systems have real time display of lines and geometries throughout edit activities, multiple window displays with edit across windows and fast pan and zoom. A good test of a geometric editor is its ability to 'edit' as opposed to create diagrams, features which allow one to insert space within an existing network for the addition of those extra gates which have been found lacking.

Above all, a graphical interface will perform electrical editing not just geometric editing, this involves features such as 'snap-connection' of lines to gate nodes and movement of gates without the need for disconnection and reconnection of connected lines. Syntaxing will also be electrical reporting of such errors as hanging connections, short circuits and illegal numbers of connections to a gate.

Finally, a graphical editor will support annotation of diagrams, with bulk text entered through a good text editor, and will allow entry of usefully long gate and signal names which are automatically qualified according to the design hierarchy.

If we return to our microprocessor example, a hierarchical logic diagram for the 'memory address register slice', created on a graphics work station, is shown in figs 5.11, 5.12 and 5.13. The register is assumed to be a serial-in, parallel-out device and is targeted for a CMOS logic array with interior NAND and inverter gates, one input buffer and one output buffer. For comparison, the textual description of this register is shown in figs 5.14, 5.15 and 5.16. The circuit activity of these logic functions involves propagation of logic 0 and 1 values around the interconnect with possible value changes at gates. Design comprehension is rather akin to timetabling problems on railway networks. Clearly it is easier to follow such activity manually from the diagrams rather than the text, hence its popularity.

5.5.2 Logic simulators

The logic simulator is the heart of a logic array design system. Its function is to model the behaviour of a design at the logic level. Its accuracy of modelling is greater than in behavioural modelling

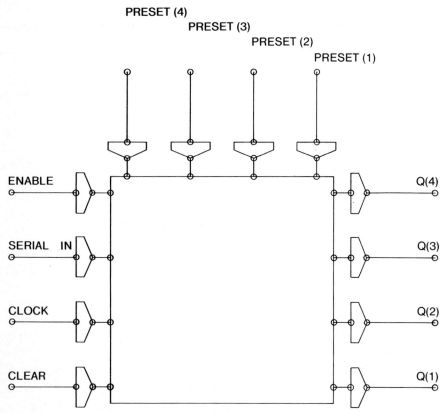

Fig. 5.11 Logic diagram of memory address register

because its input is a detailed logic level description of the function. Indeed, for logic arrays it forms the ultimate detail of electrical description. More detail still is possible through a circuit level description involving transistors, resistors and capacitors which can then be simulated with AC analysis tools such as SPICE. Logic arrays are however constructed such that 'legal' use of the basic logic elements will ensure that they behave identically to the idealised logic models which form the basis of logic simulators. We will return to the question of legal use of arrays later.

A logic simulator, in its simplest form, works as follows; at time zero logic values of 1 or 0 are applied to the inputs of a design. Each of these inputs connects to a logic gate and such affected gates might therefore change the logic level of their outputs. All such gates are analysed and their outputs changed at a fixed time later to the logic value, 1 or 0, appropriate to the logic function. Now these new signal values effect the inputs of yet another set of gates and the cycle of

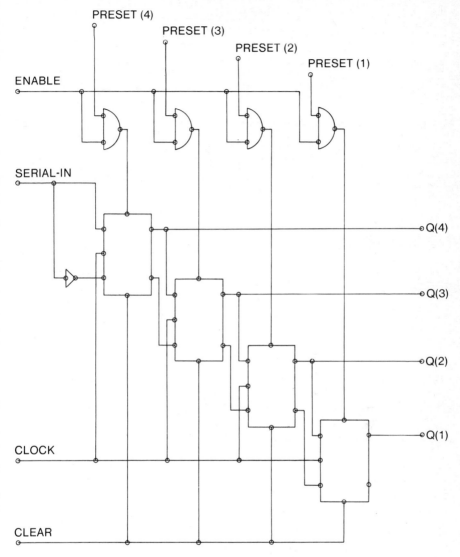

Fig. 5.12 Logic diagram of 4-bit shift register

gate analysis and output value setting restarts. This cyclic process continues until all activity in the circuit has ceased when the design outputs will hold their response. Such simulators are called 'event driven'; a name which reflects the driving force of the simulation cycle, namely signal changes or events.

This description of logic simulation is rather simplified. In reality, arrays of physical 'logic' elements do not behave so ideally. Interconnect takes time to charge to a logic 1, logic gates switch only

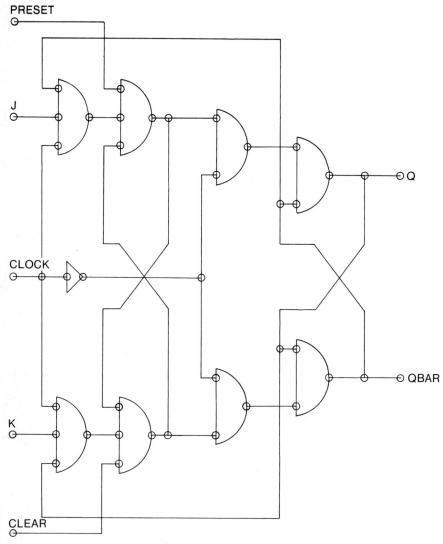

Fig. 5.13 Logic diagram of master-slave flip-flop

after signals have reached transistor switching threshold, logic values on nets in certain bipolar technologies are dominated by drains so a logic value of 1 requires majority votes from all net drivers, etc. To model this behaviour logic simulators have the following features:

1. Gate delays:
   This is the simplest additional accuracy which is added to logic simulators. It allows unique delay times to be specified for the logic gate transitions corresponding to their discrete circuit activity

```
(*          DESIGN REGISTER        *)
(*                                 *)


BLOCK REGISTER @ DESIGN;

PRESET(1 TO 4)  @ INPUT;
PRESET_ENABLE   @ INPUT;
SERIAL_IN       @ INPUT;
CLEAR           @ INPUT;
CLK             @ INPUT;
Q(1 TO 4)       @ OUTPUT;
PRESET_INTERNAL(1 TO 4) @ LOCAL;
Q_INTERNAL(1 TO 4)      @ LOCAL;



STRUCTURE
(*                                 *)
(*          DESIGN BUFFERS         *)
(*                                 *)
INPUT_BUFFERS(1 TO 4) : NINB PRESET(1 TO 4),
                    PRESET_INTERNAL(1 TO 4);
INPUT_BUFFER5 : NINB PRESET_ENABLE,
                    PRESET_ENABLE_INTERNAL;
INPUT_BUFFER6 : NINB SERIAL_IN, SERIAL_INTERNAL;
INPUT_BUFFER7 : NINB CLEAR, CLEAR_INTERNAL;
INPUT_BUFFER8 : NINB CLOCK, CLOCK_INTERNAL;
OUTPUT_BUFFERS(1 TO 4) : NINBO Q_INTERNAL(1 TO 4),
                    Q(1 TO 4);
(*                                 *)
(*          DESIGN INTERIOR        *)
(*                                 *)


COMPONENT : '4-BIT SHIFT REGISTER'
   PRESET_INTERNAL(1 TO 4), PRESET_ENABLE_INTERNAL,
   SERIAL_INTERNAL, CLEAR_INTERNAL, CLOCK_INTERNAL,
   Q_INTERNAL(1 TO 4);
```

Fig. 5.14 Hardware description of register

time. Typically, simulators use different times for 1 to 0 and 0 to 1 transitions on the output and have nominal, minimum and maximum options for modelling technology variations.

2. Net wired functions:
   This feature is necessary to model technology features such as the '0' dominance of the bipolar technologies STL and LPS. In these cases signals on the inputs to nets are ANDed together before

```
(*   4- BIT SHIFT REGISTER    *)


BLOCK '4-BIT SHIFT REGISTER';

PRESET(1 TO 4)  @ INPUT;
PRESET_ENABLE   @ INPUT;
SERIAL_IN       @ INPUT;
CLEAR           @ INPUT;
CLK             @ INPUT;
Q(1 TO 4)       @ OUTPUT;
PREBAR(1 TO 4)  @ LOCAL;
K(1 TO 4)       @ LOCAL;



STRUCTURE

SHIFT1  : NAND2 PRESET(1),PRESET_ENABLE,PREBAR(1);
SHIFT2  : NAND2 PRESET(2),PRESET_ENABLE,PREBAR(2);
SHIFT3  : NAND2 PRESET(3),PRESET_ENABLE,PREBAR(3);
SHIFT4  : NAND2 PRESET(4),PRESET_ENABLE,PREBAR(4);


SHIFT5    : INV  SERIAL_IN,K(4);

SHIFT6    : 'MASTER SLAVE FLIP-FLOP'
              PREBAR(4),CLEAR,CLOCK,SERIAL_IN,K(4),Q(4),K(3);


SHIFT7    : 'MASTER SLAVE FLIP-FLOP'
              PREBAR(3),CLEAR,CLOCK,Q(4),K(3),Q(3),K(2);


SHIFT8    : 'MASTER SLAVE FLIP-FLOP'
              PREBAR(2),CLEAR,CLOCK,Q(3),K(2),Q(2),K(1);


SHIFT9    : 'MASTER SLAVE FLIP-FLOP'
              PREBAR(1),CLEAR,CLOCK,Q(2),K(1),Q(1),UNUSED;


END '4-BIT SHIFT REGISTER';
```

Fig. 5.15 Hardware description of 4-bit shift register

```
BLOCK 'MASTER SLAVE FLIP-FLOP';

PRESET  @ INPUT;
CLEAR   @ INPUT;
CLOCK   @ INPUT;
J       @ INPUT;
K       @ INPUT;
Q       @ OUTPUT;
QBAR    @ OUTPUT;


STRUCTURE

MSFF1 : NAND3 QBAR,J,CLOCK,SIG1;
MSFF2 : NAND3 Q,K,CLOCK,SIG2;
MSFF3 : NAND3 PRESET,SIG1,SIG4,SIG3;
MSFF4 : NAND3 CLEAR,SIG2,SIG3,SIG4;
MSFF5 : BUF2  CLOCK,CLOCKBAR;
MSFF6 : NAND2 SIG3,CLOCKBAR,SIG5;
MSFF7 : NAND2 SIG4,CLOCKBAR,SIG6;
MSFF8 : NAND2 SIG5,QBAR,Q;
MSFF9 : NAND2 SIG6,Q,QBAR;

END 'MASTER SLAVE FLIP-FLOP';
```

Fig. 5.16 Hardware description of master–slave flip-flop

propagation to the outputs of the net. NMOS also requires wire ANDing, whilst PMOS requires wire ORing. Static CMOS generally requires that only one transistor drive a net so net fan-in would be an error.

3. Net delays:
   Logic gates within an array are physically wired together with metal interconnect and sometimes a mixture of metal and diffusion. The primary effect of metal interconnect is to add a capacitive load whilst diffusion adds both capacitive and resistive loading to the gates. Contacts between interconnect material also predominately add capacitive loading. All these gate loads will increase the gate delay time. Good logic simulators will model these loadings with pre-layout default net interconnect delay values, and a facility, after layout, to accept the actual interconnect lengths and number of contacts and convert them to effective gate delay times. Such conversion usually only models capacitance, resistive analysis is much harder to do. As in the case

of gate delays, net delays would have technology nominal, minimum and maximum values.

4. Unit delay:

   Net and gate delays are good for increasing the accuracy of logic simulation, they add a degree of timing analysis into the simulation; however they do slow down simulation speed by as much as 50%. During the initial stages of logic design the main emphasis is on correct synthesis of gate combinations to produce required functions. To cater for this design stage simulators often have a mode called 'unit delay'. This is a crude form of simulation which has no net delays and where all transitions of all gates occur in one time unit.

5. Switch level models:

   Simulation at the logic gate level can, under certain circumstances, become inaccurate. We have already mentioned the problems of timing accuracy, which lead to feedback paths going into oscillation, or race hazards, whereby circuit functioning is critical on, for example, setup and hold times. Gate and net delays are usually successful at solving these problems. However, for some technologies used in certain ways logic level simulation is basically incapable of modelling circuit activity. An example of this is dynamic CMOS design. Here logic levels are stored on inter-connect as charge and drive output gates only for a period of time. After a finite time, charge leakage reduces the voltage level below threshold and the logic information is lost. The problem with logic simulation is that all gates and wires have a unidirectional flow of logic values or charge. In MOS technologies, transistors can have bidirectional flow of charge and interconnect has memory: neither of these are modelled in conventional simulators. Many simulators have features for modelling MOS type behaviour with various degrees of success. Typically instead of the basic logic levels of 0 to 1, a strength/value pair is used for net values, thus allowing such states as driven or floating 0s, 1s or unknowns. Together with these more complex net states are added uni- and bidirectional transistor models. Such simulators are termed 'switch level' and are considered to be essential for MOS designs; i.e. CMOS logic arrays.

Use of a logic simulator is similar to that of a behavioural simulator. Basic activity is the user application of input signal values, simulation propagation of these values through the circuit and finally, viewing of the circuit activity via waveform displays of input and output and possibly selected interior signals. Again, just as for behavioural simulation, good features include:

1. A comprehensive simulation control language.
2. Support for hierarchical or structured design.
3. Incremental compilation of design blocks.
4. Mixed simulation at behavioural and logic levels.
5. Circuit initialisation aids; such as the forcing of internal signals.
6. Suppression of oscillations after user-defined times. In an event driven simulator, oscillation would cause indefinite simulation so it is important to detect any accidental oscillation.
7. Gate input constraint checks such as flip-flop setup and hold conditions.
8. Good use of graphical logic diagram interface.

The use of a logic diagram interface by a simulator has been one of the key innovations of recent CAD products. Such interaction allows one to use the logic diagrams to select a subcircuit for simulation, attach input stimuli, point at the nets for which waveform traces are required and then set the simulation into activity. During simulation, waveforms may be viewed and simulation control overridden to halt when simulation is complete, or if an error condition has been spotted in the waveforms. Any error conditions such as ambiguous logic values can also be indicated graphically upon the logic diagram.

Eventually, as a design grows in size, simulation speed slows to where it becomes a batch, rather than interactive activity. Logic simulators typically run ten million times slower than real logic arrays; or put another way, 200 μs of real circuit activity, representing say 2000 testpatterns run through a logic array of 1000 gates, will take approximately an hour to simulate on a computer. Such batch simulations would be run as a background activity and the results analysed with a good waveform display system. These systems, often called virtual logic analysers, have features for displaying selected signals, finding places where combinations of signals have selected transitions and generally simulate the manual activity of probing a circuit with an oscilloscope. Such a tool is an invaluable aid in turning a simulator into the design debugging tool which is its prime function.

Finally, we can illustrate logic simulation with our microcomputer register using the simulation control instructions of fig. 5.17, and the resultant waveform display of fig. 5.18. The simulation control instructions illustrate the tracing of various signals, circuit initialis-

```
(*            DECLARE VARIABLES *)
INTEGER LOOP_COUNT;

(* SET UP DISPLAYS *)

TRACE    VAR = (CLOCK,SERIAL_IN,Q),OUTFORM = TABLE;
TRACE    BLK = REGISTER.COMPONENT.SHIFT6,
         VAR = (SIG3, SIG4), OUTFORM=TABLE;
TRACE    BLK = REGISTER.COMPONENT.SHIFT7,
         VAR = (SIG3, SIG4), OUTFORM=TABLE;
TRACE    BLK = REGISTER.COMPONENT.SHIFT8,
         VAR = (SIG3, SIG4), OUTFORM=TABLE;
TRACE    BLK = REGISTER.COMPONENT.SHIFT9,
         VAR = (SIG3, SIG4), OUTFORM=TABLE;

(* INITIALISE FLIP-FLOPS WITH CLEAR AND PRESET ENABLE *)

SET PRESET_ENABLE : = CLOCK : = CLEAR : = L'0';
RUN UNTIL STEADY;

(* RUN THROUGH SEQUENCE OF CLOCKING 0101111 THROUGH REGISTER *)

SET PRESET_ENABLE : = PRESET : = L'0';
SET CLEAR : = L'1';

CLOCK VAR = CLOCK, PATTERN = B'101',
             HOLD0 =600, HOLD1 =600;
SET SERIAL_IN : = L'0';
RUN FOR 1200;
TESTPATTERN;
DISPLAY OUTFORM = TABLE1;

CLOCK VAR = CLOCK, PATTERN = B'101',
             HOLD0 =600, HOLD1 =600;
SET SERIAL_IN : = L'1';
RUN FOR 1200;
TESTPATTERN;
DISPLAY OUTFORM = TABLE1;

CLOCK VAR = CLOCK, PATTERN = B'101',
             HOLD0 =600, HOLD1 =600;
SET SERIAL_IN : = L'0';
RUN FOR 1200;
TESTPATTERN;
DISPLAY OUTFORM = TABLE1;

SET SERIAL_IN : = L'1';
FOR LOOP_COUNT : = 1 TO 4 DO
    CLOCK VAR = CLOCK, PATTERN = B'101',
                 HOLD0 =600, HOLD1 =600;
    RUN FOR 1200;
    TESTPATTERN;
    DISPLAY OUTFORM = TABLE1;
END FOR;
```

Fig. 5.17 Control of memory address register simulation

ation via the 'run until steady' command, a clock definition statement, a fixed time simulation via the 'run for 1200' command, and testpattern output. This control program simply initialises the register then clocks a pattern '0101111' serially into and through the register. Notice the utility of the 'for' loop in repetitious situations. The waveform display output clearly shows the pattern marching from $Q(4)$ through to $Q(1)$. Also shown is the successful operation of the master and slave flip-flops after the rising and falling edges of the clock and within the high and low half periods respectively. This waveform display would immediately show bad signal values and also enables circuit timing to be measured. Detailed scrutiny of the flip-flop signals will reveal a minimum clock period of 630 time units, somewhat faster than the 1200 units used for the simulation and an

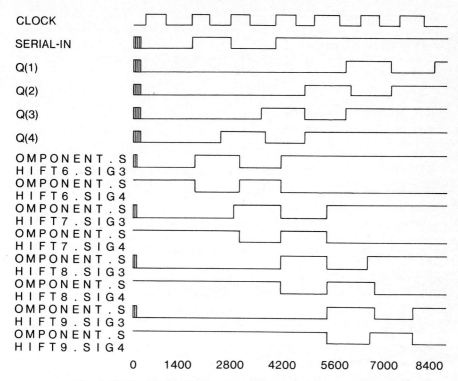

Fig. 5.18 Waveform display output from register simulation

upper limit for the frequency of operation of the register. Any higher frequency would violate the 'setup' and 'hold' requirements of the flip-flops and destroy the register action. The testpattern output is shown in fig. 5.19, we will return to this later with regard to test.

5.5.3 Timing analysers

The correct operation of logic requires not only the correct connection of logic gates but also the satisfaction of signal timings. Whilst both of these may be verified using a logic simulator, even modest sized designs will take many minutes to simulate and such simulation will only test those paths associated with the input signal test sets. A static timing analyser is a tool which, without actually simulating a design, can verify the correct timing of all paths within the design. Not only can it analyse all paths, but it manages this at between ten and one hundred times faster than a timing simulation. It therefore represents a useful step in the design process to be used in conjunction with logic simulation.

The simplest form of timing analyser comprises a critical path analyser. These typically partition the logic into sequential and

```
CONNECT SHIFT4,  VAR = (PRESET(1),PRESET(2),PRESET(3),PRESET(4),
PRESET_ENABLE,SERIAL_IN,CLEAR,CLOCK,Q(1),Q(2),Q(3),Q(4)),
DEFPIN=( IN 8,  OUT 4);
CLOCK VAR = CLOCK,  PATTERN=101,  HOLD0=600,HOLD1=600;
SETR SHIFT4  :=T'LLLLLLLL0000';
SETR SHIFT4  :=T'LLLLLLLHC0000';
SETR SHIFT4  :=T'LLLLLHHC0001';
SETR SHIFT4  :=T'LLLLLLHC0010';
SETR SHIFT4  :=T'LLLLLHHC0101';
SETR SHIFT4  :=T'LLLLLHHC1011';
SETR SHIFT4  :=T'LLLLLHHC0111';
SETR SHIFT4  :=T'LLLLLHHC1111';
SETR SHIFT4  :=T'LLLLLHHC1110';
SETR SHIFT4  :=T'LLLLLHHC1100';
SETR SHIFT4  :=T'LLLLLHHC1000';
SETR SHIFT4  :=T'LLLLLHHC0000';
SETR SHIFT4  :=T'HHHHLLLL1111';
```

Fig. 5.19 Testpattern output from register simulation

combinational parts. The combinational partitions have all their paths analysed as follows: Commencing with the input signals, which are defined to arrive at time zero; signal arrival times are propagated throughout all paths in the circuit using both gate 0 to 1 and 1 to 0 delay times and interconnect delays. Both minimum and maximum technology values are used to cover the spread of real working conditions. This dual timing delay propagation takes no account of the logical functioning of the circuit but does give a best and worst case timing value for partitions of the logic. Such values have to be manually sorted for the meaningful paths but are able to detect real timing errors.

An extra degree of sophistication can be added to these analysers if they are restricted to use on synchronous sequential logic. Such logic is characterised by activity being controlled through a set of generic clocks which determine all signal activity. Under normal functioning any specific signal will be changing for a portion of the clock cycle, otherwise it is stable. Such circuits will also have a set of setup and hold requirements for registers and latches etc. Now if for any block of logic all the input clocks have defined timing and all other input signals have assertions regarding their stable and changing time periods, it is possible to determine statically the stable and changing time periods of all signals in the logic. Once this has been done, violations of the setup and hold type can be checked. The SCALD timing verifier is an example of such a program and is capable of analysing a 1000 gate logic design in a few minutes. (SCALD is a trademark of VALID Inc.) It circumvents some of the problems associated with the non-comprehension of the logic functioning of the circuit by performing case analysis. This analysis involves choosing specific paths for analysis based on the actual logic value of, for example, control signals. Such features are a significant advance on the simple critical path analysis tools and will eventually allow these analysers to replace logic simulation as the tool for timing design.

5.5.4 Electrical design

It has already been mentioned that whilst logic design stays within the bounds of legal array usage the logical model of circuit activity is accurate enough to guarantee performance of the finished product. For bipolar technologies the rules for legal circuit usage are those of limiting the gate input connection fan-in, the total gate input fan-in and the gate fan-out. These checks are made by programs called 'loadcheckers' using a simple static analysis of the logic network. These programs are extremely fast to execute and therefore provide a useful design verification step during logic design.

For MOS technologies checking of gate fan-in and fan-out is less useful since, for instance the effect of increasing fan-out will be primarily to slow the performance of the device. MOS technologies must by and large have such things tested by logic simulation. As previously mentioned, logic simulation of MOS can eventually break down through not modelling charge storage and bidirectional gates. Under these circumstances true electrical design must be done using AC analysis tools such as SPICE. Such recourse to the electrical level of design is however very rare for logic array designs.

5.6 Test generation

As a logic array is designed the main attention is directed at the correct functional performance, there is, however, the equally important question of how the array will be tested after fabrication. First, arrays have to be tested at the end of the production process and for economic reasons these tests must be as cheap as possible and therefore not time consuming. Secondly, during the lifetime of the array, a malfunction of its parent system must be quickly and easily found. If the array is easy to test, it can quickly be eliminated from suspicion or found guilty of the error.

The electronic functions which are now being integrated into logic arrays used to be built with anything from 10 to 100 SSI or MSI chips. Such board systems are relatively easy to fault diagnose as many of the interior signals are accessible with scope or logic analyser. Upon integration into a logic array, however, 90% or more of these signals become accessible only through the 20 to 200 logic array inputs and outputs! Fault diagnosis becomes the tricky business of controlling and observing interior signals 'at a distance'.

The complexity of this test problem causes it to impact the design stage. Before fabrication of a logic array, it must be established that the array can be thoroughly tested. This problem is, therefore, an exercise in the generation of tests and measurement of their effectiveness in fault finding. Meanwhile methodologies are emerging which make ICs easy to test by design, so called 'design for testability'. Some of these can be helped with new computer aids.

5.6.1 Test generation and test coverage

The problem of test generation is one of creating a set of testpatterns which will thoroughly exercise the logic array and can therefore be used to detect errors. We distinguish here between design errors and physical errors. An example of the former is the oversight of a combination of input stimuli, which cause design outputs, for example, to become illogical or undefined, oscillating or undriven. An example of the latter is a production failure due to bad processing such as misaligned masks causing shorts between signals. Both these error classes must be detected wherever possible with the test set. To aid this activity there are two main products available, fault simulators and automatic testpattern generators.

A fault simulator answers the question, 'how thorough is a test set?'. It can also be used to direct manual generation of test sets. It works by modelling physical faults at the logic level. Many of these physical faults cause logic arrays to behave as if a signal node was stuck high or low; additionally, in MOS technologies, faults will show up as though transistors were stuck on or off. A basic fault simulator will simulate a testpattern using the correct logic model and then, for all of the possible stuck faults, repeat the simulation with each fault present. If any of the faulted simulations have outputs which differ from the good circuit simulation then the fault is classified as detected. A whole testpattern set may be processed in this manner and the final result is a coverage number giving the percentage of all possible model faults which are detected by the pattern set. Such a fault grade can range from 1% to 100%. It is interesting to observe that functional testpattern sets have graded at anything from 20% to 80%. It cannot be taken for granted that functional testpattern sets cover all possible array functions and exercise all parts of the actual logic implementation! Logic array vendors will often require a testpattern set as well as the logic description and layout for an array procurement. The testpattern set will also be required to meet a level of fault grading; often over 90%.

The fault simulator just described is a serial fault simulator and, due to its operation mode, takes excessive time to execute. Times of the order of 1000 times slower than logic simulation are possible for quite modest arrays of up to 1000 gates. Commercially available fault simulators typically use improved methods. Parallel fault simulation is where between one and sixteen fault circuits are simultaneously simulated, using the trick of packing multiple circuit values into whole words and using word operators. The other most popular type is concurrent simulation, where typically fifty fault circuits are simultaneously simulated, but the overhead of describing fifty such circuits is virtually eliminated by the technique of using good circuit–bad circuit difference information only. Parallel fault simulators are approximately ten times slower than logic simulators whilst concurrent fault simulators can approach the speed of logic simulators.

Another feature of fault simulation is that, as simulation proceeds through a testpattern set, the rate of fault detection gets exponentially slower. Figure 5.20 shows this effect for a 500 gate STL logic array modelling 3000 stuck at 1 and stuck at 0 faults as 1000 functional patterns are simulated to give a final coverage of just over 60%.

Finally, a good feature within a fault simulator is the technique of random fault selection. Whatever the type of fault simulator, the fewer the modelled faults, the faster the grading. It has been found that taking a random subset of faults gives coverage figures remarkably close to those for the complete fault set. Figure 5.21 shows the fault coverage of the above STL logic array for random samples of 100%, 10% and 3% of the faults. The grade figures are all within 5% but the 3% random fault grading was seven times faster than that for the 100% sample!

To demonstrate the action of fault simulation, the testpattern set derived from the register design simulation above, which initialises the register and then shifts the bit pattern '0101111' through the register, gives a coverage of 65% or 221 out of the 340 stuck at 0 and stuck at 1 faults. The undetected faults are shown in fig. 5.22. Clearly, to increase the coverage further tests must be added to exercise the flip-flop presets and more of the internal flip-flop states.

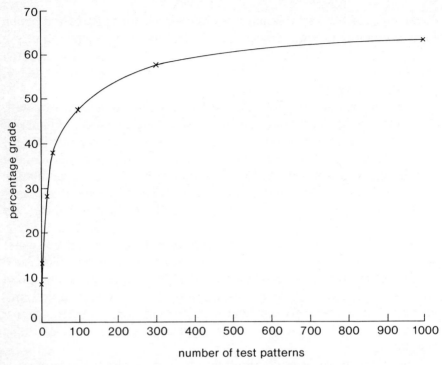

Fig. 5.20 Accumulation of fault detection

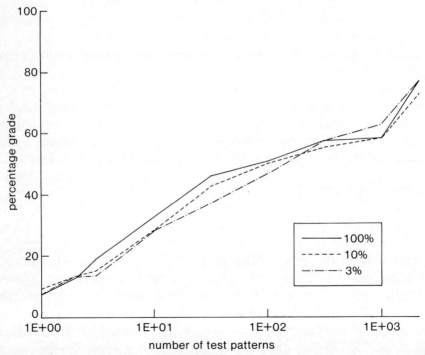

Fig. 5.21 Random fault selection

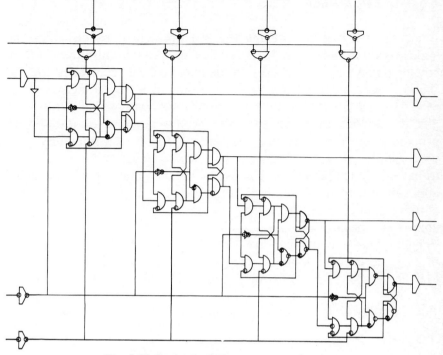

Fig. 5.22 Fault simulation coverage of register

In this manner, testpattern sets which have been generated during behavioural and logic design can be enhanced to obtain a high fault grading.

There are a number of automatic testpattern generators, mostly based on Roth's D algorithm which can be used to generate complete test sets for combinational logic and, less successfully, for sequential logic. These are used in combination with a fault simulator in the cycle: direct test generator to exercise a part of the design, measure coverage by fault simulation, identify those parts of the circuit not covered and use test generator on these, etc. Note, that although it is quite feasible to generate testpattern sets using only the logic description and a test generator, such sets will only verify the correct silicon implementation of the logic description. There is still the need for a functionally significant set of patterns generated, either manually, or with the aid of behavioural simulation. Often this functional set will form the basis for a complete test set and a fault simulator is used with a test generator to achieve the requisite 90–95% coverage.

5.6.2 *Design for test*

A productive way of reducing the test problem is by designing the logic array with test in mind. The key aim is to minimise the depth of any logic network so that every node may be easily controlled to logic 1 and 0, and such control may be observed at the design outputs. SCOAP-type programs have the ability to analyse any design and identify regions of a design which would be hard to test. These programs give a measure of the 0 to 1 controllability and observability of all the design signal nodes. Design inputs are defined to have a controllability to 1 and 0 of 1, this models the single signal application which is required to accomplish such control. Design output signals are defined to have an observability of 0, modelling the ability to measure such signals without the need to apply any input signals. These controllability and observability values are then propagated into the logic network using simple transfer functions for logic gates. The equations for a 2 input NAND gate are as follows:

Controllability (0) of output = minimum (controllability (0) of input a,
controllability (0) of input b)

Controllability (1) of output = controllability (1) of input a +
controllability (1) of input b

Observability of input a   = observability of output +
controllability (1) of b

Observability of input b   = observability of output +
controllability (1) of a

To control the output to 0 requires only setting one of the inputs to 0 thus the controllability to 0 of the output is the minimum of the controllability to 0 of the inputs, etc. The resulting controllability and observability figures when combined gives a 'lower limit' to the number of input signal applications necessary to test each signal. These figures are generated extremely rapidly, in a matter of seconds for a 1000 gate array, and enable one to identify nodes with high controllability and observability numbers. One is then able to redesign the logic to increase the overall testability.

The register example is a little small in demonstrating the utility of Scoap-type programs. Figure 5.23 shows the distribution of testability numbers showing that one signal stands out, and four others have significantly high testability numbers. These signals are the K input to

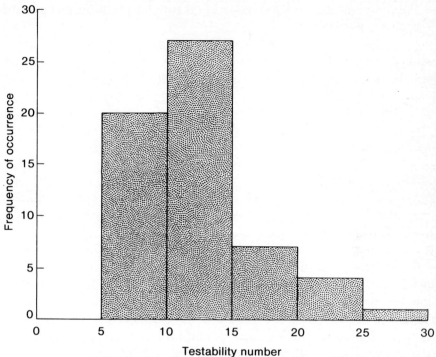

Fig. 5.23 Testability histogram for register signals

the first master–slave flip-flop, and the output of the K input NAND gate on the four master–slave flip-flops. The K input signal has an observability problem in that its sequential depth from Q(4) to Q(1) rises rapidly, whilst the other four are both hard to observe and control to 0. One wouldn't normally consider adding test logic to such a small circuit, but a few extra gates and an output could be added to observe the K input signal at an overhead of less than 10% in the gate count.

Other software aids to design for test are emerging, the LSSD method of design for test can be helped by means of automatically exploding the design out to enable test generation on the purely combinational partitions of the logic. Such test design involves the following stages:

1. Selection of the combinational circuit partition to be tested.
2. Identification of the scan paths to and from the inputs and outputs of the partition.
3. Generation of the design input controls or testpatterns which both load up the partition inputs from the design scan path inputs and unload the partition outputs to the design scan path outputs.

4. Fault simulation and test generation for the partition using these access testpatterns.

Step 3 is amenable to automation once scan paths and their operation have been defined to a computer.

5.7 Layout

The logic description and test program for a logic array form two of the three components of a complete design description, the third is the layout. Being programmable devices, the only layout which is required for a logic array is the interconnect. This is typically one or two levels of metal with inter-level contacts, or one level of metal with one level of diffused material plus inter-level contacts. Such layout is simple compared with that of the actual gates of an array and the prime target of layout is to produce a computer database representing the geometries of this interconnect so that the logic network is identical to the logic description of the design. There are two approaches to this, manual layout and autolayout; generally manual methods are cost effective for arrays of less than 1000 gates whilst larger arrays pay off the extra investment of autolayout software.

5.7.1 Manual layout

A good manual layout setup for logic arrays will be little different from the drawing of logic diagrams. The array is plotted on mylar as a symbolic grid of interconnect routes with the gates represented by black boxes. Layout is then accomplished by drawing the horizontal and vertical stick connections between gates. Common functions such as flip-flops often have paper doll stick-ons which quickly produce the interconnection of basis NAND and inverter gates. Such a manually produced layout must then be captured into a computer database using a digitiser, then cycled round the verification and edit loop until all errors are eliminated.

Layout editors are not dissimilar from the logic diagram editor described previously. As well as the features discussed for the latter, a layout editor benefits enormously by having colour and area fill capabilities. Visual comprehension of individual interconnect routes is made much easier with these features.

5.7.2 Autolayout

Many logic array layout systems provide autolayout programs. These will take a logic description of the design and generate the correct interconnect layout with guaranteed schematic correctness and without violation of any layout rules. An example autolayout flow has the following steps:

1. Partitioning:
   This is the gathering together of groups of gates within the design which are tightly connected; an operation which reduces the final length of the interconnects and eases the problem of autorouting.
2. Placement:
   This is the process of placing the partition groups physically onto the array of gates. Algorithms are used which try to place together groups which have many connected signals. Again in an effort to minimise interconnect length and the difficulty of autorouting.
3. Autorouting:
   This is the generation of interconnect for connecting all gates together. It usually proceeds with inter-group signals first and then processes intra-group signals.

During the process of autolayout, there is normally a degree of user control. The overriding concern during autolayout is length of interconnect, for the longer it is, the slower will be the final device. Two types of control are available for layout flows as described above. First, partitioning can be manually overridden so that groups of gates will be forced into close proximity and their interconnections consequently minimised. Secondly, the concept of critical signals is used whereby the user specifies a small subset of the design signals to be critical. During autorouting such signals are processed first, and therefore benefit from the routing algorithm's choice of the best available paths. Such controls are very helpful for designs which push the technology to its limits. Indeed so critical is this problem that one has, not infrequently, to resort to direct manual placement of parts of an autorouted logic array.

Autolayout has the ability to complete 100% of the layout of a logic array, but human nature being what it is, the norm is less than 100% due to engineers cramming as much logic into a single array as possible. When gate utilisation goes over 90% autolayout will begin to fail to route some of the interconnect. Indeed a useful feature of a logic array design entry program is to keep a check that array utilisation does not exceed 100%! When failures occur they must be either reduced by a manual adjustment of the layout group placement, or manually entered on a graphics editing station. One is then back into the manual edit and verification cycle.

Finally, an illustration of autolayout is shown in fig. 5.24 where our register design has been automatically layed out onto a double-level metal CMOS logic array. For illustrative reasons the placement was constrained into one corner of the array and thereby caused two routing failures.

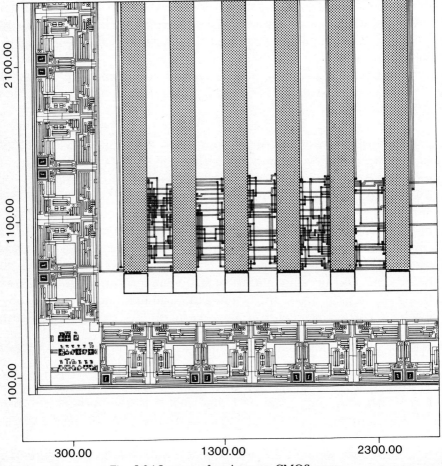

Fig. 5.24 Layout of register on CMOS array

5.8 Design verification

With a package of logic description, testpattern set and layout, a logic array design is complete and ready for final verification prior to commitment to silicon. Design verification comprises layout verification, schematic verification and post-layout simulation.

5.8.1 Layout verification

During the fabrication of an integrated circuit the correct physical structure is critically dependent on the alignment of the masking patterns. These alignments have a tolerance which, if not met, will lead to malfunctions, such as short or open circuits on the metal interconnect levels. Such tolerances impact the layout of integrated circuits by imposing layout rules such as the minimum width of interconnect and interlevel contact to minimum spacing. These layout rules are usually not verified at the point of layout edit and so all manually generated or edited layout must be checked by a layout verification program and corrected.

5.8.2 Schematic verification

The manual edit of layout can also create errors which have the effect of varying the layout network from the required logic network. A missing interconnect or unwanted extra interconnect causing an extra connection are examples. One hundred per cent complete autolayout will be free of such errors otherwise the extra manual completion is also suceptible. Such errors are called schematic errors and only recently generalised programs have become available for checking them. Schematic verification programs take as input the whole logic array layout and the logic description. By using sophisticated pattern recognition techniques, the layout is translated into a logic network, then a graph comparison program compares the layout network with the logic network and reports any deviations. The output from such schematic verification will often need careful interpretation, but such verification is essential if first-pass success is to be had with any design.

5.8.3 Post-layout simulation

The last design verification which can be performed is a resimulation of the logic with the actual interconnect lengths and contact numbers used for each of the design signals. Such lengths are typically converted into a capacitive loading and its effect comprehended during logic simulation. This check is a vital prefabrication verification.

5.9 Logic array design systems

Having reviewed the computer aids which are available for logic array design we next consider their integration into design systems. There are presently three ways of accessing software: direct use of the logic array vendor's software on the vendor's computer, use of the vendor's software on the customer's own computer and use of third party software on specific hardware. For customers with no access to any computer the first option is cost effective if only a few logic arrays are to be designed, if more than about four designs are contemplated then option three becomes cost effective. For customers already having computers the second option should be considered first. Wherever the software is accessed what is needed is a design system as opposed to a collection of design tools. The latter will allow the job to be done, but a good design system will allow the job to be done much faster and with a much greater degree of accuracy and success. The characteristics of a design system are as follows:

1. A good user interface:
   Computers are basically hard to use. Frequently a user initiates some process and the result is at best an unexpected response from the computer, or at worst a disastrous loss of data. A good user interface minimises the gap between user expectations of a computer's response and the actual response. It should also be forgiving of user mistakes; treating inaccurate instructions with intelligent responses so that it does what the user wants; not what he or she says. Computer programs are usually run via operating system instructions, these instructions are typically obscure and hard to enter correctly. A user interface will hide such technicalities from users, providing them with, for example, a simple menu driven interface where simple questions and answers are the means of gathering user instructions. Error messages are another good measure of the user interface. Messages such as 'ERROR IGG0AC4' will interrupt the user; forcing him to refer to his manuals.

2. A uniform user interface:

   It might seem trivial to mention uniformity of user interface, but too many software systems are a collection of interfaces where simple tasks, like entering a line of input, are different. It is most confusing if one has been busy pressing the 'return' key for entering information when suddenly it becomes unresponsive and one has to learn and remember to use the 'enter' key for this application.

3. An integrated organisation:

   Another obstacle to the efficient use of computers is a disjointed set of programs which have been cobbled together with a set of translation programs to produce a design 'system'. Typical of the problems one encounters with such systems is the interruption of waiting for translation utilities to run and different naming conventions in the programs. This latter feature will require the original source to be changed for compatibility or require use of name cross reference when reading the new application program output. Systems which minimise these problems often have a single design database.

4. Logic array specific aids:

   Logic arrays have much simpler requirements of computer aided design systems than, for example, full custom integrated circuits. The best logic array design systems take advantage of this fact having features which would otherwise be considered impractical for general integrated circuit design. Some of these features are:

   a. Logic array library information:

      A library of information on the logic array data for the logic arrays to be used. For successful logic array design a whole library of information is needed concerning the logic array; the simulator will need gate and interconnect delay data, a manual layout system will need the basic layout of the array, etc. . .

   b. Online schematic verification:

      The logic and layout of arrays is simple enough to allow intelligent interaction between the two. Layout is done after logic design and logic information can be used to actually prompt the layout activity, telling the user which gates need to be connected. This logic information can also be used to prevent erroneous layout connections; thus providing online schematic verification, or rather eliminating the verification step to produce layout which is correct on entry!

   c. Online geometric verification:

As well as online schematic correctness, logic array interconnect editors are also constructed such that layout errors are
disallowed on entry.

d. Design management:
   The simplicity of logic array designs allows practical and helpful
   design management features, such as the constant monitoring
   of array utilisation, simple feedback from the layout data to the
   simulation tool for post-layout simulation and output of the
   final design procurement package in the format required by the
   logic array vendor.

These are, then some of the features which make up a logic array
design system. Unfortunately, it is not possible to gauge such systems
just from sales information. Wherever possible 'hands on experience'
is the best way of measuring the effectiveness of such systems.

Finally, logic array design systems which are built into stand alone
engineering workstations must be mentioned here. Such systems
represent the best form of design systems for logic arrays, as they
have sufficient computing horsepower for the job, combined with
most of the desired design aids all integrated into a system.

A typical configuration would comprise:

* colour graphics tube
* typewriter keyboard for text entry
* Data pad for schematic and layout edit
* Fast raster plotter
* 1–2 megabytes of memory
* Several 16- or 32-bit processors
* 10's to 100's of megabytes of Winchester disk
* A floppy disk drive

A software logic design system resident on such a machine has all
the advantages of specific software plus the absence of resource
degradation often encountered in multiple user mainframe computer
installations. Figure 5.25 shows such a system being used for logic
array layout.

5.10 The future of semi-custom design systems

Logic arrays form one point in the spectrum of customisable
semiconductor products, ranging from microcomputers through logic

Fig. 5.25 Engineering workstation showing logic simulation. (Courtesy of Daisy Inc.)

arrays, to standard cell devices. Movement is towards more customisable integration, so that eventually full custom design becomes available for every electronic product.

Already the impact of these developments is being seen on semi-custom design systems. Standard cell devices require silicon compilers for their programmable ROMs, RAMs and PLAs, bar planners for cell placement, autolayout systems featuring advanced post-layout compaction. The capability of such compilers will slowly advance from their current limitations and eventually encompass the whole of design creation!

The new step from standard cell devices is that which enables the customer to design his or her own 'standard cell'. Such design will need the support of a custom design layout editor and access to the electrical level of design via such tools as SPICE.

Customisable products with hardware features for design testability will become more common as integration levels rise into the tens of thousands. Such products will feature computer aids for manipulating these test features during test design.

As the semi-custom market matures, a standard design description language will emerge, and ease the current problems of multiple standards, which exist today.

Finally, some of the newer computer hardware and software developments will migrate into the engineering workstation products. Natural language interfaces, originally developed within the artificial intelligence community, will further ease the human problems of computer interaction. Looking further ahead, parallel processors will significantly speed simulators and there will be a continuing symbiosis of software design aids breeding hardware which helps these design aids, leading to the economic production of pure hardware design functions such as verification boxes and simulation engines.

5.11 Further reading

For readers interested in a deeper discussion of design automation the following three books form a classic reference set:

Breuer, Melvin (ed.) 1972. *Design Automation of Digital Systems*, Vol 1, 2 and 3, Englewood Cliffs, NJ: Prentice-Hall.

Modern work on design automation is best reviewed via conference proceedings and the following set are recommended for this:

Proceedings of the Nth Design Automation Conference, IEEE, 19XX.

where 1983 saw the 20th proceedings, 1982 the 19th, etc.

For those interested in up to the minute news on design automation the following magazine is recommended as providing an efficient monitor of international activity in a highly readable and intelligible manner:

Werner, Jerry (ed.) *VLSI Design*, CMP Publications Inc., Manhasset, New York, USA.

There are regular conferences catering specifically for the semi-custom community and the following proceedings provide information on both semi-custom products, semi-custom design automation and real customer experiences:

The 1st international conference on semi-custom ICs 1981.
The 2nd international conference on semi-custom ICs 1982.
The 3rd international conference on semi-custom ICs 1983.

All published by Prodex, London.

Chapter 6

Gate Array Manufacturing and Packaging

STEPHEN E. McMINN

American Microsystems Inc.

6.1 Introduction

Once a gate array design has been completed and verified via whatever software tools available, it then moves out of the realm of simulation and is fabricated and packaged. Ordinarily, this handoff between design and manufacturing occurs only after exhaustive checking and logic simulation have been performed in order to guarantee a high probability of working silicon the first time the circuit is manufactured. In this chapter, the manufacturing considerations that make a circuit 'fast turn' will be looked at as well as a summary of the different stages of fabrication through the base and programmable levels. Present packaging capabilities and the future trends for high pin count packages will also be discussed.

6.2 Why 'fast-turn'?

The essence of appeal for using gate array implementation is the fact that it not only provides a low cost alternative to full custom circuits for development expenses, but can be designed and fabricated in a short period of time. Whereas full custom circuits can frequently take up to a full year to implement, gate arrays (depending on circuit size and complexity) can be produced in as little as 3 weeks from the time a logic diagram is received. Much of this time saving results from factors discussed in earlier chapters, such as design cycle shortening caused by decreases in the time required for layout and circuit simulation. However, a major factor in reducing development spans for gate array circuits lies in the processing methodology. The customisation for the circuit is implemented in most cases on only one level. (Some more sophisticated processes involve customising or 'patterning' up to four levels. These will be discussed later.) Because of this an inventory of base wafers is able to be maintained which already have proven processing and are able to be quickly patterned and shipped. This accounts for the short processing cycles that gate arrays are able to enjoy. Whereas most custom circuits require a complete set of masks and a 3–6 week cycle time in fab, the gate array has one 'custom' mask and can usually be processed inside of a week. Let's take a look at some of the predominant processing technologies being used currently to produce gate arrays, and the outlook for the future.

6.2.1 Which technology?

The digital integrated circuit market can roughly be divided into two technologies – MOS (Metal Oxide–Semiconductor) and bipolar. MOS offers higher levels of integration as a result of its extremely low power consumption, and has been a major factor in the development of VLSI ICs. Bipolar is mostly used for applications involving high speed circuitry and is at a lower level of integration than MOS. The smaller scale of integration is caused by the greater power requirements of bipolar devices, and by circuits which demand high speeds. This would seem to indicate that because of the particular attractive points of each technology, they both have appropriate applications.

Within the realm of MOS, CMOS (Complementary MOS – the name is derived from the fact that transistors within a CMOS structure always appear in pairs – one NMOS and one PMOS transistor) is emerging as the dominant technology because its low power consumption enables it to attain very high levels of integration. The fact that transistors occur in pairs is the key to its low power consumption. Because of the complementary nature of a P- and an N-channel device, in a stable condition one of the transistors is always off. This prohibits current flow and thus provides for very low power. The only time that current flows is when switching occurs. An illustration of the switching characteristics of a CMOS invertor is shown in fig. 6.1. Since the power is so low, CMOS lends itself very well to 'shrinking' which will increase speed and eventually result in CMOS which will be as fast, if not faster, than bipolar.

However, in recent years bipolar technologies have been developed that offer fairly high speed performance with only modest power requirements. These include low power Schottky and I^2L

a)

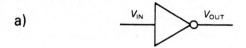

b)

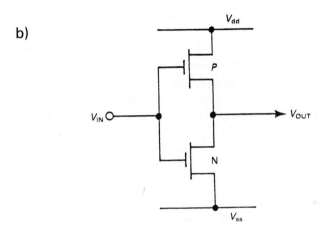

c)

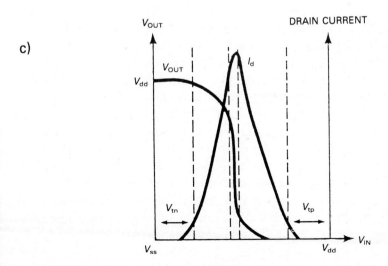

Fig. 6.1 CMOS invertor characteristics: a) logic symbol; b) circuit schematic;
c) switching characteristics

(integrated-injection logic).

One of the goals of every manufacturer is to continue to develop the capability to put more and more functions on a chip. This can be accomplished in two ways – by decreasing the size of a function or by increasing the area of the chip. Reducing a device's linear dimension by a factor of two (i.e. from a 6 μm drawn line to a 3 μm line) reduces the chip area by a factor of four. In addition, the speed of the device will be approximately doubled while the power consumed is reduced by a factor of four. Current state of the art production processing employs drawn dimensions of 3 μm for critical levels with 2 μm processing available in a prototype environment. By 1985 the line widths will shrink even further to 1.25 μm and actually becoming sub-micron (<1 μm) by 1990.

Taking into account the above factors, it is evident that the dominant technology which will be used to implement gate arrays is CMOS. Its combination of high level of integration coupled with its extremely low power requirements make it the ideal process for the future. However, before the fabrication point for a design is reached, several steps must be taken to develop the 'tooling' required to process the device.

6.2.2 PG tape to customisation level

The typical point in the development cycle at which design 'hands-off' the circuit is at the pattern generator (PG) tape. This is a tape which contains 'flashes' or small rectangular shaped boxes which are flashed onto a photosensitive piece of glass to create what is known as a reticle. These flashes are obtained by running a program on the design which will take the geometries in a layout and segment them into individual flashes which will accommodate a predefined aperture opening. The PG tape is mounted on a tape drive which is connected to a large camera. The camera takes commands from the tape and flashes images on a piece of glass (the actual glass material may vary depending on resolution and thermal expansion properties required). The size of the flash is controlled by an aperture opening on the camera. The chuck on which the glass is mounted moves back and forth under the lens opening until all of the required flashes have been performed. A checkpoint at this stage of development is to ensure that the actual number of flashes developed on the glass is the same as the number the designer input on his tape.

The reticle produced from this activity is normally a scale of 10× which means that the image on the piece of glass is ten times the size of the actual circuit. This image is then optically reduced down to get the circuit to its intended size. The reason these reticles are made at a size this large is simple. Any particles which can cause destructive defects (i.e. dust, hair, grease) are shrunk to $^1/_{10}$ their normal size and thus become much less of a problem on the actual circuit. However, a limiting factor on how large-scale reticles can be made is the size of the die being made. In 1978, the largest reticles which could be made measured 2.6 inches (66 mm). This meant that circuits larger than 260 mils (6600 μm) had to be manufactured from 5× reticles. The increased die size coupled with the exponential yield loss because of defect density seriously hampered efforts to obtain die larger than this. However, state-of-the-art photolithography equipment is now capable of producing perfect (defect-free) masks at a 10× scale in excess of 400 mils (10 200 μm).

At this point in the cycle, we become a little less general depending on the level of technical sophistication present. Most processes require a set of 1× masks to be made. These masks are used in the fab for projecting the image of the layout onto a wafer which is coated with a light-sensitive material called photoresist. This masking is achieved in one of three ways. First is contact printing in which the mask actually comes into contact with the wafer. This method is not widely used as the masks tend to have defects rapidly introduced on them as a result of the constant contact and are usually only good for approximately seventy-five exposures before excess defects warrant them unusable. Second is proximity printing which is similar to contact printing except that the mask does not come into contact with the wafer and thus is able to be used much longer. The third type is called projection printing. It is the most precise and allows for an infinite number of exposures because the masks are rarely touched and never come into contact with the wafer. One drawback of projection printing is that the intense heat generated by the projection aligners requires that the masks produced have an extremely low coefficient of expansion. This draws the price of masks for this method of processing to a point where projection printing is only used on those processes with mask geometries small enough to demand the precision this alignment method offers. The typical point at which projection is required is for drawn geometries less than 3 μm.

Many manufacturers are skipping the entire 1× mask generation completely and are now using direct step on wafer (DSW) in which the reticles are optically reduced to 1× directly on the wafer thus allowing 1× masks to be bypassed. This method dramatically reduces defects and allows uncanny precision, but is expensive. Contemporary steppers can cost in excess of $1 million. Another method which will probably gain wide acceptance in the mid to late 1980s is called direct-write-on-wafer. This process uses an electron beam to etch the pattern in the photoresist from the PG tape. It is evident that as the technology evolves, the push is to eliminate steps in the processing of masks. Every time a step is eliminated in masking, it not only cuts down on the time involved, but reduces the chance for damaging defects.

6.3 Process flow

As mentioned earlier, the reason that a gate array circuit provides such fast turnaround times through the fabrication area is the fact that the customisation of the circuit is not done until the next to last step of the process (the metal mask). At this point, 'base' wafers are usually inventoried to ensure that an adequate amount of wafers exist to handle the volume requirements of any device. The masking steps used in a typical process (in this case, 3 μm CMOS) are shown in fig. 6.2 with an explanation of each.

1. P-well implant:
   Before N-channel devices can be diffused, a P-type substrate must exist. In the process used at AMI, an N-type starting material provides the substrate for P-channel devices and this 'well' is diffused for the complement to exist. Many fabricators also use 'N-well' processes in which P-type starting material is used or even 'dual-well' in which both are diffused. The eventual direction of the industry has not yet been determined. Once the P-well area has been defined, the field mask is used.
2. Field:
   This mask defines where diffusions for sources, drains and diffused interconnect will exist on a circuit. It actually defines areas in which field oxide will not exist, which will allow the diffusions to penetrate down into the substrate.
3. N- channel field implant:
   This mask is used to enhance the field doping in the P-well areas (N-channel transistor areas).
4. P-channel field implant:
   This mask is used to enhance the field doping in the N substrate. The mask used is the same as mask 3, but the polarity is opposite.

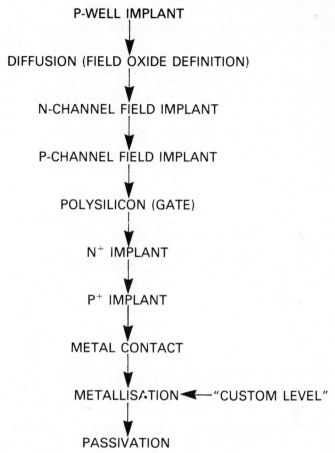

P-WELL IMPLANT

DIFFUSION (FIELD OXIDE DEFINITION)

N-CHANNEL FIELD IMPLANT

P-CHANNEL FIELD IMPLANT

POLYSILICON (GATE)

N$^+$ IMPLANT

P$^+$ IMPLANT

METAL CONTACT

METALLISATION◄——"CUSTOM LEVEL"

PASSIVATION

Fig. 6.2 Masking steps for a typical CMOS gate array process

5. Polysilicon:
   The polysilicon masks form the area in which all transistor gates and poly interconnect are made. Any time that polysilicon passes over our previously defined field mask, a transistor results. It can now be seen that even before the 'customisation' layer for a gate array is applied, all of the transistors exist. It is just a matter of hooking them up to reflect the logic being implemented.
6. N$^+$ implant:
   This mask defines areas of heavily doped N-type material and is used to dope all of the N-channel transistors. The usual doping material used for this step is either phosphorus or arsenic, both of which make their diffused areas 'electron heavy'. This mask is very nearly a duplicate of the P well because all of the N-channel transistors must be within the boundaries of the P well.

7. P$^+$ implant:
   This mask defines the areas for P diffusions to form the P-channel transistors. The normal dopant material is boron.
8. Contact:
   Somewhere in all of these levels of processing, the capability must exist to form contact between different levels. Such is the function of the contact mask. The contact masks define areas in the oxide in which small holes (for a typical 3 μm process, the holes cut would be 3 μm × 3 μm) are etched to allow for electrical connections to be made between the metal and polysilicon or the metal and diffusion areas.

This completes the levels which are needed to get base wafers to a staging point where they can be customised by adding the metallisation. Staging refers to the point in the process at which wafers are inventoried in an uncommitted state to wait the application of the customised level. (For a discussion on staging and inventory levels required to support production requirements, see opposite page.)

A prime area of concern is determining whether or not the wafers being staged have indeed been correctly processed. The explanation for this is obvious; to stage several hundred wafers in order to meet production commitments and then find out at the wafer testing stage that they are all bad could be disastrous. This can result in missed shipments and in the end, unhappy customers. Some method needs to be devised to qualify the goodness of the wafers at the customising stage, but yet not commit them to a particular pattern. The solution lies in the use of a test insert which is standard for the particular process being used. These inserts (frequently called PCMs for Process Control Monitors) are stepped into each wafer at anywhere from two to five sites and are used to obtain parametric data from wafers. The attractive point of these PCMs is that they can contain several test structures which can find flaws in processing that a conventional small test site inserted into the custom chip cannot. If the data obtained from probing these inserts can be applied towards other wafers in the same fabrication lot, then samples can be taken from each lot and the results used to determine whether or not the base wafers are good. As an example, suppose a lot of fifty wafers is started. These wafers would ordinarily go through all steps of processing at the same time. This would include ion implantation, time in the diffusion furnaces and all etching steps. Once the wafers reached the metallisation point, it could be assumed that all wafers

Staging

In order to accomplish as little as a one week cycle time in fab, base wafers have to be 'staged' or inventoried at the point of metallisation. A necessary step in this process is to determine the number of base wafers which must be staged at any one point to guarantee that production requirements can be met. This requires not only co-ordination from a planning group to meet orders already received, but an accurate forecast from the sales and marketing groups as to the level of business expected over the next 12 months, so that capacity can be set aside. Yields must be determined from the final testing done on the parts, back through assembly and wafer level testing, and finally to the fabrication area itself in order to determine how many wafers must be started to result in a needed shipment. An example is shown below to illustrate exactly the staging of base wafers required to support an order of 1000 pieces per month of a gate array which is approximately 150 × 150 mils (381 × 381 μm) in size.

REQUIREMENT:	1000 pieces per month	
* ASSUMPTIONS:	Final test yield	90%
	Assembly yield	95%
	Wafer sort yield	40%
	Fabrication yield	75%

Final chips: 1000
Final test: 1000/90% = 1111 (required out of the assembly area)
Assembly: 1111/95% = 1169 (die required out of wafer sort)
Wafer sort: 1169/190 die per wafer = 7 (wafers out of wafer fabrication)
Wafer starts: 7/75% = 9 wafers starts

*Note: In most manufacturing areas, 'model' yields are established to aid in the planning of the number of wafer starts needed to meet a certain requirement. Based on historical trends, yields for varying die sizes and technologies can be derived. The historical information used in the above example was taken for a 150 mil/side die in 3 μm CMOS using a 4 inch wafer. Based on a gross die per wafer of 475 die and using the assumed model yield of 40%, this means that 190 good die from each wafer tested at the wafer sort point can be expected.

Therefore, to maintain a 1000 piece shipment, nine wafers would have to be started (based on model yields). Since the staging area is approximately 85% of the way through processing, an inventory of about eight wafers should be brought up to the point of metallisation each month to satisfy this particular order.

would possess nearly the same process characteristics. A sample of three wafers could then be processed with the custom metal mask of a circuit with existing backlog and data taken from the PCM to determine the quality of the wafer run. As an added safeguard, the three wafers could then be tested to determine if they will yield the model number of die. If so, the three wafers could be further processed to result in shippable parts, and the remaining wafers from the lot of fifty could be inventoried with a high degree of certainty that they have correct processing up to the metallisation point.

6.3.1 Metal mask

Now that the mechanics of how a mask is made and the processing which takes place prior to customising base wafers have been discussed, what exactly happens to make the 'fast-turn' appeal of a gate array achievable?

Once the design is completed and the PG tape is handed to the mask shop, the responsibility for getting finished units out of the door lies in the hands of the manufacturing organisation. The metal mask is processed in the manner discussed earlier and is transported to the fab area where it is scheduled to be exposed on as many wafers as necessary to meet the commit. The time to get a mask completed from PG tape and into the fab area is usually about three working days. The wafers are patterned with the metal mask of the custom gate array, etched, and then sent on to the passivation layer. This level is a coating of protective silicon nitride which covers all of the die except for the bonding pad areas in order to keep contamination off the die once it leaves the wafer tab. After passivation, the wafers are tested parametrically to ensure that all of the process parameters have been met. From this point, the wafers are backlapped, gold-backed, and shipped to the wafer test area. Backlapping is an operation performed on all wafers which effectively 'sands' or laps the back of the wafer down to a thickness of 8–10 mils. The reason for this is twofold – it improves the thermal characteristics of the die and also rids the wafer of unwanted impurities diffused into the backside of the wafer during the normal fabrication steps. The gold backing is done to insure good contact to the package substrate when the die is being assembled. The time span for the fabrication steps is usually in the area of four working days.

The above example is for a process which only has available one customisable level. However, a double metal process includes the option to customise up to four layers. These layers are the two metal levels plus a contact level called the *via* mask which allows for interconnect between the two layers of metal. Some processes may require the metal to poly/diffusion contact mask also to be 'programmable'. The attractive point of the dual metal process is a significant improvement in speed because most of the interconnect is achieved with low resistivity metal. The single metal process requires interconnect in one direction (either horizontally or vertically) to be polysilicon which has a resistivity of 20–35 ohms per square and can significantly slow a part down.

An illustration of the architecture of a gate array using one layer of interconnect is shown in fig. 6.3. This is an array containing 2500 gates where a gate is defined as an equivalent two-input NAND. The

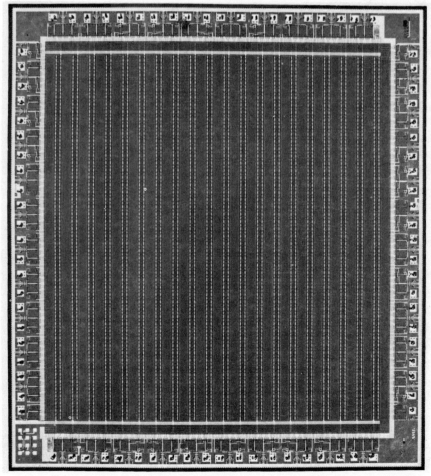

Fig. 6.3 Photograph of a 2500 gate, 3 μm CMOS array

metal bus in the outermost chip area is the external V_{dd} supply which is 60 μm wide. Concentric with it is a 75 μm wide V_{ss} bus, and the area between the power lines is occupied by the peripheral cells which extend all the way around the chip. The core cells are arranged in a fifty column by twenty-row matrix with polysilicon routing being vertical and metal interconnect running horizontally across the chip. Note the marks on each of the bonding pad areas which indicate that this chip has already been 'probed' or tested at the wafer level.

From this point, the wafer moves into the test area where the good die are sorted, and shipped to the assembly area. Assembly will ordinarily take about 5 days if done domestically. Most semiconductor companies have their primary production assembly in the Far East which can take 2–3 weeks from the time the die are shipped and received back. An additional 3 days is then needed to finally test and ship the product.

A detailed chart showing the time required for each operation is shown in fig. 6.4.

6.4 Manufacturing problems

As beneficial as gate arrays are to the user community and as much of a success as they have been to semiconductor companies, the fact still remains that from a manufacturing viewpoint gate arrays can cause problems. Newer start-up operations tend to have less trouble adapting to gate array requirements since they have never had to switch their operation from one handling huge volumes of a few circuits to one shipping small volumes of a large number of circuits.

Handling small volumes constitutes one of the greatest problem areas. A company practised in starting 10 000 wafers per week to support a 16K RAM will have trouble realising that for many gate arrays, two wafers may handle all of the required shipments for a month on a particular circuit. This is further illustrated by the graph shown in fig. 6.5. This cost v. volume alternative graph shows that for a CMOS device of 1000 gates, the gate array solution is cost effective only for volumes under 10 000 pieces per year. This is because the gate array per-part cost is higher even though the initial development cost is lower than a standard cell ($20 000 v. $40 000). Time spans aside, this differential in piece part price begins to make a standard cell more attractive costwise once a run rate of 10 000 parts per year is obtained. The result of this is that for a typical spread of circuits, the maximum number of shipments for a gate array would be of the

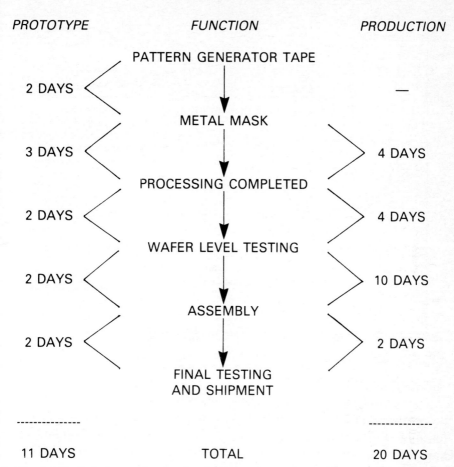

PROTOTYPE   FUNCTION   PRODUCTION

PATTERN GENERATOR TAPE

2 DAYS   —

METAL MASK

3 DAYS   4 DAYS

PROCESSING COMPLETED

2 DAYS   4 DAYS

WAFER LEVEL TESTING

2 DAYS   10 DAYS

ASSEMBLY

2 DAYS   2 DAYS

FINAL TESTING
AND SHIPMENT

11 DAYS   TOTAL   20 DAYS

Fig. 6.4 Typical time-scales for development, processing and testing of a 500 gate array

order of 1000 parts per month. Naturally, there are exceptions, the two most prevalent being (1) the customer is willing to pay a higher price for the quick turn, and (2) the customer may be unsure of his volume requirements and is thus getting his circuit developed for the lowest cost option available (gate array at $20 000).

This clearly points up a need for manufacturing organisations to realise that concessions have to be made in order to facilitate moving many products through a production area fast. Testing procedures need to be streamlined and as much of the testing as possible standardised. This could include universal test cards for wafer level testing and standard performance boards for final device testing (a performance board is the hardware required to interface a device-under-test (DUT) to the tester itself). Quality levels should be examined. While it is commendable to want to achieve a goal of zero

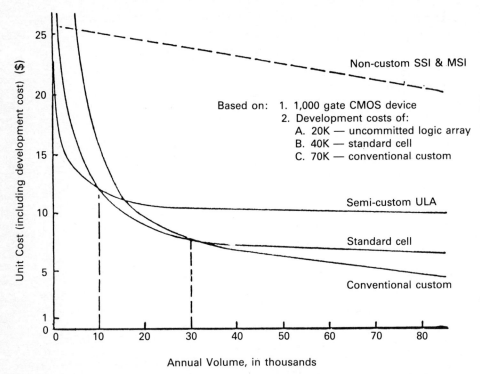

Fig. 6.5 Gate arrays prove to be most economic at volumes under 10 000 pieces per year when the cost v. volume alternatives plot is examined

defective parts being shipped, in many cases it is not economical or feasible. For example, even though most gate array manufacturers have software which will 'automatically' generate a test program, very few are capable of guaranteeing that 100% of the nodes or paths in a circuit are being tested. More often the number is in the area of 80–95%. To spend the extra time and money required to test out all of these failures which will surely be a small number does not make sense. The economics which first drove the customer to the gate array will disappear very quickly. The solution is to make all parties aware of the limitations of the test and to obtain an agreeable solution for any failures which may come up.

Another problem area lies in the staging of product. As mentioned above, two wafers may supply a full month's requirement. Since most manufacturers run a minimum of five to ten wafers at one time, several months inventory must be stored unless provisions are made to 'stage' product at one point after the wafer fabrication and then continue on with the cycle once the next order comes due. Procedures need to be set up to determine where these staging points occur and how to control them.

These are just a few of the problems that can occur when producing gate arrays. Many other areas more subtle than these exist such as the question of just how to number the circuits. Many manufacturers prefer to assign a base circuit number and then call each gate array of that particular base design – a pattern which is similar to the approach used for a ROM. (A 7594 base gate array may have circuit numbers 7594-001, 7594-002, etc.) While this approach is viable, the circuit is still not a ROM and should not be treated as such. All of these areas of trouble can be overcome with careful planning and above all, communication between the groups affected.

6.5 Packaging

Two important trends are being encouraged by the cost reduction move in the IC industry – single PCB solutions and a move toward planar mounting. The standard dual-in-line package (DIP) is proving to be increasingly inefficient for more complex ICs with the need to drill holes in the PCB to take the leads into the board. Some alternative packages which have been developed include leadless chip carriers which mount on the surface of the PCB. Such planar or surface mounting packages allow a greater density of integrated circuits on a PCB, and because the need for many of the drilled holes on the board is removed, the PCB can be more efficiently used. With the increasing demand, surface mounted packages are falling to prices lower than DIPs. This is because in most cases they are smaller and contain less material. Moreover, because of the reduced area taken by the chip on the PCB, the entire system cost is reduced. Also, being able to mount all the components on a single PCB board offers savings in inter-PCB connection, enclosure size and testing. Clearly the use of surface mounting makes a single PCB solution much more attainable. Gate arrays, in particular, are leading the packaging industry towards more complex, higher pin count packages.

The standard package used in the IC industry at present is the DIP, available in fully hermetic ceramic, CerDIP, and plastic post moulded formats. The plastic DIP is the least hermetic, but its low cost has led to its dominant position among IC packages. (Approximately 70% of all ICs are currently packaged in plastic DIPs.) They are restricted to a temperature range of 25–85°C and suffer from moisture problems. This results in a package that is not suitable for military or critical industrial applications. CerDIP is an intermediate package which offers greater hermeticity than the plastic DIP, but at less cost than the ceramic package. It is made of ceramic halves with a lead frame sandwiched between them. The lead frame, however, is still susceptible to moisture problems.

All types of DIPs are readily available with up to forty pins, but for forty to sixty-four, the ceramic DIP is the only one able to achieve any reliability.

Since the mid-1970s, new packages have been developed, mainly to cope with the ever increasing I/O requirements of VLSI ICs. Of prime importance to gate arrays are the chip carriers and pin grid arrays (PGA).

The chip carrier is foremost among a group of surface mounting components, each much smaller than the DIP, and promises high density electronics and significant cost reductions through reduced PCB area and more efficient assembly. Built on the same concept as the highly reliable sidebraze ceramic package, it is made of three layers of ceramic, refractory metallisation and gold plating. The chip carrier also offers contact pads equally spaced on all four sides of the carrier resulting in increased package density, better electrical characteristics and a more cost effective method of packaging devices. The package comes with a gold/tin eutectic sealed metal lid or the low cost glass sealed ceramic lid creating a standard hermetic cavity. A diagram of a typical chip carrier is shown in fig. 6.6. While the multilayered ceramic chip carrier has found the widest use to date with large pin count gate arrays, the plastic post-moulded is expected to replace the plastic DIP as the number one IC package in the late 1980s.

Pin grid arrays (PGAs) have been used by computer mainframe

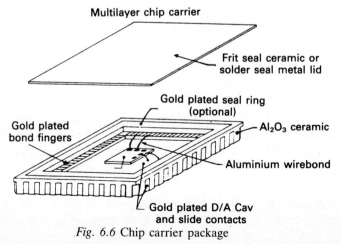

Fig. 6.6 Chip carrier package

Table 6.1 Gate array package options

PACKAGE TYPE	LEAD COUNT	Θ Ja (°C/W)	Θ Jc (°C/W)	SPACING (MILS)	MAXIMUM CHIP WITHOUT DOWN BOND (MILS x MILS)	GA-500	GA-1000	GA-1500	GA-2000	GA-2500	GA-1000D	GA-2000D	GA-3000D	GA-4000D	GA-5000D
						3μm Si-Gate Single Metal					3μm Si-Gate Double Metal				
PLASTIC	14	121.8	47.0	100	140 x 170	•									
	16	114.8	39.5	100	140 x 210	•									
	18	125.1	57.5	100	140 x 210	•									
	22	—	—	100	220 x 240	0	•	•			•				
	24	102.1	42.5	100	290 x 280	0	0	0	0	•	0	•			
	28	82.1	31.2	100	250 x 240	0	0				0				
	40	79.9	31.9	100	340 x 330	0	0	0	0	0	0	0	0	•	
	48	—	—	100	250 x 260	X	0	0	•		0				
	64	64.1	39.5	100	315 x 305	X	0	0	0	0	0	0	•		
CERDIP	22	65.0	18.6	100	200 x 280	•	•	•			•				
	24	51.6	15.8	100	250 x 390	0	•	•	•	•	•				
	28	50.0	15.8	100	250 x 390	0	0	•	•	•	0				
	40	38.3	10.1	100	260 x 345	0	0	•	•	•	•	•			
CERAMIC SIDE-BRAZED	16	58.3	18.1	100	245 x 255	0	0	•	•		0				
	18	63.1	17.2	100	145 x 300	•									
	22	56.5	11.1	100	220 x 260	0	•	•	•	•					
	24	42.5	9.0	100	270 x 280	0	0	0	•	•	0	•			
	28	40.9	6.9	100	280 x 290	0	0	0	0	•	0	•			
	40	37.1	8.2	100	320 x 360	0	0	0	0	0	0	0	0	•	
	48	37.8	8.6	100	310 x 320	X	0	0	0	0	0	0	•		
	68	37.7	5.7	100	295 x 305	X	0	0	0	0	0	0	•		
MINI FLATPACK	18	96.2	37.1	40	200 x 190	0	•								
	22	96.2	37.1	40	200 x 190	0	•								
	24	96.2	37.1	40	200 x 190	0	•								
	28	96.2	37.1	40	200 x 190	0	•								
	40	116.9	35.3	40	240 x 230	0	0	•			0				
	44	116.9	35.3	40	240 x 230	X	0	•			0				
	68	92.1	—	40	240 x 230	X	0	•			0				
LEADLESS CHIP CARRIER	24			50	205 x 215	0	•				•	•			
	28			50	220 x 230	0	•	•			•				
	40	40.5	—	40	270 x 280	0	0	0	•	•	0	•			
	44			50	270 x 280	X	0	0	•	•	0	•			
	48			40	320 x 330	X	0	0	0	0	0	0	0	•	
	64			50	320 x 330	X	0	0	0	0	X	0	0	X	
	68	25.4	—	50	370 x 380	X	0	0	0	0	0	0	0	0	•
	84			50	360 x 370	X	X	X	0	0	X	0	0	0	•
PIN GRID ARRAY	51			100	230 x 240	0	•				•				
	68	27.8		100	271 x 261	X	0	0	•	•	0	•			
	84			100	380 x 370	X	X	0	0	0	0	0	0	0	•
	100			100	330 x 320	X	X	X	X	X	X	X	•	•	
	120			100	413 x 403	X	X	X	X	X	X	X	X	X	0
	144			100	442 x 452	X	X	X	X	X	X	X	X	X	0
CERAMIC FLATPACK	42	53.9	14.7	50	196 x 206	0	•								

Legend: 0 = Gate Array Implementable in that Package
X = No. of Pads < No. of Pins
• = Consult factory regarding down bond option and die orientation.

manufacturers since the early 1970s. Comprised of a ceramic body with a solid matrix of pins for thorough mounting, the PGA is a more familiar concept to PCB manufacturers and users alike than the surface mounting chip carriers. However, PGAs are expensive and their pin concept requires a costly PCB design. The PGA offers the highest I/O per unit area of all packages. PGAs are already on offer by gate array suppliers for pin counts above sixty-four.

Table 6.1 summarises and details the currently available package options. Dice up to 450 mils per side can be accommodated with lead counts up to 144 pins. The chart is applicable to the present AMI 3 μm single and double metal CMOS process, but can be extended to other gate array families as well.

For a more graphic view of the types of package being used today, fig. 6.7 shows a layout of all package technologies offered today. The left side of the photo contains plastic, ceramic, and cerDIP DIPs with the right side being an assortment of pin grid arrays, mini-flatpacks, and leaded and non-leaded chip carriers. As can be seen, a wide variety exists to choose from when packaging a gate array design.

6.5.1 Pin count reduction?

Increased pin counts require more expensive packages and it seems as if the problem of handling ever-increasing numbers of pins will never go away. However, the opposite will occur once the point is reached at which whole systems of large functional blocks are able to be implemented on single chips. The pin counts tend to be highest when a small part of the system is integrated, especially if parallel transfer of data on data buses is employed.

Fig. 6.7 Many package options are available to gate array designers

Chapter 7

Testing Gate Arrays

J.D. TONGE

British Telecom

7.1 Introduction

A fundamental requirement of any manufacturing process is the ability to verify that the finished product will successfully carry out its design function. This testing activity should be sufficiently rigorous to demonstrate that all facets of the product's design requirement will be met. In general, the more complicated the product, the more difficult it will be to devise a rigorous test that will prove beyond doubt that the product is fault free, and furthermore, will function correctly under all anticipated conditions of operation.

In the case of present day digital integrated circuits (ICs) where well over 100 000 transistors may be incorporated onto a silicon die less than 10 mm square, it can be an extremely difficult problem simply to determine that the circuit logic is functioning correctly. In addition to this, it is of course necessary to establish that both AC and DC performance criteria will be satisfied over the full range of electrical and environmental conditions specified for the circuit.

Although gate arrays are by no means the most complex ICs currently being fabricated, they are nevertheless sufficiently complex to make the task of defining an adequate test far from easy. An additional problem germane to gate arrays is the short timescale in which they are usually required to be developed. This means that far less time will normally be available for test programme development than, for example, in the case of a full custom IC development. This problem may be exacerbated further as it is often the customer himself who is responsible for this task. Although this may pose no unexpected difficulty for an experienced customer, someone cutting his teeth for the first time, even on an array of only one or two thousand gates, may well find the problem of test programme development considerably more difficult than at first anticipated.

The main role of the test programme for an array which is procured in quantity will undoubtably be at production test. It is also well worth considering, however, other areas where the test programme may be of value. It may be necessary, for example to debug prototype devices if these are found to exhibit some systematic failure mode, thus indicating either a design fault or systematic fabrication defect. This will be more easily accomplished if the programme has been structured in such a way as to enable meaningful information about the nature of the fault to be deduced from the test equipment. It may on the other hand, be required to obtain characterisation data on the device under test, for example for reliability studies or quality assurance programmes. Again, this may only be possible if the programme has been designed to facilitate the extraction of the relevant data. A further area where the programme can be of value is that of maintenance and diagnostics at system level. Depending upon the nature and complexity of the system into which the gate array is to be incorporated, it may be possible to use the test programme either directly or indirectly to test the device within the system environment. This, however, is unlikely to be a realistic approach unless the device can be thoroughly exercised with a relatively small number of test vectors.

It is now clear that there are a number of sometimes conflicting considerations to be kept in mind on the subject of gate array testing. We require the test to be rigorous, yet often time will be limited, or the test programmer may be inexperienced. We require the test programme primarily to detect faulty devices at production test, yet we may also wish to use it in alternative roles such as prototype debugging, obtaining characterisation data or for maintenance procedures at system level. It should be noted that unless these considerations are borne in mind right from the start of a particular development, it may be impossible later on to extract the desired performance from the test programme without making extensive modifications to it. In extreme cases, the design of the gate array itself may need to be modified to enable the required test procedures to be carried out.

Unfortunately, there is no universal formula which can be applied to provide all the answers to the testing problem, as each development will be undertaken under differing circumstances. It is hoped, however, by discussing the various considerations involved, that the prospective gate array user will be helped to decide on the optimum test philosophy for his particular development, and it is with this aim in mind that this chapter has been written. Before moving on to examine these considerations in more detail, however, it is useful to look first at where our sights should be set, and in this context examine the concept of the *ideal test*.

7.2 The ideal test

The ideal test will possess three main attributes. It will be:

(a) easy to define
(b) easy to use
(c) of maximum effectiveness.

Maximum effectiveness here refers primarily to the ability of the test programme to unambiguously differentiate any faulty or potentially faulty devices from those which can be expected to perform reliably over the range of specified operating conditions. Unfortunately, a test programme developed to be of maximum effectiveness is likely to be complex, and may consequently be less easy to define and use. In practice, therefore, a compromise will normally have to be reached, where effectiveness is sacrificed somewhat to allow the programme to be developed within the time and other resources available.

It should be noted that any such compromise to the test programme effectiveness will almost invariably lead to certain disadvantages later on. These relate mainly to production test costs, as well as device and system reliability, and are more fully discussed later.

How then can we try to ensure at the outset of a gate array development that the effectiveness of the test programme will be compromised by the minimal amount? Assuming that the timescale is fixed, we could first try to ensure that an experienced test engineer is assigned to the task, backed up by the latest computer simulation tools. In practice, however, an experienced engineer may be unavailable, and although it is extremely difficult to do without the appropriate simulation tools, there is still one factor which has an overwhelming effect on the difficulty of defining the test, namely the intrinsic *testability* of the device itself.

7.3 Device testability

The testability of a gate array design can be considered to be an *a priori* measure of how easy it will be to develop a test programme of maximum effectiveness for the device using existing techniques. In general for a digital device, the main problem in defining the test programme will be in arriving at a set of logical test vectors which can be shown to exercise the circuit in such a way as to make any of *a defined set of postulated faults* detectable at the device outputs. This logical set of test vectors is referred to as the *functional test*. It is necessary to restrict our attention to a defined set of faults as it would be an almost impossible task to develop a test programme which would detect any *conceivable* fault. The difficulty here is that no matter how clever the test programmer is, the device can always be more capricious!

Take, for example, a gate array in a microprocessor interface application. It is possible to imagine a timing fault on the array which only manifests itself after a particular sequence of microprocessor instructions. This need not be a hard logical fault, but perhaps a leaky or high impedance transistor which manages to do its job for most of the time, only giving rise to circuit misoperation under a specific set of circumstances. It may even be that the fault only causes misoperation to occur around a certain junction temperature. This implies that not only would the functional test need to be almost arbitrarily long, but in addition, the test would need to be conducted at several different tempratures even to give a chance of detecting this particular fault. In practice, therefore, the general policy is to develop a functional test which can be shown to detect a more manageable subset of all possible faults. This test is then applied to the device in such a way as to maximise the chances of detecting other classes of faults which have not been specifically focused on. An example of this technique would be the use of the functional test to exercise the device at elevated temperature, and at maximum designed clock rate, in an attempt to expose timing faults.

The most widely used subset of possible faults used for developing the functional test for digital ICs is the *single stuck-at* fault. Using this fault model, it is assumed that under fault conditions one of the internal nodes of the circuit becomes stuck at either a logical '1' or '0' condition. A set of test vectors is then developed which, when applied to the device under test, gives rise to a different set of conditions at the primary outputs of a faulty device than for one which is fault free. Computer fault simulators are an essential tool for such development work, and these are more fully discussed in section 7.7.1.5.

There is at present some doubt as to the effectiveness of the single stuck-at fault model, particularly with regard to MOS circuits. [7.1,7.2] There is also the problem that a test developed to detect single faults may fail to detect multiple faults.[7.3] In practice, however, the single stuck-at fault model has been found to be an extremely useful tool in developing high quality functional tests, and until such time as an improved model is developed which gains wide acceptance, it will undoubtably continue to be the standard by which most functional test programmes are evaluated.

We can now, therefore, consider the testability of a gate array design as being primarily concerned about the ease with which a functional test programme can be developed that enables 100% of single stuck-at faults to be detected. Our objective is therefore to influence the design of the gate array logic in such a way as to maximise its testability in this respect. Before we move on to examine how this might be achieved, however, it is useful to consider first some of the disadvantages which can arise in the case of a circuit design which is difficult to test.

7.4 Disadvantages of a design which is difficult to test

A gate array design which is difficult to test may lead to one or more of the following disadvantages:

(a) Long test programme development timescale.
(b) High test programme development cost.
(c) Higher production test costs.
(d) Poor system reliability.
(e) Difficulty in board or subsystem testing.
(f) Higher system field repair costs.

Before these points are discussed in more detail it is worth noting that the last four disadvantages continue to affect the system throughout its operating lifetime. This alone would seem sufficient justification for endeavouring to improve device testability, quite apart from the fact that any efforts expended in this direction are likely to be more than amply repaid during the test development alone.

7.4.1 Long test programme development time-scale

The test programme for a gate array which is difficult to test will obviously take longer to develop than for one which is easily testable. For a relatively complex gate array with testability problems, it is quite likely that the time required to complete the test development will represent a disproportionately large amount of the overall IC development timescale. In cases of severe difficulty, the test programme may not be ready by the time prototype devices become available, thus causing additional delay before these can be formally approved.

7.4.2 High test programme development cost

The longer it takes to develop the test programme, the more this development will cost. It is not just a question of the man-hours expended, however, as computer simulation costs must also be taken into account. For a gate array which is difficult to test, and which consequently requires a long functional test, fault simulation costs can quickly rise to prohibitive levels. As an example of this, the author has recently been concerned with a 2400 gate array development which required around 8000 test vectors to achieve reasonable fault cover. Using a fast parallel fault simulator (HILO-2) on a VAX 11/780 computer, the final fault cover assessment alone consumed over 130 hours of CPU time!

7.4.3 Higher production test costs

There are two ways in which poor device testability can result in increased production test costs. The first concerns the execution time of the programme on the production tester, whilst the second relates to the increased costs of fault detection which may result if programme quality is compromised.

7.4.3.1 Production test execution time

Difficulty in testing certain designs may lead to the requirement for very large numbers of input clocks or test vectors to exercise the circuit fully. In extreme cases, this may lead to additional production test costs, if, for example, the programme takes longer than a few seconds to execute on the production tester.

7.4.3.2 Fault detection costs

In cases where severe testing difficulties are encountered, it may be that the only way in which test programme development can be completed within the time or other resources available is by compromising the effectiveness of the programme. This will inevitably result in a greater chance of faulty devices being passed on in error for inclusion in the system.

It has often been claimed that the costs of detecting a faulty IC go up by a factor of ten for every increase in the level of the system hierarchy.[7.4] Thus if it costs £0.10 to detect a fault at the chip level, it will cost £1.00 to detect the same fault once the chip has been embedded on a printed circuit board, and £10 to do so once the board has been assembled into the system. Once the system is in use, it may well cost in excess of £100 to find the same fault if a field repair has to be carried out.

It can therefore be seen, that any compromise in the quality of the test programme will result in higher production costs as a greater number of faulty devices pass on up the system hierarchy, where the costs of detecting the same fault may eventually be several orders of magnitude higher than at the single IC level.

7.4.4 Poor system reliability

Another characteristic which may suffer as a result of any compromise to the test programme effectiveness is the reliability of the system in question. This happens when, as a result of inadequate testing, a faulty IC becomes included in the system, but where the system testing itself fails to expose the defective component. Subsequent system problems can be notoriously difficult to diagnose, as even if the faulty device is suspected, removed and retested, it will still pass the test programme! (Similar problems can also arise with 'marginal' devices when inadequate AC or DC parameter testing is carried out as explained in section 7.7.2. In certain cases, such faulty devices can continue to plague the system throughout its operating life, undiagnosed failures being put down to misoperation by the user, mains spikes, or other 'gremlins in the works'.

7.4.5 Difficulty in board or subsystem testing

A device which is difficult to test in isolation will almost certainly become even harder to test once it has become embedded in a printed circuit board. Boards containing several such ICs may consequently be extremely difficult to test, and as a result, the quality of the test programme for the board itself may have to be compromised. Indeed, this disadvantage, together with those discussed in section 7.5.2 will affect all levels of the system hierarchy. Thus a system whose components are difficult to test will itself require protracted and expensive test development. Furthermore, the difficulty of achieving adequate subsystem test quality may lead to a further reduction in system reliability, in addition to that caused by inadequate testing at the device level as discussed in section 7.4.4.

7.4.6 Higher system field repair costs

As discussed earlier, IC designs of poor testability can lead to systems which are difficult to test as well as being less reliable. Such systems will obviously attract higher field repair costs throughout their operational lives than those of an easily and completely testable design.

It is thus apparent that a number of disadvantages may be experienced as a result of poor testability at the device level. Several of these disadvantages have repercussions at all levels in the system hierarchy, and may eventually lead to the end product acquiring a poor reputation, with consequent loss of competitiveness. It is of crucial importance, therefore, that every effort is made, as early as possible in the design cycle of the end product, to ensure that good testability at the component level is achieved. Let us return, therefore, to the question of testable design, and consider how the testability of a proposed gate array might, if necessary, be improved.

7.5 Achieving a testable design

Much has already been published about improving the testability of printed circuit board design.[7.5-7.7] Not all of this information, however, is of direct relevance to the gate array designer. For example, considerable emphasis is placed on diagnostic routines for boards to enable faults to be *located* and thus repaired. An IC, on the other hand, is generally impossible to repair, and this is certainly true for gate arrays, although an interesting exception does exist in the case of large memory chips, where laser programming is used to switch in redundant memory cells when faulty cells are detected.[7.8,7.9] In the case of the gate array, then, we are more concerned with fault *detection* than fault location, although, as mentioned later, some ability to determine the nature of the fault is always to be preferred, and can be particularly useful at the prototype debugging stage.

A further, more obvious difference between boards and single ICs concerns access to internal nodes. Whereas, in the case of a circuit board it is often quite easy to probe internal circuit nodes, an IC must be fully testable from its package pins alone.

In general, therefore, our aim in the case of a gate array is to design the circuit in such a way that as well as fulfilling its design function, it is also possible for the internal nodes of the circuit to be easily *controlled* from the primary inputs and *observed* via the primary outputs to facilitate testing.

7.5.1 Testability analysis

The concept that the testability of an IC is related to both the *controllability* and *observability* of its internal nodes has led to the development of software tools to perform testability analysis.[7.10-7.13] Such tools allow the testability of a given design to be assessed before any IC development work is commenced. Areas of poor testability can thus be identified, and appropriate measures taken to improve matters.

Although testability analysis programs can be useful in cases where the circuit design is presented as a *fait accompli*, it is preferable if the need for last-minute modifications to the circuit can be avoided altogether by designing the logic to be testable in the first place. The remainder of this section indicates how this might be achieved by describing first a number of specific testability hazards which should, if possible, be avoided. Later, a number of techniques are presented by which the testability of a given design might be improved.

7.5.2 Specific testability hazards

7.5.2.1 Inaccessible circuitry

Inaccessible circuitry is by definition difficult to test. The application of one or more of the techniques described in sections 7.5.4 and 7.5.5 should enable a more testable design to be achieved.

7.5.2.2 Feedback loops

Circuits incorporating feedback loops can be extremely difficult to control. Initialisation can be a particular problem unless a master reset has been included. Controllability can be further improved by the inclusion of a gate to break the feedback path during testing.

7.5.2.3 Complex interconnected functions

Complex interconnected functions which cannot be independently controlled can also be extremely hard to test. Blocking gates can be used to improve controllability as described in section 7.5.4.4.

7.5.2.4 On-chip power-on-reset circuits

Some gate array manufacturers are now including power-on-reset circuits on chip. Unless these can be externally controlled, however, it is impossible to know whether the power-on-reset circuit has been effective, or whether initialisation has occurred by chance.

7.5.2.4 On-chip clock oscillators

Once again, unless these can be controlled externally, it may prove impossible to synchronise the test machine to the device under test.

7.5.2.5 Asynchronous circuitry

Although there may be occasions where asynchronous circuitry can be used to reduce the utilisation of a gate array, synchronous design principles are always to be preferred. Asynchronous circuitry, by its very nature, is more difficult to control, and in addition, its use may lead to other timing hazards such as races or decoding spikes, unless extreme care is exercised by the circuit designer to avoid these.

7.5.2.6 Monostables

Monostables, like asychronous circuits in general, are inherently difficult to control. In addition, under test conditions, the output pulse period may bear no relation to the speed of the test machine clock. Unless provision can be made during test for all monostables to be both controlled and observed externally, they are best avoided in favour of a fully synchronous solution.

7.5.2.7 Redundant circuitry

Redundant circuitry should be avoided as certain types of fault on a redundant path will automatically be masked. Where redundancy is a design requirement, provision should be made to examine the paths independently during test.

7.5.2.8 Long counter/divider chains

Long counter or divider chains can require an excessive number of clock pulses to exercise them fully. Consideration should therefore be given to the modification of these features during test as described in section 7.5.4.3.

So much for the kind of circuit features which should be avoided. What then are the options open to us to ensure that testable designs are specified in the first place? Broadly speaking these fall into two categories: *ad hoc* and structured techniques. Before we move on to examine these in more detail, however, it is important to consider first how the circuit will be initialised.

7.5.3 Initialisation

In order to ensure predictable and repeatable operation of the circuit under test conditions, it is first necessary to initialise the internal logic such that every node is driven to a defined state regardless of its 'power-up' condition. For a combinational circuit, this will happen as soon as the inputs have been defined. For a sequential circuit, however, a complex sequence of test vectors may be required before this can be achieved. For this reason, it is well worth considering the inclusion of a master reset line, accessible directly from the primary inputs, to enable all storage elements to be initialised together. Such an input can also prove invaluable at the board test stage, where developing procedures to initialise a board full of ICs can otherwise be a real problem.

A further advantage of the master reset is the avoidance of difficulties with computer simulators, particularly those which include an 'X' state (unknown) in addition to the usual logical '1' and '0' values. These may be unable to demonstrate successful initialisation in sequential circuits with feedback, even if it can be demonstrated pragmatically that initialisation would, in fact, be successful. Figure 7.1 shows an example of this problem where a divide-by-seven counter is required. Although we can be sure that within eight clock pulses at the most, the decoded signal will be produced, the simulator may be unable to make such inferences, and will therefore continue to propagate the initially assumed unknown values around the feedback loop *ad infinitum*.

7.5.4 Ad hoc techniques for testability improvement

Under this heading are grouped an assortment of techniques which are aimed at improving the testability of an existing circuit design. There are, by definition, a great variety of such techniques, and several of the more common approaches have therefore been selected for discussion as examples of the principles involved.

More radical methods, generally referred to as structured design techniques, which involve constraining the way in which the circuit can be constructed, are dealt with in section 7.5.5.

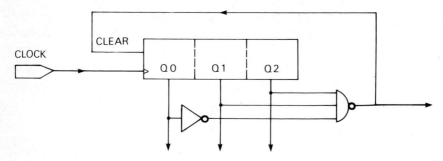

Fig. 7.1 Synchronous divide-by-seven counter

7.5.4.1 Test points

This term is normally used to describe additional primary outputs which are connected to deeply embedded nodes to improve the observability, and thus the testability, of the surrounding area of circuitry. Fortunately, such test points are often the most effective way of improving circuit testability, as in general, nodes are more difficult to observe than they are to control. This is because of the difficulty which is often encountered in setting up (or sensitising) a path from the node of interest to a primary output, to allow it to be observed.

Test points should always be buffered by an output stage to preserve the internal noise immunity of the logic.

7.5.4.2 Tristate buffers

Tristate input/output buffers can be used to good effect where it is required to improve both the observability and controllability of a particular circuit node. Figure 7.2 shows the use of such a buffer in the feedback loop of a complex section of sequential logic. Note that as well as the output pin, an additional input pin is also needed to control the buffer.

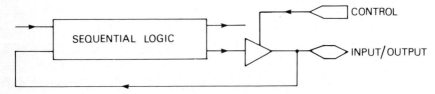

Fig. 7.2 Use of tristate buffer to break feedback loop

7.5.4.3 Multiplexers and decoders

Multiplexers may be used to increase both controllability and observability. The latter can be enhanced, for example, by multiplexing highly embedded nodes onto more easily observable nodes, or alternatively, directly onto additional primary outputs. Figure 7.3 shows how a single 2:1 line multiplexer might be connected in such an application.

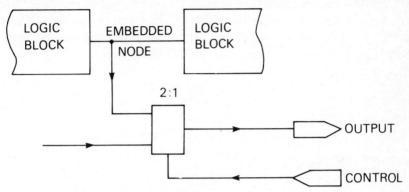

Fig. 7.3 Use of multiplexer to increase observability

An allied technique to the use of multiplexers to increase observability is that of test point condensation.[7.14] Here, gating structures are used to concentrate or *condense* a number of internal nodes onto a single output pin.

Multiplexers may also be used to improve controllability as shown in fig. 7.4. This arrangement can often be advantageously used to reduce the number of test vectors required when long counter or divider chains are encountered, particularly when further sequential logic is driven from the later stages. One technique here would be to clock the counter round once only using the system clock input. Once correct operation had been established, the multiplexer could then be switched to allow direct access to the later stages from either the system clock or an additional 'test clock' pin.

For very long counter chains, say twelve stages or more, it may

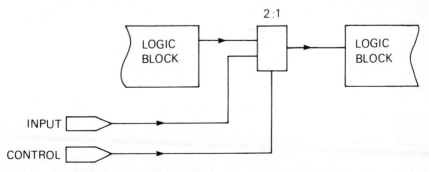

Fig. 7.4 Use of multiplexer to increase controllability

well be undesirable to have to clock the counter right through its total sequence even once, as this test alone would involve more than 4000 clock cycles. One possible solution to this problem is provided by the use of a 1:2 line decoder as shown in fig. 7.5. This technique allows long counter chains to be split up and tested in sections. Stage 'A' is first checked by using the CONTROL input to connect QNA to the TEST OUT pin. Stage 'B' may then be stimulated by first setting QNA high and then clocking the CONTROL input.

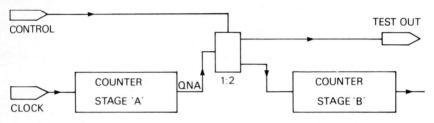

Fig. 7.5 Use of decoder to increase testability of long counter chains

In all these examples an additional price has to be paid in terms of extra input and output pins, and in each case, any additional circuitry must itself be fully tested.

7.5.4.4 Blocking gates

Blocking gates may be used to improve both controllability and observability, for example by inhibiting feedback loops, or by functionally isolating complex logic blocks during test as shown in fig. 7.6. An additional primary input is again required, and the blocking gates themselves must be testable.

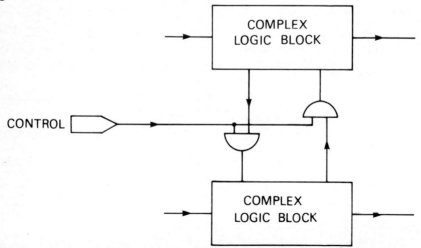

Fig. 7.6 Use of blocking gates to increase controllability

7.5.5 *Structured design techniques for testability improvement*

Although *ad hoc* techniques have been used successfully in many gate array designs, once circuit complexity exceeds approximately 1000 gates, they may no longer prove to be adequate. A more generalised solution to the problem of design testability is thus required for more complex circuits. Structured techniques are an attempt to provide such a solution, by establishing design constraints intended to ensure that circuits of testable design result. Three examples will be discussed. The first, Test State Registers, is really a stepping stone between *ad hoc* and structured techniques aimed at facilitating manual test programming. The other two examples are, however, aimed at automating the test generation process altogether. Scan Design achieves this by making the circuit susceptible to computer test generation, whilst Built In Logic Block Observation (BILBO) allows the IC to test itself. It is worth noting that the latter two techniques also allow the internal logic of the chip to be functionally tested from just a few primary inputs and outputs. This is likely to become an increasingly important factor at probe test, where it is becoming more and more difficult to make reliable probing jigs, as the number of connections to the chips continues to grow together with the gate count.

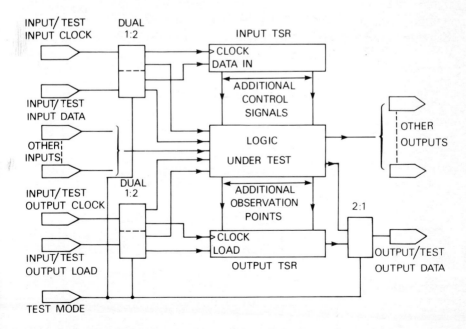

Fig. 7.7 Use of test state registers (TSRs) to improve testability

7.5.5.1 Test state registers

The use of Test State Registers (TSRs) allows a more generalised solution to be found to the problem of enhancing the testability of an existing circuit design. The arrangement is shown in fig. 7.7. It should be noted that the inclusion of decoders to switch the inputs, and multiplexers to switch the outputs allows all test operations to be carried out at the expense of a single additional TEST MODE pin. Under normal system operation, all primary inputs and outputs are connected to the gate array logic. Under test conditions, however, use of the TEST MODE pin allows additional control signals to be clocked into the input TSR by redefining two of the primary inputs for this purpose. The same technique allows the states of additional observation points to be latched into, and then clocked out of the output TSR, in this case via a redefined primary output.

It may, of course, be possible to reconfigure existing storage elements on the chip to act as TSRs under the control of a test mode pin. This technique can often lead to savings in the additional test circuitry required, and it is an extension of this idea which leads on to the concept of scan design.

7.5.5.2 Scan design

There are a variety of allied techniques which come under this heading ranging from the basic *Scan Path* concept [7.15] where all bistables are chained together for testing purposes, to the full design

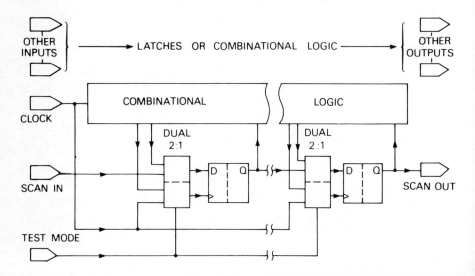

Fig. 7.8 Simplified representation of scan testable logic

discipline of *Level Sensistive Scan Design (LSSD)* developed by IBM.[7.16] The aim of all these techniques is to enable the circuitry to be reconfigured for testing in such a way that the development of test vectors reduces effectively to the problem of testing combinational circuitry only. Once this has been achieved, techniques such as the D-algorithm[7.17] can be employed to assist with, or fully automate test generation.

A simplified diagram of logic designed to be scan testable is shown in fig. 7.8. With the TEST MODE pin inactive, normal system operation is accomplished with the bistables interacting with the combinational logic in the required manner. With the TEST MODE pin active, however, all bistables are connected together as a continuous shift register, allowing test data to be clocked into the chip via the SCAN IN pin. By further control of the TEST MODE and CLOCK pins, the resulting output signals from the combinational logic can be latched back into the shift register, and clocked out of the chip via the SCAN OUT pin, for examination by the test equipment.

Such techniques inevitably lead to some increase in chip area which may be as high as 20%[7.16] although in certain cases it may be possible to deploy some of this additional logic usefully in the system configuration.[7.18] An additional problem may be encountered with the length of the test programme for complex chips which have been reconfigured as long shift registers. In such cases the storage requirements for both the stimulus and response vectors may become excessive.[7.19] Some improvement can be effected by dividing the scan register into several sections which may then be tested in parallel. An alternative approach would be to establish rules limiting the complexity of the combinational logic allowed between the latches. This would reduce the number of test patterns required to be clocked through the scan register to test the combinational logic fully.

Despite these disadvantages, the overwhelming advantages of achieving a circuit design that is 'testable by construction' make such techniques extremely powerful, and a gate array has recently been announced which has been specifically designed for scan path testing.[7.30] An additional advantage of scan design arises at the sub-assembly or board testing level. Here, a number of units may be connected in series as shown in fig. 7.9, thus retaining all the advantages of component level scan testing. Indeed, such techniques may be extended right to the top of the equipment hierarchy, greatly facilitating the development of maintenance and diagnostic procedures at the system level.[7.18]

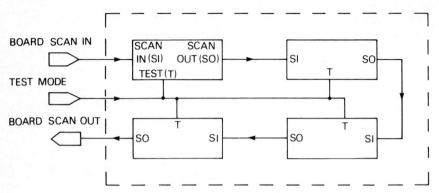

Fig. 7.9 Application of scan testing at board level

7.5.5.3 Built in logic block observation (BILBO)

The discussion of scan design methods in the preceding section hinted at the problems which can arise in handling the large quantity of test data which may be required. BILBO[7.20] has been proposed as one way in which this problem may be overcome, principally by arranging for the IC to test itself. The technique makes use of the BILBO register as shown in fig. 7.10. With the A and B control inputs at '1' and '0' respectively, the register can be used either as a pseudo-random sequence generator with Z1 to Z8 inhibited, or as an 8-bit parallel input signature analyser with Z1 to Z8 enabled. Further combinations of the control inputs allow the register to be reset, configured as a shift register, or used as a system latch. By arranging the chip logic as shown in fig. 7.11, the device can be tested by using BILBO 1 to generate pseudorandom input data, while BILBO 2 is used as a parallel input signature analyser to capture the response data.

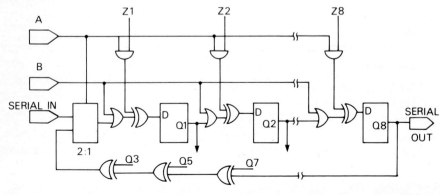

Fig. 7.10 Eight-stage BILBO register

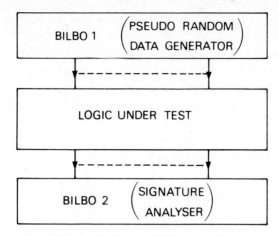

Fig. 7.11 Application of BILBO to IC self-test

In a system designed using several such ICs, an alternative mode of operation allows the intervening interconnection and circuitry to be tested by reversing the roles of the two BILBO registers, while at the same time isolating them from the internal chip logic. It is interesting to note that at least one gate array has already been developed specifically with these techniques in mind.[7.21]

The chip self-test mode depends to some extent upon the ability to run the test at maximum circuit speed in order to ensure that adequate fault cover is achieved within a reasonable test time. The resulting large quantity of test input data tends to preclude the use of fault simulation techniques to determine the fault cover accurately, and a statistical approach is therefore usually adopted. Although this may be justified where the logic between the BILBO registers is combinational and of low fan-in[7.22] it remains a weakness of the technique that it is in general very difficult to predict fault cover accurately, and indeed, this may be totally impractical where sequential logic is concerned.

A further, though admittedly smaller problem is the difficulty in arriving at a reference signature where the computational requirement to determine this is excessive. In such cases the only alternative will be to derive the signature from a working model of the proposed IC, where one is available.

The advantages of BILBO are nevertheless, considerable, offering as they do the prospect of both component and system level self-testing, albeit with limited diagnostic capability.

Perhaps the optimum way forward will be to combine the techniques of scan design and BILBO in such a way as to reap the advantages of both. One such proposal has already been made to combine the LSSD structure with signature analysis.[7.23] Here LSSD may be used with its greater diagnostic capability for prototype device development or system field diagnostics, and signature analysis can be used when a simple go/no-go test is required, for example during chip production testing or for system self-test.

7.6 Device testability – summary

Section 7.5 has summarised the principles of testable design. A number of specific testability hazards have been described, and examples of various testability enhancement techniques have been discussed. These have ranged from the simplest *ad hoc* methods, to structured techniques which call for a more radical reappraisal of both the circuit design methods and the way in which the test data is generated. Although structured techniques at present are used for only a small proportion of gate array developments, it seems inevitable that they will become increasingly common as gate arrays themselves continue to grow in complexity, and the need to find a more manageable solution to the testing problem becomes more urgent. In the meantime, however, I would like to return to the problem of defining the functional test by manual or interactive methods, and discuss the techniques involved and the tools which are available to assist with this task.

7.7 Developing the test programme

Sections 7.5.3, 7.5.4 and 7.5.5 discussed at some length various techniques for enhancing the testability of a digital gate array design. This was justified on the basis that the functional test is frequently the most difficult part of the test programme to develop, particularly if circuit testability is not considered prior to attempting to write the test vectors. However, it is not just the logical functionality of the array which is of concern, but also the DC interface and AC timing performance. Indeed, as far as the system is concerned, a failure in any one of these three areas would be of equal significance. A good test programme should therefore be designed to check both AC and DC parameters in addition to simply checking out the logic, and it is the purpose of this section to discuss these three facets of test programme development. First, let us return to the problem of defining the functional test and consider the ways in which this problem might be tackled.

7.7.1 The functional test

The functional test for a gate array can be tackled in one of two basic ways. These are referred to as the *behavioural* and *non-behavioural* approaches.

The behavioural approach involves the development of test vectors which cause the circuit to behave in a similar way to its intended system function. Although this often appears the most straightforward way to proceed, particularly when the test programmer is familiar with the overall function of the device, an inefficient test set can sometimes result if this approach is followed too blindly. Such inefficiency would arise, for example, where the circuit had been designed to execute a number of independent functions at separate time intervals. In such a case it would obviously be desirable to shorten the programme by the parallel operation of these functions, as far as this could be achieved.

It is an extension of this thinking that leads on to the non-behavioural approach. Here the circuit is conceptually broken down into a number of easily identifiable sub-units, which need bear no specific relation to the overall behaviour of the circuit. The test programmer then concerns himself with the task of testing each of these sub-units separately. This method is naturally made much easier if testability aspects are considered prior to freezing the circuit design, thus ensuring that access to both the inputs and outputs of the sub-units is easily arranged from the primary inputs and outputs of the device. Once again, it may be possible to exercise more than one sub-unit in parallel, thus decreasing further the total number of test vectors required. An additional advantage of the non-behavioural approach is that the test programmer need have no prior knowledge of the circuit's intended application.

In practice, the best solution is usually to be found in a combination of the two approaches. This is because it is often beneficial to have some appreciation of the circuit's overall function in order to identify most effectively the optimum sub-units, and then determine how best to stimulate and observe them.

Whichever way it is decided to proceed, the next thing which should be considered is the overall structure of the test programme. In the same way that software engineers have found advantages in structured programming, and hardware engineers derive benefit from using structured or hierarchical design methods, so too, the test programmer can more effectively carry out his task by deciding on an appropriate overall structure for his test programme. This is because there are several factors which should be taken into account besides the basic objective of testing the device, if problems are to be avoided later on. These include:

(a) how to achieve initialisation quickly
(b) how to minimise the mean time to fault detection
(c) how to provide the maximum of diagnostic information
(d) how best to enable the test programme to be understood by others.

These requirements will be discussed in more detail below.

7.7.1.1 Initialisation

As discussed in section 7.5.3, it is important to initialise the circuit as quickly as possible at the start of the test programme. Failure to achieve this can result in problems during test programme development as well as later on at the board test stage. If a master reset has been included as recommended, then it is simply a question of first setting this to the appropriate condition. In the absence of such a signal, the maximum effort should be made to initialise all nodes within the circuit with the minimum number of input test vectors.

7.7.1.2 Mean time to fault detection

Although this is unlikely to be significant in the case of a test programme which executes quickly, it could be an important factor for one which takes more than a few seconds to run during production test. This will be of particular importance for circuits which are expected to be manufactured in high volume, where the per-device cost will be far more sensitive to production test costs. It is therefore desirable in such cases to exercise as much of the circuitry as quickly as possible once initialisation has been achieved. This is far better, for example, than concentrating first on small areas of circuitry which can be accessed more or less independantly of the rest, and only much later in the programme moving on to stimulate the remaining circuitry, perhaps for the first time. By using the former technique, the test programme can ensure that the maximum percentage of possible faults are flushed out as early in the test sequence as possible, thus minimising the mean time to fault detection together with the associated production test costs.

7.7.1.3 Obtaining diagnostic information

Although this, again, is generally of secondary importance, it can be extremely useful when debugging prototype devices if the programme has been structured in such a way as to furnish some diagnostic information. The ability to localise faults on the chip to some extent, also allows data to be more easily collected and analysed for any subsequent reliability or quality assurance programmes.

In general, it will be far easier to diagnose faults on a circuit of high testability. There are however, two further techniques which can be used to improve the diagnostic capability of a given design.

First, the programme should specify liberally the points at which the test machine compares the circuit outputs with those predicted. Fortunately, this is extremely easy to do using logic simulators, which can be used to predict each output state for every input test vector.

Secondly, the structure of the programme should be arranged in such a way that at any given point, a clearly identifiable area (or areas) of the circuit is being exercised. Fortunately, again, it is just this kind of structure which is most easily comprehended by others.

7.7.1.4 Facilitating understanding by others

The most important factor in enabling one person to understand another's test programme is undoubtably good documentation (see section 7.8). However, it is also a prerequisite that the programme has a clearly discernable structure, as discussed above, which allows sections of the test code to be easily associated with identifiable subunits of the circuit under test.

Bearing these various points in mind, the task of writing down the test vectors themselves is commenced. How far any particular test programmer can go using purely manual techniques, will depend largely on his experience, and the complexity of the circuit in question. Sooner or later, however, for all but the most trivial of circuits, a fault simulator will be required to measure the effectiveness of the proposed test set, and if necessary, to assist with its further development.

7.7.1.5 Fault simulators

A fault simulator is basically a logic simulator to which additional features have been added to enable the effects of certain types of faults to be determined. By far the most widely used fault model at the present time is the single stuck-at fault discussed in section 7.3. There are several different types of fault simulator ranging from those which simulate just one fault at a time to more complex and efficient varieties which allow many faults to be simulated in parallel.[7.5] The basic objectives of any fault simulator, however, remain the same. These are:

(a) To measure the number of postulated faults covered by the functional test.
(b) To draw attention to the outstanding faults which remain.
(c) To assist with the development of further test vectors to mop up the outstanding faults.

The fault simulator achieves these objectives by comparing the response of a fault-free model of the circuit with that of a separately simulated model to which a fault condition has been applied. If the latter response (which must be observed at the primary outputs of the device) differs from that of the fault-free model, then that particular fault is deemed to be covered.

It can be seen that the amount of simulation involved may be considerable (as illustrated in section 7.4.2). Take, for example, a 2500 gate array design with a functional test of 4000 vectors. If the circuit is modelled at the two-input gate level, and each gate terminal is tested for both stuck-at '0' and '1' conditions, then 15 000 separate simulations of the circuit will have to be carried out to ascertain the fault cover. Each simulation may not necessarily require the whole 4000 input vectors to be applied. Indeed, if the programme has been structured along the lines suggested in section 7.7.1.2 to minimise the time to fault detection, then we would hope many of the faults would be detected relatively early on in the test sequence.

A further reduction in the computational requirement can be achieved by removing faults from the faults list which are logically equivalent. This process, known as *fault collapsing*[7.24], can typically result in a 20–30% reduction in the number of faults to be simulated.

Nevertheless, a formidable amount of computation may still remain, and for this reason alone it is desirable to generate as good a set of test vectors as possible prior to commencing fault simulation, in an attempt to avoid the additional cost of any false starts to the programme development. As mentioned earlier, the experience of the programmer will play a significant part here, but by far the most important factor in achieving a good initial test set will be the inherent testability of the circuit design.

The use of the fault simulator is indicated diagramatically in fig. 7.12. Here it can be seen that the simulator is used to derive a figure

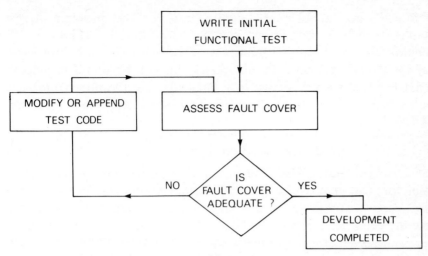

Fig. 7.12 Use of fault simulator to develop functional test

for the fault cover of the initial functional test. If the fault cover is insufficient, the programme is modified and reassessed for fault cover until a satisfactory figure is reached. During the early phase of test programme development, it may be quite acceptable to restructure or otherwise modify the existing test code in order to try to improve the fault cover. Once a fairly high figure has been reached, however, it is generally better to append additional code rather than interfere with the existing programme. This is because any modification to the exiting programme will necessitate a complete re-run of the entire fault list in order to reliably establish the new fault cover. Appended code, on the other hand, requires only the simulation of the outstanding faults in order to establish the new figure. As to what is meant by the term '*adequate* fault cover' in fig. 7.12, this will depend very much upon the circumstances of the particular gate array development. Ideally, of course, we would like to establish 100% cover for single stuck-at faults, as even achieving this figure by no means guarantees that all possible faults will be detected, as discussed in section 7.3. In practice, however, the cover that can be achieved for a particular development within the time and resources available will once again depend largely upon the testability of the design.

7.7.1.6 Fault dictionaries

Many fault simulators enable a *fault dictionary* to be compiled for the simulated circuit. This contains a list of the disparate output vectors associated with the various faults in the faults list. Reference to the dictionary thus enables the likely cause of the problem to be established when a faulty device is encountered. Although this technique was developed primarily to allow faulty circuit boards to be diagnosed and repaired, the dictionary can also be useful in helping to localise faults on defective ICs, particularly if the programme has been structured with this in mind as discussed in sections 7.7.1.3 and 7.7.1.4.

7.7.1.7 Advanced fault simulation techniques

It was mentioned earlier that even the use of fast parallel fault simulators can give rise to excessive demands on computer resources once gate array designs of a few thousand gates or more are encountered. This has stimulated the development of advanced techniques in an attempt to maintain the feasibility of fault simulation as designs become ever more complex. Concurrent or deductive fault simulators, for example, make use of algorithms which reduce the amount of computer processing required to ascertain the fault cover.[7.5]

An alternative approach makes use of special-purpose simulation 'engines', specifically designed to carry out hardware simulation tasks as quickly as possible. A recent IBM paper, for example, describes the development of such an engine which is claimed to be able to carry out more simulation in just eight hours, than an IBM 370/168 can perform in an entire year.[7.25]

Another technique involves the use of classical statistics to obtain a figure for fault cover by simulating a randomly chosen subset of faults from the faults list. Using such techniques it has been claimed, for example, that for a fault population of 10 000, only 1000 need to be simulated to give an answer with 90% confidence, that lies with ± 2.5% of the true value.[7.26]

Finally, a different method has recently been described which claims to reduce the amount of processing involved to deduce fault cover. This uses a path tracing algorithm rather than simulating the faults directly.[7.29]

All of these techniques are aimed at maintaining the feasibility of fault simulation or allied techniques in the face of increasing circuit complexity. An alternative philosophy, however, is to avoid the interactive use of such techniques altogether, by generating the functional tests automatically.

7.7.1.8 Automatic testpattern generation

Automatic testpattern generation (ATPG) is already possible using structured design techniques such as LSSD, as discussed earlier. It would also be of great value, however, to be able to generate the functional test automatically for circuits of less constrained design. Unfortunately, at the present time, all available techniques deal effectively only with combinational logic.[7.27] Much research is, however, being directed towards the development of 'intelligent' ATPG tools that will deal with arbitrary mixes of combinational and sequential logic. Indeed, recently reported work suggests that such tools may be available in the near future.[7.31] It remains to be seen how useful this type of approach will prove to be, especially for the much more complex gate array families now being developed.

It is also interesting to reflect upon a further consequence of such developments, as structured design methods, such as LSSD, as well as offering the advantage of ATPG today, can also offer the further advantages of hazard-free design and simple timing analysis due to the rules that must be adhered to by the designer. The removal of this design methodology 'safety net' by the greater freedom of design that intelligent ATPG will bring, may, in some cases, present more problems than it solves!

7.7.2 The parametric tests

In addition to the functional test which is primarily aimed at verifying that the circuit logic is working, it is necessary also to ascertain that the device will operate within any AC timing or DC interface parameters which may have been specified. It is important that all critical AC and DC parameters are checked by the test programme. Furthermore, any such tests should be designed to demonstrate that the circuit will operate successfully over the recommended supply voltage and ambient temperature ranges. Failure to carry out the parametric testing thoroughly can lead to the penetration of marginal devices into the system. As in the case of inadequately functionally tested ICs, such devices can give rise to problems which are extremely difficult to diagnose, as even if the faulty device is suspected and removed for retesting, the programme will again fail to expose the faulty parameter.

The parametric tests are often 'woven' into the functional test, which may be temporarily suspended, for example to allow input or output currents to be measured. A general feel for AC performance can be obtained by running the functional test at speed where the test machine allows this. Further parameters, such as set-up and hold times on inputs, or propagation delays on outputs will need to be measured separately. This can sometimes be arranged by choosing an appropriate point in the functional test code, and programming the test machine to measure the relevant parameter. Alternatively, some additional test code may need to be written in order to 'expose' an elusive parameter.

Precisely which tests are specified will depend upon the nature of the application and the facilities which can be offered by the gate array vendor. It is, however, a fundamental requirement to be able to measure all DC parameters on each signal input and output pin of the device, as well as monitoring power supply currents. It is also highly desirable to be able to measure at least those timing features of the array that are in any way critical. Ideally, of course, AC parameters should be confirmed for all signal pins of the device, although this does demand a fair degree of sophistication from both the test programme and the test equipment. Until relatively recently, AC measurements were often impossible, or at best, extremely costly to arrange with gate array vendors. Fortunately, however, many are now better equipped with general-purpose automatic test equipment (ATE) and this allows both sophisticated AC and DC measurements to be taken much more easily.

As mentioned earlier, it is important to ensure that the device will operate reliably under any combination of specified conditions. Ideally, therefore, we would like an 'idealised tester' which would logically operate the device at maximum speed, measuring both AC and DC parameters as it did so, while continuously varying any environmental factors such as supply voltage and ambient temperature. In practice this is an impossible task, and we normally have to settle for operation at a few selected temperatures and, say, maximum and minimum supply voltages. Even this can be relatively costly and many gate array vendors will therefore offer as standard the ability to make measurements only at room temperature. In this case it is important to ensure that any temperature dependence of the parameters is taken into account and allowed for in the values specified in the test programme.

For example, a device may have a critical propagation delay which must be met over the temperature range 0°C to 70°C, and over the supply voltage range 4.5 to 5.5V. If testing can only economically be arranged at room temperature, say 25°C, then the value of the delay to be measured will have to be recalculated to allow for the temperature dependence. If the delay is known to increase with rising temperature, but decrease with rising supply voltage, then the best course of action would be to specify a recalculated or 'offset' value of delay to be measured with a 4.5 V supply. In the above case, for a maximum specified delay of 100 ns, and where the temperature coefficient of delay was 0.5% per °C, this would mean ensuring that the programme was written to reject any device exhibiting a delay of more than about 80 ns. Alternatively, a measurement could be made at nominal (5 V) supply voltage, this time offset by a larger amount to take into account the variation of delay with both temperature and supply voltage.

In addition to offsetting any AC parameters, it is, of course, necessary to offset any DC parameters similarly, or the clock frequency of any functional speed testing, when these are not assessed under 'worst case' conditions.

This kind of modification to the specified parameters can only be carried out with a detailed knowledge of the characteristics of the process used to fabricate the array. Sometimes this information is included by the gate array vendor in a design manual. In this case the customer is able either to specify his own offset parameters, or alternatively, to ensure that the correct offsets have been applied by the test programmer. Certain vendors, however, provide only approximate information of this kind, and undertake to write the parametric part of the test programme themselves, working directly from the specification. In such cases, the customer should insist on a copy of the vendor's test programme documentation, together with a synopsis of the conditions under which the tests are to be applied to the device. An attempt can then be made to confirm that any necessary offsetting has been correctly carried out, by comparing the figures in the specification with those written into the test programme.

7.7.3 Developing the test programme – summary

There are clearly many factors to be taken into account when developing the full test programme for a gate array. Ideally we would like to aim for a programme which could unambiguously detect any conceivable kind of fault. In practice this is impossible. In the case of the functional test, this compromise may be brought about by poor design testability or the inadequacy of the fault model used for fault simulation, whereas the parametric testing may be compromised due to limitations of the test machine or because of the expense, for example, of testing at anything other than room temperature. In addition, for any IC development there will be a practical limit imposed on the resources available to develop the test programme, and for a gate array, where speedy development is of the essence, this limitation is of particular significance. It is important to bear in mind that the circuit testability is by far the most important factor in determining how good a test programme can be developed in the time available. Any effort expended to improve testability is thus likely to be more than amply rewarded both during and after the test programme development phase.

One final point relates to the dynamic (AC) testing of gate arrays which have been reconfigured for testing purposes. Certain *ad hoc* and structured techniques involve altering the circuit arrangement for testing, from that of its system configuration. Under such conditions, the verification of logical and DC performance presents no problem. The AC parameters which can be measured under such conditions may, however, bear no resemblance to those that the device will exhibit in its system environment. For a rigid design discipline such as LSSD, supported by comprehensive design automation tools, it may be acceptable to rely on the results of timing analysis, and perhaps simply measure output rise and fall times in addition to running the scan test at high speed. For less rigorous approaches however, it may be necessary to include some additional behavioural code, with the device in its system mode, where it is necessary to verify critical timing requirements.

7.8 Test programme documentation

Much gate array design work, including test programme development, is carried out not by the array vendor himself, but by the customer. This situation has been brought about largely by the vendors, who have encouraged customers to carry out their own difficult and complex design work where possible, in order to avoid the design bottleneck that would otherwise result. In certain cases, the customer's systems engineer may find it more convenient to ask a third-party gate array specialist to do the necessary design work. This could mean the involvement of either a captive design facility in the case of a large company, or in the case of a smaller company, the use of an external specialist. A captive design facility may again choose to subcontract part of the work, perhaps because the required timescale cannot be met due to pressure of existing work.

It is thus imperative, with the possibility of so many different people involved, that clear and comprehensive documentation is compiled on all aspects of device development, and nowhere is this more important than for the test programme. Good test programme documentation, in addition to facilitating good communication between the various parties involved, can also be invaluable:

(a) to assist with test programme development
(b) to assist with troubleshooting at the prototype device stage
(c) to enable useful characterisation data to be obtained during production or reliability testing
(d) to provide good engineering back-up should it be required on some future occasion to modify either the device or its test programme.

7.8.1 *Assisting with test programme development*

An easily understood, concise representation of the proposed tests can be an invaluable asset even while the programme itself is being evolved. Figure 7.13 shows one form of test summary sheet or 'schedule'. On it are plotted the input stimulus changes for the functional tests, and, in the corresponding output columns, the anticipated circuit responses. Separate columns for control signals, such as clocks, allow these to be easily discerned. A unique test reference number is allocated sequentially to each new input vector, with the possible exception of large numbers of clock pulses which may be grouped together for conciseness. Prior to logic simulation, only those outputs of immediate concern need be inserted. If required, the unknown responses can be added later once simulation has been carried out. Comment columns adjacent to the vector columns allow the inclusion of explanatory notes which should preferably be used liberally to explain the nature of the functional testing being carried out. These columns also allow suitable points in the functional test to be picked out for the specification of parametric measurements. The test schedule may be written manually, or derived from computer aids such as simulators which offer appropriate data formatting facilities. Of the two, the latter is to be preferred as it is less error prone.

The great advantage of such a form of test summary is the relative test machine independence of the representation. It thus provides a common basis for systems engineers, gate array designers, test programmers and array vendors to discuss the proposed test procedures without reference to the details of a specific test machine. This is of particular importance in the field of gate array development where there is as yet no standardisation of test equipment, and a

DEVICE CODE : ICXXX															SHEET 1 OF 7
ISSUE NO : 1															
DATE : 30·2·83															

PIN 9 = 5 V
PIN 1 = 0 V
⎍ CLOCK PULSE SHOWING ACTIVE EDGE

* = PARAMETRIC TEST
PIN NO. AND REF.

COMMENTS	TEST NO.	CKA	CKB	CKC	RST	DIN	A	B	C	R1	R2	R3	R4	D	E	COMMENTS
		6	7	8	2	3	4	5	10	15	16	14	13	12	11	
	1	0	0	0	0	0	0	0	0	X	X	X	X	X	X	* MEAS IIL ALL I/Ps
	2	1	1	1	1	1	1	1	1	X	X	X	X	X	X	* MEAS IIH ALL I/Ps
RESET	3	0	0	0		0	0	0	0	0	0	0	0	0	0	* MEAS VOL ALL O/Ps
																CIRCUIT INITIALISED
	4				0											
	5					1										
	6	1								1						CHECK POSITIVE
	7	0														EDGE OPERATION
LOAD REGISTER	8	⎍									1					
	9	⎍										1				
	10	⎍											1			
SET COUNTER	11		1													CHECK NEGATIVE
	12		0											1	1	EDGE OPERATION * MEAS VOH ALL O/Ps
RESET	13				1					0	0	0	0	0	0	
	14		0													
	15		1												1	CHECK POSITIVE
CLOCK COUNTER	16		0													EDGE OPERATION
	17			⎍										0	1	
	18			⎍										1		
	19			⎍										0	0	
	20					1										

Fig. 7.13 Example of a functional test schedule

good variety of different testers are likely to be encountered if more than one vendor is used.

As well as assisting the test programmer himself to marshall his thoughts regarding the structure and philosophy of the test procedure, such a schedule can also be of great assistance during any programme debugging which may be carried out prior to the sampling of prototype devices, for example, by using a breadboard of the proposed gate array circuit. Such diagnostic work will be much easier if the programme has been structured in such a way as to facilitate this, as described in section 7.7.1.3.

7.8.2 *Troubleshooting prototype devices*

By the time that prototype devices become available, the test programme has normally been debugged by the use of either a breadboard of the circuit or a logic simulator. In the latter case, however, errors may be introduced when the programme is mounted on the vendor's test equipment (see section 7.9). Further difficulties may arise if the small prototype batch has been affected by low yield, and none of the devices are in fact defect free. Worse still, a design fault may have propagated unnoticed to the customisation masks causing a proportion of the devices to exhibit some systematic failure mode.

In each of these cases, access to good test programme documentation, such as a well-commented test schedule, is of great assistance in helping to diagnose the cause of the problem.

7.8.3 *Compiling characterisation data*

The test programme is considered by many to be primarily a means by which good devices may be separated from bad ones at production test. Although this is undoubtedly true, the test programme can also play an important role at the same time by providing feedback to the fabrication process. This information can then be used to enable the process to be adjusted to minimise the defect rate.[7.28] Such data will again be most easy to extract where the test programme has been well structured and is well documented, and for which a fault dictionary has been compiled during fault simulation. Even without the use of a fault dictionary, however, a good, well-documented programme will allow a certain insight to be gained as to the cause of a particular fault, simply by reference to the point in the programme at which the failure was detected. In either case, further follow-up work will be necessary to determine the precise nature of the fault.

For an application where more detailed characterisation work is required, and where modern sophisticated ATE is available, the programme can be written to measure precise values of AC or DC parameters rather than simply perform a go/no-go test. Once again, a well-documented programme will allow the results to be interpreted with maximum efficiency.

7.8.4 *Providing engineering back-up*

There are a variety of reasons why subsequent re-engineering may need to be carried out on an existing gate array or its test programme. It may be decided at a later date, for example, to extract more characterisation data from an existing device, or alternatively, to carry out detailed reliability studies on samples of a particular design. In either case it may be necessary to add further tests to the existing programme. Such modifications will be much easier to carry out if the test programme documentation is easily understood.

As to the gate array itself, small improvements to devices may be requested by systems engineers once they have had a chance to look at the prototypes and how they behave in the system. Subsequent evolution of the system itself may, on the other hand, require the circuit function to be altered slightly, or an allied system function may be satisfied by a new version of an existing array. As long as the required modifications are of a minor nature, it may be preferable to modify an existing device rather than start again from scratch. In each case, the test programme will have to be modified to accommodate any changes which are made to the circuit specification. Although this may be of little concern if the same engineer who originally developed the test programme is asked to effect the modification, where it is not possible to arrange this, it may only be feasible to modify the existing programme successfully where clear and comprehensive documentation has been recorded.

7.9 Verifying test programme implementation

By the time that the test programme is ready for implementation on the vendor's ATE, a good deal of time, effort and money will have been spent on its development. It is thus of paramount importance that the programme is correctly and accurately implemented at the test site.

Many large customers will have access to their own CAD tools, and may therefore use these for expensive preliminary tasks such as fault simulation. One problem which then arises is how to translate the resulting test vectors into a form acceptable to the vendor, without introducing errors. One solution would be for the customer to develop a further software facility which would automatically translate his own CAD output into a form suitable for mounting directly into the vendor's ATE. This, however, is unlikely to be a solution for many customers due to the costs involved in generating such software.

An alternative solution exists in the case of a vendor who offers simulation tools which interface directly to his own ATE. A model of the circuit logic must first be coded up and submitted to the vendor's simulator. This may appear at first sight to be duplicating effort, however this activity is in any case becoming more frequently necessary, as more vendors introduce facilities such as logic to layout checks, autoplacement and autorouting. Next, the customer-developed test vectors must be translated manually into a form suitable for input to the vendor's simulator. A single unfaulted simulation of the circuit is then carried out to check that the logic and the test vectors correspond. As a single 'good circuit' simulation is relatively cheap, the need to perform this additional check in no way detracts from the cost advantage of the customer using his own CAD to perform the more expensive fault simulation.

In the absence of suitable vendor CAD, and where it is still necessary to translate the test programme, the only way of verifying this prior to the arrival of sample devices will be to use a model of the proposed gate array in association with the vendor's test equipment. As this is often difficult to arrange, this will normally mean that the programme cannot be debugged before prototype devices arrive. This is an extremely undesirable state of affairs as, if a test failure occurs, it may prove difficult to determine whether the programme or the device itself is at fault.

Further problems may be encountered in implementing any parametric testing which may be required. As this activity is normally carried out by the vendor, it is necessary for the customer himself to ensure that suitable checks are carried out to confirm that this work has been carried out correctly. As discussed earlier, this may also involve ensuring that all parametric measurements have been suitably offset in cases where it is not planned to carry out testing under worst case conditions.

Ideally, a means is required whereby test programmes of various origins can be automatically mounted onto the test equipments offered by different gate array vendors.

One possible solution might perhaps be found in the development of a standard test programming language, together with appropriate software translators to generate the machine test code. Until a solution is found, however, it will unfortunately continue to be necessary for the gate array user to verify by some means that the test programme is eventually mounted at the test site precisely as intended.

7.10 Summary

Gate arrays undoubtedly offer a unique opportunity for equipment designers to incorporate all the advantages of a higher level of circuit integration into their products. It is thus of paramount importance that the economic advantages of using these devices are not put at risk by testing problems. Despite the complex software tools which have been developed to assist with test programme development, severe difficulty may be experienced where the testability of the circuit design has been neglected. In cases where this difficulty results in the quality of the test programme being compromised, the economic penalties will have to be borne throughout the lifetime of the product.

Other problems may arise when the test programme is mounted at the test site, and until more formalised procedures are evolved, it will remain necessary for the gate array user to verify that the programme has been correctly implemented.

It may be, however, that time will prove all of these difficulties to be of an ephemeral nature, as further advances in design automation enable test programmes to be generated automatically. Perhaps structured design techniques are already pointing towards the time when the chips, and indeed, their target systems, will be designed in such a way as to test themselves comprehensively.

Until such times, it is hoped that the contents of this chapter will help prospective gate array users to develop and apply high quality test programmes to these most useful devices more effectively.

7.11 Acknowledgement

Acknowledgement is made to the Director of Research, British Telecom, for permission to make use of the information contained in this chapter.

7.12 References

7.1   Banerjee, P. and Abraham, J.A. (1982) 'Fault characterisation of VLSI MOS circuits'. *Proceedings of 1982 IEEE Conference on Circuits and Computers* 564–8.

7.2   El-ziq, Y.M. (1983) 'Failure analysis and test generation for VLSI physical defects'. *Proceedings of 1983 IEEE Custom Integrated Circuits Conference* 300–303.

7.3   Agarwal, V.K. and Fung, A.S.F (1981) 'Multiple fault testing of large circuits by single fault test sets'. *IEEE Transactions on Circuits and Systems* **CAS-28**, (11), 1059–69.

7.4   Williams, T.W. and Parker, K.P. (1982) 'Design for testability, a survey'. *IEEE Transactions on Computers* **C-31**, (1), 2–15.

7.5   Bennetts, R.G. (1982) *Introduction to Digital Board Testing*. London: Edward Arnold, New York: Crane Russak.

7.6   Lelivre, D. and Smith, K. (1980) *Designing Digital Circuit Boards for Testability*. Application Report, Membrain Ltd.

7.7   Mittelbach, J. (1978) 'Put testability into PC boards'. *Electronic Design* 128 *et seq.*

7.8   Moench, J. *et al.* (1983) 'A sub 100 ns 256K DRAM'. *Proceedings of 1983 IEEE International Solid State Circuits Conference* 230–31.

7.9   Natori, K. *et al.* (1983) 'A 34 ns 256K DRAM'. *Proceedings of 1983 IEEE International Solid State Circuits Conference* 232–3.

7.10 Goel, D.K. and McDermott, R.M. (1982) 'An interactive testability analysis program – ITTAP'. *Proceedings of 1982 IEEE Design Automation Conference* 581–6.

7.11 Grason, J. (1979) 'TMEAS – a testability measurement program'. *Proceedings of 1979 IEEE Design Automation Conference* 156–61.

7.12 Goldstein, L.H. and Thigpen, E.C. (1980) 'SCOAP: Sandia Controllability/Observability Analysis Program'. *Proceedings of 1980 IEEE Design Automation Conference* 190·96.

7.13 Bennetts, R.G. et al. (1980) 'Computer-aided measurement of logic testability – the CAMELOT program'. *Proceedings of 1980 IEEE Conference on Circuits and Computers* 1162–5.

7.14 Fox, J.R. (1977) 'Test point condensation in the diagnosis of digital circuits'. *Proceedings of the IEE* **124**, (2), 89–94.

7.15 Funatsu, S. *et al* (1979) 'Easily testable design of large digital circuits'. *NEC Journal of Research and Development* (54) 49–55.

7.16 Eichelberger, E.B. and Williams, T.W. (1978) 'A logic design structure for LSI testability'. *Journal of Design Automation and Fault Tolerant Computing* **2**, (2), 165–78.

7.17 Roth, J.P. (1966) 'Diagnosis of automata failures: a calculus and a method'. *IBM Journal of Research and Development* **10**, (7), 278–91.

7.18 Stolte, L.A. and Berglund, N.C. (1979) 'Design for testability of the IBM System/38'. *Proceedings of 1979 IEEE Test Conference* 29–36.

7.19 Lindbloom, E. *et al.* (1982) 'VLSI testing, diagnostics and qualification'. *Proceedings of 1982 IEEE Conference on Circuits and Computers* 341–5.

7.20 Konemann, B. *et al.* (1979) 'Built in logic block observation techniques'. *Proceedings of 1979 IEEE Test Conference* 37–41.

7.21 Resnick, D.R. (1983) 'Testability and maintainability with a new 6K gate array'. *VLSI Design* 34–38.

7.22 Agrawal, P. (1975) 'Probabalistic analysis of random test generation method for irredundant combinational logic networks.' *IEEE Transactions on Computers* **C-24**, (7), 691–4.

7.23 Komonytsky, D. (1982) 'LSI self-test using level sensistive scan design and signature analysis'. *Proceedings of 1982 IEEE Test Conference* 414–24.

7.24 McCluskey, E.J. and Clegg, F.W. (1971) 'Fault equivalence in combinational logic networks' *IEEE Transactions on Computers* **C-20**, 1286–93.

7.25 Denneau, M.M. (1982) 'The Yorktown simulation engine'. *Proceedings of 1982 IEEE Design Automation Conference* 55–9.

7.26 McDermott, R.M. (1981) 'Random fault analysis'. *Proceedings of 1981 IEEE Design Automation Conference* 360–64.

7.27 Muehldorf, E.I. (1981) 'LSI logic testing – an overview'. *IEEE Transactions on Computers* **C-30**, (1), 1–17.

7.28 Mahoney, M. (1982) 'Closing the loop – an expanded role for ATE in semiconductor manufacturing'. *Proceedings of 1982 IEEE Test Conference* 12–21.

7.29 Abramovici, M. *et al.* (1983) 'Critical path tracing – an alternative to fault simulation'. *Proceedings of IEEE 1983 Design Automation Conference* 214–20.

7.30 Grierson, J.R. et al. (1983) 'The UK5000 – successful collaborative development of an integrated design system for a 5000 gate CMOS array with built-in test'. *Proceedings of IEEE 1983 Design Automation Conference* 629–36.

7.31 Warton, D.J., Robinson, G.D. and Maunder, C.M. (1983) 'The Hitest test generation system' (3 papers). *Proceedings of IEEE 1983 Test Conference* 302–32.

Chapter 8

Using and Designing with Gate Arrays

Part 1
Application Considerations

MERVYN A. JACK

University of Edinburgh

8.1 Gate array selection, guidelines and comments

The decision to apply a dedicated gate array chip to a specific market is partly based on objective scientific reasoning and partly based on subjective assessment. The reasons *why* a gate array design might be suitable to a given product range, either existing or projected, will be predominantly based on marketing and commercial considerations with technical performance as a secondary impetus in most cases. Similarly the decision *where* a gate array might be used in products or product ranges, and in which markets, will be largely based on cost-effectiveness considerations relating the potential advantages to the overall costs, be it in military systems, in 'original equipment manufacture' (OEM), or in large scale production (consumer) markets. Trade-offs in the selection of gate array, standard cell or full custom design approaches have been presented in earlier chapters. The discussion here centres on the selection of possible gate array alternatives.

Having established the likely viability of a gate array design there then arises the more detailed decision of *when*, and at what level of technical development, an engineering specification is to be released to potential (selected) gate array suppliers. The timing of this release will be a function of the type of product involved, as well as the technical competence – imagined or otherwise – of the customer involved.

This level of technical competence will also be measured by the ability to establish *which* of a range of gate array technologies is most suited to a given requirement. It is at this level of decision that good relationships between customers and potential suppliers need to be fostered in order to fully appraise arguments from a variety of suppliers as to the suitability of their individual technology or technologies, or the types of gate array that they offer.

Having established communications with a range of possible supliers to discover the advantages of particular technologies to particular applications, the dialogue can be expanded to consider *how* the gate array design will actually be carried out in terms of available computer-aided design software and *how* the final designs will actually be manufactured.

Finally, the decision as to *who* is actually contracted for a specific gate array design can be made, based partly on an objective assessment of capabilities and partly on a subjective assessment of credibility.

In this chapter, an attempt will be made to catalogue some of the details which might influence the objective assessment of a given supplier and technology. In addition, some background details which would be considered in a subjective assessment will be included as an indication of possible features to examine. The chapter then continues with details of some specific findings from gate array users.

8.2 Reasons for choosing a gate array

Traditional product and system design approaches, involving standard, off-the-shelf, ECL, TTL and CMOS integrated circuits soldered onto printed circuit boards, are increasingly being replaced by their present-day equivalents in custom and semi-custom integrated circuits, and gate arrays in particular.

In essence the gate array, which can include both linear (analog) and digital components, serves as a direct replacement for several small- to medium-scale integrated circuits by incorporating extremely complex circuitry on a single large scale integration (LSI) gate array chip. The gate array thus allows the production of a single chip to fulfill a specific customised requirement and one such LSI gate array chip can be used to replace more than 100 off-the-shelf chips.

Manufacturers become involved with producing a dedicated gate array chip for a specific product in a particular market for one of two reasons – marketing or technical. In the case of an existing TTL/CMOS product, especially, the marketing advantages in terms of an up-graded product which can be advertised as exploitng 'the latest microchip technology' will be significant in creating a 'high technology' image for a product. This new gate-array based product might serve to augment the overall product range by offering a series of functional or performance features not previously achievable. For example, a typical microprocessor-based product normally consists of a printed circuit board on which are mounted the microprocessor chip, one or more memory chips and several other medium-scale integrated circuits for control, display and general 'random logic' functions. These random logic circuits, which may comprise up to 70% of the manufacturing complexity of the product, are ideally suited to 'logic replacement' by a gate array chip. This gate array option therefore offers a number of distinct advantages. First, product reliability will be significantly improved as a large number of components, wires and solder joints are eliminated. The single gate-array chip will have basically the same reliability as just one of the components that it replaces. This feature in itself will tend to minimise the warranty costs of the product. The overall system manufacturing costs will similarly be reduced by the elimination of several components (reduced inventory, storage costs) and by the elimination of assembly costs of printed circuit boards, back planes or wiring looms. In addition, the gate-array based system will offer reduced size, and possibly reduced power consumption, thus offering the potential for hand-held, battery powered products in some markets such as portable data logging products.

The use of a gate array chip will also improve product security as the product will become significantly more difficult for a competitor to copy, or 'reverse engineer', allowing the product to maintain a market lead for longer. This feature is especially important in markets such as security systems where the advantage of greatly improved resistance to tampering by criminals would be of benefit in marketing.

The savings in space, power consumption, materials inventory, assembly costs and the enhancement of reliability which can be achieved by incorporating gate arrays can thus serve to produce a more viable and cost effective product in the market place.

The second motive for considering gate arrays, namely technical enhancement, would be of more pronounced importance as part of the development of a new product, or possibly a product with extended performance. Here the considerations already discussed still apply. However they assume slightly different aspects. For example, the development costs and time-scales involved in developing a custom gate array chip would be roughly comparable with those of a printed circuit board equivalent. Thus, with an existing design, where the 're-design' costs involved in retro-fitting a gate array to the product would be amortised over the remaining product lifetime, for a new product, the start-up cost would have to be tolerated with either the gate array option or the printed circuit board option. Many of the personal or home computer systems presently available, employ gate array chips for these reasons.

Technical motivation assumes a dominant role in cases where it is clear that the achievement of specified performance would be difficult without recourse to a gate array. Here such features as improved speed of operation may be important where, by reducing the physical dimensions over which logic signals must propagate, signal delays can be reduced. The gate array might also offer technologies or technological features and circuit functions not otherwise obtainable from off-the-shelf components. Examples might include the very high processing speed of ECL, the constant speed-power product of I^2L or the low power consumption of CMOS.

In general terms therefore, the gate array can now be considered as a cost-effective replacement for off-the-shelf circuits. However, in the vast majority of cases, the reasons for adopting a gate array design in a given product, either existing or projected, will be predominantly based on marketing and commercial considerations; technical considerations would be taken secondarily.

8.3 Where to apply the gate array

A variety of customisation techniques are available for an integrated circuit design (fig. 8.1). These range from the full custom approach which involves detailed designing (and manufacture) of all of the circuit features required, through the standard cell (library) design approach based on a (software) library of tried and tested cells, to the gate array which is essentially a matrix of pre-processed circuit elements, or logic gates, whose main interconnections (in metal) can be customised (fig. 8.2). In general terms, the gate array and cell library approaches offer small trade-offs only in terms of performance and technology, and the full capabilities of silicon can only ultimately be exploited by custom design. Full custom and cell library design techniques differ significantly in the degree of engineering effort and design automation required. Standard cell options which offer large LSI blocks of memory or analog functions are readily available.

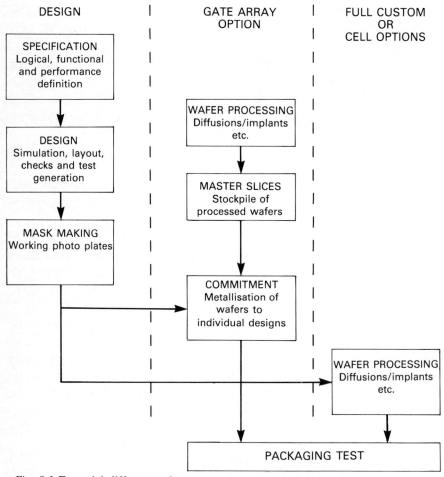

Fig. 8.1 Essential differences between gate array and full custom or standard cell approaches: with gate arrays, wafer processing can take place during, or prior to, design activities

The custom design approach to producing integrated circuits represents the optimum choice in terms of highest performance, maximised production yield and minimised per-unit cost for large scale production. This approach demands manual and highly skilled engineering design and layout. However, the attendant high design costs, coupled with a relatively long development cycle, restrict this full custom approach to circuits for very high volume production, (greater than around 100 000 parts per year, see fig. 8.3), or to circuits which require premium performance (very high speed, very low power) and can afford the development overhead. However as design automation software tools become more capable and more widely used, the design time and cost for such custom designed

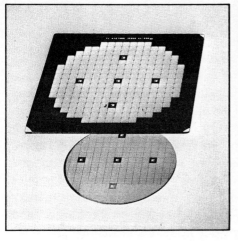
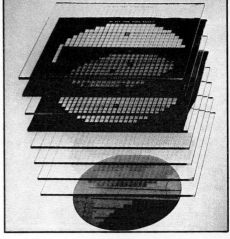

Fig. 8.2 Mask levels: cell-based designs require up to ten mask levels; gate array designs require only one or two. (Photographs courtesy of Racal Microelectronic Systems Ltd)

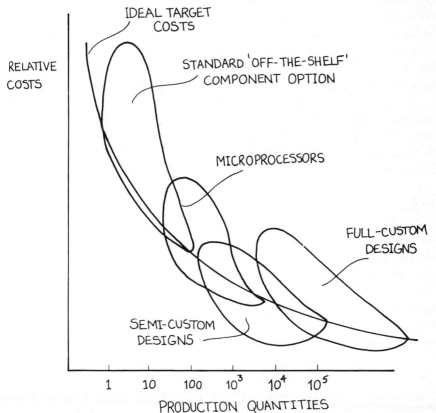

Fig. 8.3 Cost-effectiveness of semi-custom design options

circuits may be reduced. The engineering design/layout and fabrication cycle for a custom integrated circuit can take from 3 months to 3 years and involve up to 20 man-years of effort, depending on the chip complexity. It follows, therefore, that the design costs of such circuits are high and, traditionally, many semiconductor companies have been unwilling to undertake such a development unless large and long-term production runs could be guaranteed. Thus, full custom design has been the realm of the very high volume component such as memories and microprocessors. In recent years, however, there has been a marked trend towards the development of integrated circuit-design capabilities within systems manufacturing companies and this division of the design and mask making/fabrication activity has been accelerated by the appearance of silicon brokerage and silicon foundry facilities which present a clear and distinct interface between design and implementation activities.

In essence, the silicon broker operates as a technical expert/-consultant who will accept individual designs either as mask sets or as layout (or pattern generator) files and acts as an independent authority to procure mask sets, fabricate wafers (possibly using silicon foundry facilities) and supply packaged chips to the individual designer. Full custom design, however, finds primary application in high performance applications where the complete capability of the technology is available to the designer, and in very high production volume parts such as microprocessors where the production yield must be maximised by reducing chip area.

Between these two extremes, the gate array or other semi-custom alternative is very attractive (Fig. 8.4), especially when the technical specification for the system is well within the technological and performance limits of the gate array itself.[8.1]

In the consumer market, where speed of entry into and capture of the market is an important criterion, a gate array approach may permit market penetration while, at the same time, an on-going full custom, (and significantly more cost-effective), design solution is developed. For normal production runs, in consumer markets, the gate array will often offer a viable commercial proposition. The sophistication of some of the simpler consumer products is however, so low, that some of the more advanced microprocessors or microcomputers can accommodate the total technical requirement. Thus the main application area for gate arrays has moved to the more sophisticated (professional) level of consumer goods – such as the home computer. Here the full cost advantages – in overall systems terms – of the gate array can be fully exploited. In addition, the

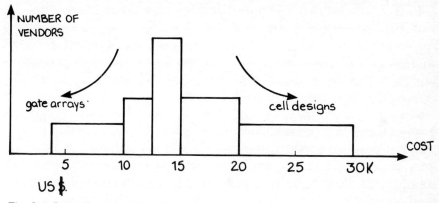

Fig. 8.4 Quoted average development costs to prototype samples. (After Hurst[8.1])

protection from industrial copying is of particular advantage in these markets. The gate array will often be used as an adjunct to a microprocessor for 'glue' logic.

At higher levels of sophistication, in the original equipment manufacture (OEM) market, the gate array approach becomes less attractive in systems savings simply because the gate array represents such a small proportion of the overall production; unless the gate array offers technological/marketing advantages as discussed previously.

8.4 When to opt for a gate array

The specific point, in the development of a product, at which a gate array option might be seriously and fruitfully considered is a function of the product itself. If the product is already on the market in some form, then the gate array option will involve consideration of marketing and cost saving elements to update the product. Here, in the absence of new features to be incorporated in the gate array version, the overall systems costs will form the dominant consideration since, especially for larger systems, the cost advantages of a gate array solution might be less marked.

Further back in the development process, for a product which has reached the level of a breadboard model, the gate array option becomes particularly attractive since the development costs and time-scales for the gate array option will be similar to those of a printed circuit board option. Thus the full technological benefits and cost-effectiveness (in reduced production costs) of the gate array will be available.

Earlier still in the development of a product, when it exists only as a concept or outline requirement, the gate array option can offer a very much higher degree of flexibility since the full potential of the technology and the gate array itself can be exploited to produce a superior product, in terms of performance and functional capability, than might otherwise have been possible.

A product must pass through a series of stages as it progresses from conception to marketplace. Having identified a potential market for an innovative product, the first stage is system/product definition in technical, marketing and production terms. Next the system specification attempts to interpret this system definition in terms of a parametric description – gains, bandwidths, word lengths, memory size. Then, in digital systems, the logic definition of the system or sub-system can be accomplished and the overall logic specification described. It is at this point that a breadboard of the system in some suitable technology would be possible, and in some cases desirable, both to prove the system concept and specification and to provide a tool for validating the final gate array.

This stage represents the ideal point at which a gate array decision can be made since the overall confidence in the design and specification is high. A further advantage at this stage is that it is possible to select an array in a technology which is generally similar to that used in the breadboard. In some cases it may prove advantageous to re-breadboard in a technology more representative of the gate array, possibly even using gate array elements – particularly so in the case of analog blocks.

For a product concept which could include gate arrays from the outset, the possibility exists to perform most of these initial steps by means of software which will accept a system description in a high level language and will interpret this description in gate array terms to compile a computer simulation of the system – as a 'breadboard'.

The latter stages of gate array design are increasingly being performed by software – conversion of the logic specification to a format suited to the gate array under consideration, layout of the gate array interconnects commitment and simulation.

The earlier the point in the development cycle at which the gate array selection is made, the more optimal will be the use of the gate array.[8.2] If the total design task is assigned to the supplier, his costs will in many cases reflect this design flexibility. If the customer is prepared to maintain an interest, at some level, in the design process, his ability to do so must be considered. The later the point of entry into the gate array route, relatively, the lower will be the costs, the higher will be the confidence in the final product, and the more divorced will the customer be from the contractor. Thus the customer's design remains more exclusive.

The design of a gate array of the order of 1000 gates will normally take about 10–12 weeks (fig. 8.5). Most companies engaged in gate array design encourage the customer to become involved in designing at the earliest possible point in product development and to remain involved for as long as possible. In the majority of cases, the original point of contact exists when the breadboard or prototype system, possibly in TTL or CMOS, has been constructed and proven. From the logic design or circuit schematics, either the contractor, or the customer (with appropriate training) must translate this specification into a form which is directly suited to the gate array system chosen – an operation known as down-conversion. In the gate array, this implies translating the circuit into the standard interconnection schemes preferred by the contractor. If the customer has assisted in this translation exercise the design will normally offer a high probability of being correct; the responsibility for this correctness rests with the customer.

It is clear from the previous discussion that gate array development will normally involve the creation of some form of contractual interaction between customer and supplier such that the overall success of the development will be a function of the contributions and the effectiveness of the individual participants.

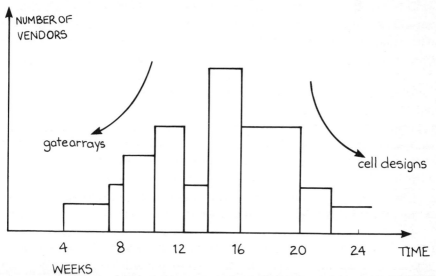

Fig. 8.5 Quoted average development times to prototype sample. (After Hurst[8.1])

Three primary classes of gate array supplier can be identified in terms of array design and manufacture or commitment service.[8.3] First there are the indigenous, large semiconductor companies who have seen their existing standard product markets eroded to a certain degree by gate arrays and have introduced gate arrays to increase their overall capability. Secondly there are the systems companies who have developed a gate array capability, initially for internal use, but can see a demand for making their gate array systems more generally available. (The suppliers involved in this second group do not generally fabricate their own gate array wafers although they may have internal commitment and test facilities.) The third group of companies essentially offer only a design service but can arrange for brokerage facilities to be made available during manufacture.

Smaller suppliers have tended to employ manual layout of lower complexity chips (up to 1500 gates) although two new trends are developing in this section of the market. Firstly, many of the smaller suppliers are negotiating franchise arrangements with larger semiconductor companies so that they can gain access to the sophisticated software used by the larger supplier. Secondly, a range of minicomputer- or microcomputer-based designer work-stations are becoming available at modest cost for use by the gate array supplier. Mostly, these systems are dedicated to specific manufacturing process rules, but we are already seeing the appearance of supplier/-technology independent workstations.

The smaller vendor will encourage customer assistance for a variety of reasons. Firstly, the smaller vendor will typically be dealing with smaller production runs and so will wish to minimise his design risk by using as much of the customer's knowledge as possible. Secondly, the smaller vendor may be more flexible than a larger supplier and as he typically has less design software available, is less guarded in exposing this software. The larger supplier generally prefers to limit customer involvement, primarily because these larger suppliers have sophisticated software available and can dispense with customer assistance; large suppliers are also, generally, more guarded with their software.

The degree of customer involvement will therefore have an important role to play in deciding when to enter a gate array design. For any planned design, which appears suited to gate array implementation, a dialogue should be established with a range of vendors to establish the degree of interaction which might be available, balancing the capabilities of the customer (possibly augmented by design manuals or design course run by suppliers) with the capabilities of the supplier (in terms of his design involvement, his production schedules and his previous knowledge in the application area).

Allowing the supplier complete control of design and development, while forming the cleanest definition of individual responsibilities, will not produce the optimum degree of first-time correctness. This first-time correctness measure will be increased if the customer has access to sophisticated design software, especially in the early stages of the design cycle.

This generalised division between larger and smaller suppliers will manifest itself in a more pronounced manner when the product specification demands performance close to the limits of the respective technology. Generally in such cases, the larger supplier, who is 'closer to the process', will be at an advantage. The customer must, however, be fully aware that pushing the technology must increase overall risk and this should be minimised as far as possible in the early stages of product definition. This risk might be minimised by attempting to realise the required performance on an alternative, possibly higher performance, process. The availability of a process which is in a state of continuous enhancement might also affect the stage at which the decision to opt for a gate array is made.

8.5 Choice of gate array technology

There are several types of gate array chip, each of which offers different performance features. [8.4] As might be expected, digital gate arrays are available in virtually all technologies – NMOS, CMOS, TTL, ECL, (see fig. 8.6). In addition, some gate array chips with intrinsically analog components are available. The actual selection of an appropriate gate array technology is dependent mainly on detailed technical considerations. However, the expected availability of the manufacturing process over the projected lifetime of the design must be included as a consideration (second sourcing).

Technical considerations may well be influenced by the technology used to implement a new product, constraining the gate array technology selected to the same technology as used elsewhere in the product. However, in more general cases, the technological considerations can be made (initially) by a process of elimination, based on the most elementary system requirements. Specification of operating voltages and operating speeds will represent the first stage in elimination – strict 5 V power supply or high speed might dictate

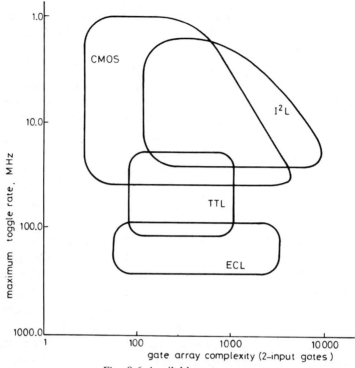

Fig. 8.6 Available gate arrays

bipolar technology such as TTL. Wide operating voltage or low power consumption might dictate CMOS. Integration level (numbers of gates per chip) will also form a factor in the selection although suppliers normally offer a range of devices of increasing complexity for a given technology.

The design and layout of the basic gate array cell forms the key to the overall effectiveness and utility of the gate array itself and several imporant features can be identified:

PHILOSOPHY: For simplicity of design, simplicity of processing and lowest cost, only the metal interconnection should be changed for each new design. Design methods based on sophisticated CAD techniques (autorouting), however, benefit from the use of multiple levels of metal interconnections for high efficiency automatic design.

FLEXIBILITY: For maximum flexibility of interconnection, cells should be approachable from as many sides as is possible, for both input connections and output connections. In addition, a high degree of cell transparency is required so that a fully utilised cell will still offer a through route for a wiring interconnect. Use of multi-level metallisation for interconnects, especially for power supply lines, or possibly differentiating between intra-cell and inter-cell connections, will improve the cell flexibility. Some (low power) arrays offer the potential for accommodating the power supply connections within the underlying gate array using diffusion or polysilicon layers thereby allowing the metal interconnect pattern to be used wholly for circuit and logic arrangements. Availability of multi-level 'cross-unders' or 'underpasses' which allow connection between metal and the underlying silicon structure within the cell, further adds to cell flexibility.

COMPLEXITY: A trade-off must be achieved between low cell complexity, which results in a requirement to interconnect too many cells together to implement a given functional requirement, and high cell complexity which demands too many interconnect tracks running to a cell. Typical cell complexities are limited to 2- or 3-input gates plus possibly an extra inverter.

CONNECTIONS: More cell connection points will permit improved flexibility in the use of the cell while fewer cell connection points will permit easier track routing and small cell size. A typical requirement would be for one input and output to be available from either direction with space for a single through-run connection.

GRID: For simplification of design, especially where CAD is employed, a grid system is required for the possible connection points.

The main features which affect the overall size and complexity of the gate array chip itself include:

YIELD: The gate array chip must necessarily be of a size consistent with an adequate production yield. Typical chip sizes are 4 mm × 4 mm.

CHIP COMPLEXITY: The total number of cells on the gate array must be sufficient to accommodate the design but not so large as to waste too much silicon area. For a two-dimensional matrix type array where (manual design) cell utilisation factors in the range 80–90% can be achieved, the chip complexity need only approximate to the design gate count. However, in row-oriented gate arrays, where (autorouted) cell utilisation factors are generally around 60%, a higher complexity gate array should be considered.

PACKAGING: In contrast to many chip applications, the gate array typically demands a very large number of input connections and output connections which in general are not suited to multiplex (bus) operations. Thus special packaging systems (such as chip carriers) must be investigated. This has been discussed in some detail in chapter 6.

PERIPHERALS: Associated with each input/output pad should be an input protection device and an output buffer/driver.

CMOS technology is increasingly becoming the dominant technology for gate arrays. Metal-gate CMOS gate arrays developed as a result of CMOS 4000 series developments have now been largely superseded by faster, and more dense silicon-gate CMOS structures (as discussed in chapter 3). In particular a range of special oxide-isolated silicon gate CMOS devices with superior packing density and switching speeds can now be obtained from a number of suppliers. Most of these CMOS arrays are fabricated with well-proven 5 μm device geometries with, typically, around 1500 gates per array.

Advances in CMOS technology mean that arrays with up to 5000 gates using 2.5–3 μm features can now be manufactured and this type of array can be expected to form the mainstay of CMOS arrays in the near future. Also, whereas single-level metallisation interconnect has been commonplace, trends are towards the use of double-layer metal interconnect, both to achieve higher on-chip densities, and to accommodate more sophisticated autorouting software packages. The main disadvantage of double-layer metal is the increased complexity required to customise the array since, typically, instead of a single mask plate being used to define the single metal layer, two additional masks are required for the two-level process. One of the extra masks provides the interconnect pattern for the second level of metal and the other mask is used to provide contacts through the insulating layer used to separate the two levels of metal. CMOS technology offers good logic noise margins and logic levels which swing between the supply rails. Since, in its static condition, the CMOS gate has zero power dissipation, the power rail distribution problem in CMOS can be minimised, and in some cases the power rails can be 'hidden' in the underlying silicon. Gate arrays in CMOS can normally interface directly with 4000 series CMOS gates and 74HC type devices, and in some cases special input/output circuits permit direct interfacing with (Schottky) TTL.

Designing with CMOS is made more difficult by the limited fan-in, fan-out capability of CMOS gates where increased capacitive loading limits operating speeds. CMOS can however offer (restricted) linear capabilities as discussed in chapters 3 and 4.

In spite of the leading position held by CMOS, bipolar technology offers some advantages over CMOS in that some bipolar manufacturing processes are significantly less complex than CMOS processes. Of more importance for gate array users, however, is the fact that bipolar technologies can offer variously similar packing densities and power consumption in comparison to CMOS. Most notably, integrated injection logic (I^2L) offers a very low power delay product which is constant over a range of operating clock frequencies. I^2L can also offer packing densities comparable to or better than those achievable in CMOS. Gate arrays which employ integrated Schottky logic – combining the simple structures and high packing density of I^2L with the high speed of Schottky TTL are also available. Two main disadvantages exist with these technologies in that although they are general purpose arrays, the power supply requirements are frequently non-standard, e.g. use of an extra negative supply rail, and the arrays in some cases do not directly interface with CMOS chips. Also, since the technology for bipolar arrays has been developed independently by gate array suppliers over a number of years, second sourcing possibilities are less well defined than with silicon gate CMOS.

ECL gate arrays are offered by several of the larger semiconductor and gate array suppliers, largely as a result of demands by mainframe computer manufacturers to have access to gate arrays in ECL for their equipment. Indeed, several mainframe computer manufacturers have developed their own (internal) ECL gate array capabilities. ECL arrays typically offer less than 1000 gates complexity with ultra fast operation (300 MHz). Note that ECL requires non-standard supply voltages, and the power dissipation of larger ECL arrays operating at high speeds can represent a severe packaging problem. A more detailed treatment of bipolar gate arrays can be found in chapter 2.

Although CMOS can be used to provide a limited linear (analog) capability, a major feature of bipolar gate arrays is their ability to offer both analog and digital functions on the same array; this is discussed in chapter 4.

When comparing arrays of differing technologies, and especially when comparing arrays in nominally identical technologies, care must be taken not to place too much emphasis on 'specmanship'. Some suppliers offer arrays with large numbers of gates, but these are simply composed of repeats of small arrays. Manufacturers will quote propagation delay time for their arrays and these times will often have been measured for a ring oscillator structure, which has been optimised in terms of fan-out and loading, etc., and may not translate directly into the speed performance for a specific circuit to be integrated. Propagation delay times can therefore only be used as a rough measure for arrays of very similar technologies. A more useful guide would be the typical (or maximum) toggle rate for a flip-flop at some specified voltage and temperature.

One aspect which should be included in any decision at device technology level should be the package types available for a given technology or from a given supplier. Packaging provides physical protection for the chip within the package, enables the circuit to be physically mounted on circuit boards and enables electrical signals to be passed into, and out of, the integrated circuit. Package technology can be very sophisticated in terms of the packaging design, the choice of materials and in the degree of automated assembly afforded by the packaging techniques. Poor assembly and packaging will adversely affect the mechanical and electrical reliability of the gate array chip. The choice of package type has an influence on the overall circuit performance and will contribute significantly to the overall cost of the product.

The dual-in-line (DIL) package has been traditionally used in gate array packaging, due largely to their wide availability, (up to 64 pin). Typically, gate array chips demand a high number of input/output pins so that although low pin-count DIL packages are used for gate arrays, the present trend is towards mounting each chip in a compact, leadless sub-frame or chip carrier and to assemble these units directly (see chapter 6). A key area-saving advantage of chip carriers is that electrical connections are made via solder joints or 'bumps' beneath the carrier rather than to the sides of a standard package which requires extra area. Further, the placement of the chip carrier in production is simplified since the surface tension of the molten solder tends to pull the chip carrier accurately into position.

8.6 How to design the gate array

A slow evolution in gate array architecture can be traced in that the earliest arrays, developed mainly by semiconductor manufacturers as a cost effective method of accessing silicon fabrication, consist of a two-dimensional matrix of gate array cells. These types of array generally feature very high cell density, high cell utilisation efficiencies and high engineering performance. The ease or difficulty of routing these arrays in the x- and y-directions is approximately equal and the design involves some degree of manual layout. Computer aids to designing with this first generation gate array are generally confined to interactive graphics packages which relieve the designer of some of the tedious data-capture of the design exercise. Design invariably involves the use of (×400) enlargements of the gate array chip to which can be affixed a series of decals or transfers to represent the preferred cell structures used to create commonly used functions such as flip-flops and basic gates. Wiring interconnect routing between these functions as well as placement of cells on the array is largely performed manually although the emergence of autorouting software for these types of array will assist with this problem. The enlarged chip design can be entered to the design computer via a digitiser board and subsequent design checks such as logic simulation, function simulation and mask tape generation can be performed.

In contrast to this type of array which optimises the utility of silicon and the performance specification, the second generation of gate array devices features an architecture which displays a row-oriented matrix of cells where wiring channels are placed between the rows of cells to carry the main interconnect wiring. The cell architecture is more ideally suited to sophisticated design automation software but gives less efficient utilisation of silicon area. The level of initial input specification to the computer for this type of gate array is increasingly in the form of a high level functional description or high level interconnection definition.

Having established that gate array architecture has evolved to exploit advanced software developments, two main classes of design software for gate arrays can be identified – computer-aided design (CAD) software which, although assisting with data capture, is primarily a tool for use in an analytic mode, and design automation which is primarily a synthesis tool. Design software of both types is used to reduce design times and costs for translating a design from specification into working parts. An advantage is the improved probability of correctness, (right-first-time designs), which is of particular importance in fast turn-around gate array designs.

8.7 Points to seek in gate array design capability

A good design system will involve a variety of component programs for design capture, editing or modification and verification or simulation. In evaluating the quality of a design software suite, particular attention should be paid to the manner and efficiency in which the component programs, identified below, interface with one another. A basic and obvious requirement, that all the required programs should reside on the same host computer, is not always achieved. (For further information on computer aids see chapter 5 and associated references.) Component programs included in a computer-aided design process are as follows:

PLACEMENT ALGORITHMS: These involve the assignment of a position on the gate array matrix to each functional block, commensurate with input/output requirements and possibly with worst-case specification of timing or wiring interconnect length. Optimised placement involves minimisation of the total wiring length while at the same time minimising the wiring congestion at any one point.

TRACKING OR ROUTING ALGORITHMS: These perform the assignment of a track or route for each desired interconnection within the constraints provided by the points of access to individual functional blocks, input and output connections, wiring channel capacities and fixed cross-under positions. Two main classes of autorouting algorithms are in general use. The first involves assigning a specific wiring channel with subsequent routing within the channel. The second attempts to sort all wires in a hierarchy and fits each wire one at a time. In general, wiring failures will inevitably result, necessitating manual intervention.

LOGIC EXTRACTION: Extraction involves converting a gate array design back to a logic format for interpretation in comparison with the original logic specification. In systems where data capture has been achieved from a logic diagram, this logic extraction exercise will be relatively straightforward. Where data capture has been achieved from a high level description language, a compatible extraction file will be generated for subsequent simulation operations.

CIRCUIT SIMULATION: Simulation involves the use of an accurate device model for the active elements used on the array. Where novel, high performance, functional blocks are being designed for the gate array, circuit simulation can prove an important tool.

LOGIC SIMULATION/TIMING SIMULATION: Logic simulation offers the opportunity to exercise (in software) the gate array design, removing the necessity for a hardware breadboard in some cases. A good simulator will permit simultaneous multi-level operations including the circuit simulator described above; a switch-level simulator where devices are modelled by simple switches; a gate level simulator based on NAND or NOR gates; and a functional level simulator, (e.g. A = B × C). The user may define which level is to be used for various parts of the gate array design and identify a set of input events or stimuli and, also, define the nodes of interest in the simulation. The responses of the required nodes can be displayed as timing waveforms or as logic functions. In most simulation exercises, it is not necessary to model time precisely and event-oriented simulators where nominal time delays are employed, generally prove adequate.

TESTABILITY: Test pattern data, available largely from fault simulation programs provides guidance on which input test states are most meaningful. Here by selecting specific test states, a fault simulator program will normally assign stuck-at faults, at random, through the design and will provide a measure of fault capture for the information of the designer. Exhaustive testing of the gate array demands that all possible logic states should be exercised. As gate array circuit complexities increase, the costs of test pattern generation and indeed of the actual test times increase exponentially. Thus the cost of testing completed chips increases exponentially unless designs have specific silicon areas for testability purposes in which case it is possible to reduce the problem to only linear increases in test costs.

8.8 Design for testability in gate arrays

A third generation of gate array architecture, where silicon area is dedicated to improve the chip testability, is already beginning to appear. Here circuit area in the heart of the gate array is used to improve testability by means of scan-path configurations or, alternatively, circuit area on the periphery of the array used for signature analysis.

The main objective in designing for testability is to increase the controllability and the observability of internal states. The scan path allows the connection of selected circuit nodes to a long shift register during the test mode. In this way the circuit nodes can be initialised at the start of the test (controllability) and these states can then be observed at the end of the test sequence (observability). The input and output of test data takes place in a bit-serial fashion with serial-to-parallel conversion during the initialisation operation and parallel-to-serial conversion in the observation operation performed by the scan-path shift register. The simplest form of scan-path design is to include, on-chip, a specific parallel-in/serial-out shift register with connections from various nodes on the chip. Clearly this involves increased circuit overhead, although the scan-path might be used to form sequential logic elements in the circuit. Alternatively, functional conversion of circuit registers to create the scan-path can reduce test circuit overheads.

The scan path provides excellent controllability and observability for a gate array but much of the actual test time is wasted in serial transmission between the circuit and the test equipment. An alternative is to build the 'test equipment' into the circuit. Pseudo-random sequences are well suited to on-chip test pattern generation since they can be generated very easily by feedback shift register techniques. Monitoring the test responses for such pseudo-random sequences can be performed using a signature analysis register which is of the same construction as the pseudo-random sequence generator with some extra feedback loops. Signature analysis effectively performs a go/no-go test and further information is required for diagnostic purposes. A detailed discussion of design for testability is given in chapter 7.

Having discussed the main features of design software and the principles of design for testability, several options can be identified as to how the gate array design might be carried out. Most suppliers will provide design packages for individual gate array families; in some cases design courses might also be available.

First generation arrays design packages will include ×400 enlargements of the array plus a set of adhesive transfers for use by the designer. Normally the designer would travel to the supplier's premises to digitise his array although recent advances in remote user work stations permit this data capture to be performed on the customer's premises. Array definition by high level description removes this stage of the design.

The choice of interface level between customer and supplier has been considered previously. Where a designer is capable of, or hopes to become acquainted with, a gate array system, a close working relationship between the customer and supplier should be established, fostered and maintained. Where the customer requires the supplier to undertake the overall design, a clear demarcation should be established and adhered to. In this case both sides must foster an atmosphere of trust and no interfaces should be duplicated. The customer should make sure that the supplier not only has access to a total design software package, but that all the components in the suite are exercised for his specific design and results are tabulated. The supplier should include some degree of design for testability on-chip. Further, the customer should initiate a full goods-inward acceptance test and not rely completely on supplier testing.

8.9 Choice of gate array supplier

In selecting a supplier for a specific gate array design, three main categories of supplier can be identified:

The indigenous semiconductor supplier, who provides a gate array service as a means of utilising his manufacturing capability to the full. The advantages of this type of supplier are that they will have a fully supported and experienced design team, they will possess a greater knowledge of the ultimate performance of their gate array processes, and they will be in a better position to influence and guarantee delivery deadlines.

The systems houses, who have developed their own gate array capability, originally for internal use but who now offer this service externally. These suppliers will have their own design teams and possibly their own specially oriented gate arrays. However, all manufacture, and possibly commitment and testing, will be carried out by subcontract to a semiconductor manufacturer or silicon foundry.

The independent design house, which can obtain access to one of a number of design systems and gate array technologies and can act, as consultants, on the customer's behalf through all of the design phases; mask making, fabrication, packaging and testing. Here all of the procurement effort is performed under subcontract.

The independent design house can act for the customer when the customer is unable to undertake his own design or when the supplier is unwilling to release design data to a 'novice' designer who may not achieve a working design which would enter production. The design house therefore acts as a convenient buffer between two opposing requirements. In principle the design house is able to provide the customer with a higher level of critical awareness in respect of choice of technology or supplier. In practice however, by the very nature of things, the independent design house will be closely tied only to one or two preferred suppliers. The customers should appraise for themselves the breadth of choice open to the design house and should furthermore ascertain the degree of experience possessed by the design house in the selected technology – in the use of the appropriate software and more importantly the method of access to this software – and the degree of supplier/design house interaction and discussion which might be possible.

The design house will also be able to achieve a degree of design optimisation which might be precluded by customer designs due to lack of experience and which might be precluded in supplier designs due to inefficient use of design resources on the design phase. An independent design house may be in a position to more fully optimise the design (in terms of performance or production yield) than the systems customer. By the same token, the independent design house may also be in a position to review the design at system level and advise on suitable improvements.

The following brief discussion is aimed at providing the customer with a framework of points to consider in selecting a foundry/-semiconductor supplier either for customer design or for supplier-design, or for independent design house contracts:

TECHNOLOGY: The supplier should possess the technology appropriate to the gate array specification created by the customer. Ideally the supplier should have a proven record in use of this technology (previously successful designs would provide a good reference) and the supplier should be involved in, or aware of, on-going developments in the technology which would improve his gate array systems. Second sourcing possibilities would form another important measure.

RANGE: The supplier should offer a range of gate arrays of increasing complexity or be able to assure the customer that a given design will not over-run his gate array capabilities.

INTERFACES: The supplier should have decided which levels of customer/contractor interfaces he is prepared to consider. These interfaces will depend on the specification since a supplier faced with a 'no-frills' design will attempt to capture most of the design work under contract. With a design which involves the most sophisticated levels of the technology or gate array, the supplier may be happy to encourage customer involvement, thereby minimising his responsibilities and risk.

SOFTWARE: The customer should check what computer aids are available for use on the design and, where it is the supplier who uses these aids, the customer should define a series of tests to demonstrate that all the required aids have been employed satisfactorily. In the case of customer usage of the design aids, the details of how the various component parts are interfaced and used, as well as an outline of how to use these, and how easy they are to use, should be sought. Of importance also is a definition of how much computer time will be available to the customer.

TOOLING: The position in respect of the tooling – i.e. pattern generator tapes or mask plates, etc. – should be established specifically in terms of second sourcing. Care should be taken in specifying the mask formats such that they are compatible with second source capabilities in terms of overall dimensions, polarity (positive or negative) and compatibility of wafer test structures. Definition of the points at which second sourcing might be involved should also be agreed.

DOCUMENTATION: The quality of supplier's design documentation is a crucial feature in selection. Take care to differentiate between sales documentation and real engineering design documentation. Check that all the design parameters are stated and have been suitably up-dated.

SPECIFICATION: The acceptance standard must be fully understood by the supplier. This standard might involve operation of the design to a specific level of functionality or speed and the standard documents should be agreed by both parties.

PROTOTYPES: The level of acceptance tests should be appreciated by the customer. Typically some fifty packaged chips tested to some agreed standard will be delivered to the customer for full characterisation.

SECOND SOURCE: The supplier should state the source of the uncommitted wafers and the supply conditions. Some gate array manufacturers may only offer gate array output at times of low demand. Similarly the source of masks should be stated. Where applicable the source of commitment packaging and testing should also be specified.

DELIVERY SCHEDULES: Details of time-scales involved in design, validation and production should be available. The accuracy of time-scale predictions should be validated by previous supplier experiences, and where applicable, the dependence of time-scales on outside suppliers should be specified.

TESTING: The supplier's attitude to testing should be appraised. Software generation of test patterns should be generally used, however, suppliers of arrays with design for testability features will offer more easily tested chips.

TRACK RECORD: Finally, but more difficult, the supplier should be able to provide some case histories of previously successful chips, ideally for customers of similar status.

It is not suggested this catalogue of various pointers to gate array selection can create a completely rationalised appraisal of this problem. Rather, by listing the various facets involved in gate array selection and implementation it is hoped that a customer will possess some degree of enhanced awareness of what to basically seek from a reliable supplier. Several of the catalogued pointers are based on subjective assessments of capabilities and the single, most important facet to gate array vendor selection must therefore be that of any purchase – to accept and balance, as much advice as possible.

Part 2

Some User Notes on Semi-custom Logic

ROBERT HEATON

Acorn Computers Ltd

The availability of dense semi-custom logic has enabled the introduction of advanced products which would not have been viable using standard logic building blocks. While products such as large CPUs have benefitted enormously from semi-custom logic it is in the area of small equipment that the impact has been greatest. The market for low cost personal computers has actually been created by the low cost complexity that this approach allows.

A good example of a product made possible by the use of semi-custom logic is the Acorn Electron, the circuit board of which may be seen in fig. 8.7. All of the random digital circuitry is integrated into one 68 pin leadless carrier of the type shown in fig. 8.8. Only the processor, memory, and some analogue circuitry is needed to

Fig. 8.7 The Acorn Electron – a circuit board using semi-custom logic

Fig. 8.8 Ferranti ULA in a 68-pin leadless carrier

complete the system.

The Acorn Electron is a sophisticated machine providing almost all of the internal features of the BBC Microcomputer which uses a combination of standard TTL logic and two semi-custom logic circuits. The Electron exemplifies a trend in the design of high volume electronic products made possible by the increasing complexity of semi-custom parts. The trend is to mop up all random logic into as few semi-custom chips as possible while leaving complex, dense functions such as memory and processors to standard devices. It is feasible to custom-integrate such functions with currently available technologies and CAD, but such standard functions tend to be relatively low cost because of the high volumes involved and the ability of large semiconductor houses to hand-craft designs for optimum cost-effectiveness. Another trend is towards device packages with larger pin counts. This is because the limitation on integrating functions is frequently not complexity but number of inputs and outputs. In some cases this has meant that circuits have been partitioned into more than one array because of pin count rather than gate count. Low cost, high pin-count packaging however, remains costly and the partitioning of logic into blocks with a cost effective I/O configuration is the first obstacle for the designer to overcome.

8.10 What kind of semi-custom?

There are a bewildering range of technology and vendor choices for the semi-custom logic designer. There are three main types of custom logic circuit available: logic array, standard cell, and symbolic/-procedural design systems.

Logic arrays are the oldest and best known type of semi-custom logic and are now available in just about every technology. They remain the safest option for the designer because their rigid constructs impose control on the design. In many cases logic arrays also remain the most cost effective approach and are the commonest type of custom logic. Their fixed logic and I/O structures minimize the number of custom layers required and allow fast prototype processing but limit design flexibility. Logic arrays with complexities of more than 10 000 gates are now available but the value of such devices is rather questionable for volume components. This is partly because of the very large die sizes (and unit costs) involved. A more significant reason is that few circuits of over 2000–3000 gates complexity do not require constructs more specialised (and more area efficient) than fixed logic gates. RAM and ROM blocks, for example, are very inefficiently implemented with logic arrays both because of increased active area required and because of the ineffective use of routing space.

Standard cell design approaches have recently become available to the semi-custom user. Since cell positions are not fixed like logic array cells, there is much more flexibility in size and I/O configuration. It is often claimed that standard cell designs are smaller and therefore cheaper than logic arrays in large volumes but this is not necessarily true. An important case is when the chip is pad bound, (i.e. the number of I/O's is such that the periphery of the chip dictates its size). Most cell systems also use very primitive macros together with even more primitive place and route programs which may not produce a smaller chip than a more mature logic array system. However many vendors are planning to construct much more complex cells such as RAM and ROM and some are preparing to offer system level components such as processors and peripheral functions as 'super cells'. These cells are frequently standard products with modified I/O cells and so are not, in principle, difficult for vendors to offer. However there are a number of copyright and technology difficulties to be resolved before comprehensive libraries can be built. In the longer term however the standard cell concept will win much of the logic array market because of its flexibility.

A lot of effort has gone into simplifying full custom chip design in recent years and this has led to the development of suites of software which bring custom chip design within the reach of logic designers. A number of vendors are now offering systems which evolved partly from a design methodology set out by Carver Mead and Lynn Conway in their popular book.[8.5]

VLSI Technology Inc supply one such system. Parameterised cell libraries allow designers to automatically build system elements such as ROM, RAM, and PLA of arbitrary size. Additionally transistors and interconnect can be placed symbolically using a 'sticks' graphical editor and auto compacted to remove redundant spaces between symbols. Such leaf cells may be connected together hierarchically to form a complete chip layout using a symbolic box graphical editor known as a composition editor. Users have access to the cell compiler language called VIP[TM] which enables the development of user parameterised cells and represents a move towards silicon compilation. (VIP is a trademark of VLSI Technology Incorporated.)

Such design techniques can produce extremely rapid layout design time compared with conventional approaches although there is a unit size and cost penalty involved. However as semiconductor device geometries reduce in size such systems will be of major importance for generating silicon systems.

8.11 Semi-custom computer-aided design systems

The increasing popularity of semi-custom logic has added impetus to the development of user-friendly software design tools. Since vendors of CMOS logic arrays and standard cells typically have very similar products to offer, special efforts have been made to entice customers with suites of powerful design tools. In the last two years almost all vendors have begun to offer closed-loop design systems which largely remove the risk of an error being introduced during the layout of the chip. These are designed to ensure that the designer gets exactly what his netlist specifies. Additionally most vendors now offer 'post layout simulation' which allows the circuit to be simulated using wiring loads extracted from the actual layout data base and allows layout aggravated race conditions to be detected. It's worth noting though, that the wiring delay extraction is often rather crude and does not usually include the distributed delay effects of the resistive wires that the designer should be aware of at the outset of the design.

Both closed-loop verification and post-layout simulation are vital to first-pass design success. Given this, the ability of the vendor to offer auto-placement and routing is less important. Indeed a manual layout based system frequently produces a smaller die size and may be able to offer lower unit costs as a result. Manual layout also allows the placement of cells and tracking to be accurately fixed which enables the optimisation of critical paths if this is an absolute necessity. Auto layout systems offer varying amounts of routing and placement fixing. The ability to at least 'seed' the auto placement of cells is important when regular structures are implemented. If an auto placement system is unable to recognise such structures, very inefficient placement and routing can result.

8.12 Getting it right

Even with perfect software the design of a semi-custom chip must be approached in a disciplined way if design recycles are to be avoided. Extra effort spent in ensuring first-pass design success is justified because debugging hardware and resubmitting a design is costly, time consuming, and disheartening for the staff involved. A more important reason for being able to plan for a first-pass working design is the knock-on effect to the target system which is usually of very high value compared to the chip itself. Simple errors in chip designs can be avoided by putting special effort into the following areas:

SPECIFICATION: One of the commonest causes of problems in chip design is that the chip performs to the specification but the specification is either wrong, misinterpreted or incomplete. If the overall functional specification for the chip is poor the logic designer may be unable to visualise the system effect of operations at a gate level. This problem can be minimised by taking the time to write a good specification for the part before attempting detailed design. This is a good practice anyway and helps dispel the Well-I'm-not-too-sure-but-we-can-always-fix-it-later method of working which is accepted to some extent in PCB circuit designs. The formulation of accurate, readable, specifications for chip designs often has a beneficial effect on the whole system design.

Some CAD systems offer a behavioural modelling language which allows the behaviour of the circuit to be put down in a computer readable form. This provides a better reference against which the logic can be verified. Such 'top down' approaches take more time at the specification stage but in the long run pay off because errors are caught earlier in the design cycle.

TEST PATTERNS: The function of a circuit is absolutely not uniquely specified by its netlist. This is a very common misconception. Only the test sequence specifies to the vendor what the circuit is required to do both at design sign-off and at final test. Many vendors include this in their contracts as a way of protecting themselves against inadequate test sequences. If circuits pass functional test sequences at speed the responsibility of the vendor for device integrity is satisfied. Thus the test stimulus should be considered at the outset of the design.

Unfortunately designers frequently leave this 'less interesting' pastime until stimulus for a simulation is actually needed. By this time the designer may well be more in tune with what his circuit does than what it is required to do. Most simulators aggravate this by not requiring the designer to predict the results in advance. The test stimulus language of many simulators is also rather poor. It is hardly surprising that designers shudder at the sight of a sea of 1s and 0s and SET statements typically presented for verification of test sequences.

The test pattern set is a vital part of the design and even with the development of auto test generation systems will remain so. It is as important to approach the design of test patterns in as planned a way as one would approach the design of a piece of software of similar complexity. The problem is how to both separate and regroup specific functional tests in such a way that all of the possible in-use functional combinations are modelled at simulation and at final test with the minimum number of test patterns. One possible method of setting about writing a test pattern sequence is as follows:

a)   Identify an extensive set of the high level functions of the chip and write a test for each. These tests always overlap somewhat. Ensure that a full range of cases for each function are covered, structuring these into sub-tests if necessary. The cases covered here are only those that will occur in the real system.

b)   Combine these functional tests in a way which is as typical of the real system as possible.

c)   Enhance these tests to take into account the testing of individual transistors and connections within that function. For example when the adder function of an ALU is tested data should be applied in such a way that the carry circuit from each bit is tested as well as any look-ahead circuitry. These enhancements require detailed knowledge of the design and can really only be done by the designer after the design is more or less fixed.

d) Ensure that buses are properly exercised. Apart from doing a thorough simulation, this tests the chip for metal-to-metal short circuits which is one of the more common processing faults. This kind of test is often called a 'zebra pattern' and tests that two bits of a bus are not shorted. This kind of fault is not implicitly modelled by fault simulators and so may pass the vendors check unnoticed.

Very few simulators offer a simulation control language (SCL) with high level language structures such as procedures, 'while' loops, and data structuring. This can make the job of writing test programs extremely tedious and time consuming. High level SCLs on the other hand allow code to be written easily and legibly. When constructs such as 'load_counter (13)' can be built, code becomes easy to debug and may be reuseable with other related circuits. It is possible to build a front end which allows the test stimulus to be written in a normal high level programming language and this is a very worthwhile activity.

Most vendors require a minimum percentage of test faults in the circuit to be tested. Care should be taken with the design so that this figure can easily be met with a reasonable number of test patterns; not only because of the tester time, though this may be important, but more because of simulation times and readability of simulation output. This latter point is most important with many systems because ultimately the integrity of the device may depend on the designer manually checking and signing off tens or hundreds of pages of test patterns – clearly not an ideal situation in which to ensure first-pass success of the design.

TIMING: Most semi-custom logic vendors only offer testing of static patterns at speed and I/O parametric testing. This is due to the high cost of writing timing enhancements to test programs manually. The designer must therefore satisfy himself of the critical timings from data sheet figures and worst-case simulations. This must be done meticulously if delivery of a percentage of dynamically marginal parts is to be avoided.

Post layout simulation is able to catch gross timing errors caused or aggravated by the placement and routing process. While this is obviously a useful check it is very late in the design cycle to find logic races and hazards which require netlist modifications and layout changes. This situation is largely avoidable if the design is approached laterally, i.e. the designer is aware of the likely variations in net delays and probable placements at the outset. He will then be in a position to guide the vendors placement.

8.13 Design stations

Most vendors offer CAD facilities which are open for the customers' use. This works well but can be expensive on mainframe CPU time, travel and accommodation. It may also require some duplication of effort in documentation. The need for frequent retraining may also impact development time.

The appearance of low cost workstations brings the possibility for in-house design capture, documentation and verification at a netlist or layout level. As integratable designs get more complex and more difficult to debug, the CAD workstation will come into its own. A number of 'low cost' workstations are already available with an impressive range of capabilities. These systems are increasingly able to offer a much wider range of software, such as full custom design suites, previously only available on minicomputers and mainframes.

8.14 Summary

In conclusion, experience shows that semi-custom logic can be an extremely cost-effective solution to the implementation of random logic. If care is taken with the design procedure and a few simple disciplines are applied it is possible to reduce the risk of a design recycle to an acceptable level. Additionally low cost design tools are becoming available which allow users to design and debug semi-custom integrated circuits in-house and reduce time-consuming technical interaction with vendors.

Part 3

Experiences of a Computer Designer

S.A. CLARKE

International Computers Ltd

8.15 Why a computer designer uses gate arrays

A computer company generally uses gate arrays to develop two different types of product. First, for new products in both processor and peripheral applications, and secondly for reducing the costs of existing products. For each of these two different requirements there will be different system performance criteria – high performance, for which we use ECL technology, medium performance, for which we use TTL technology and lower performance/low power for which we use CMOS technology. Any one computer product may well have a mixture of these three technologies depending on the particular performance constraints of each particular section of system design. We will now examine the reasons for wishing to use gate arrays in each performance area in turn.

In the design of a large powerful mainframe, the computing power of the machine, measured in Millions of Instructions Per Second (MIPS), is of critical importance, and ECL would be the preferred technology. We have, however, reached the stage where delays due to the interconnect are more significant to overall system performance than the intrinsic gate delays on the chip. By using an ECL gate array, rather than standard SSI/MSI ECL parts, we are able to pack very much more logic into a single chip, thus greatly reducing delays due to interconnect and improving system performance.

The large mainframe computer market is extremely competitive and the requirement to produce designs through to manufactured products in the market place using the latest and fastest technology rules out the luxury of full custom LSI design. This is because of the long time-scales – one to two years – necessary for this sort of development should full custom design be used.

Computer design engineers have for years now been designing with SSI/MSI type components and thus have a great wealth of skills in this style of logic design. These skills can be very quickly adapted to designing with gate arrays as the cell library functions available are very similar to the SSI/MSI functions. In effect we have moved one level up, the SSI/MSI components become the cells in the cell library, the printed circuit boards become the gate array and the backplane becomes the new printed circuit board.

If we now consider cost reductions of a high performance machine then the same reasons why gate arrays should be used in new designs still apply. This is because, when a production machine is cost reduced we aim to make maximum use of the performance and reliability benefits that gate arrays can give.

For designs which require a medium performance technology, i.e. where very high performance ECL is not required but speed constraints necessitate something faster than current CMOS technology, then TTL gate arrays are used. These include, for example, designs for peripheral handlers, interface couplers and store control systems. In these types of application, both for new designs and cost reductions, the amount of logic that can be packed into one device coupled with adequate performance is the main benefit. It may now be possible to have the entire required function on one device. When we desire to produce a medium performance computer (half to one MIPS) we have the option of using a medium performance technology and a low performance design or a low performance technology and a very high performance design.

A high performance design is achieved with the main expense of requiring many more gates than equivalent low performance designs. Since CMOS gate arrays can now be produced with up to 10 000 gates on one array, the high performance design approach is possible. Another feature of CMOS which makes it particularly alluring to the computer designer is the ability to 'shrink' the process and thus reduce the array's intrinisic delays. When the physical geometries of the device are shrunk there is a corresponding increase in speed. Thus a machine built out of CMOS gate arrays today could have its performance increased by using chips which are essentially the same but are produced from the shrunk process of tomorrow. Life is not that simple of course as system performance is also dependent on such things as memory access time; however, this is also getting faster.

The problem of heat dissipation and cooling must be considered as we are packing more and more logic into a smaller space. With high performance ECL arrays, although the overall system heat dissipation may be lower than for an SSI/MSI solution, the individual device or package heat dissipation is considerably higher than for the previous generation of components. As long as it is less than about 5 watts per device then heat fins and forced air cooling can cope, but for higher heat dissipations liquid cooling must be employed.

However, CMOS arrays have a very low heat output and even arrays of 8000 gates or so still dissipate less than 1 W which means that even forced air convection may not be required.

Computer systems currently have a three-fold product cost reduction every five years and this trend is expected to continue. If we, as a company, expect to double our revenue within the same period then we must deliver six times the current volume. We must therefore take advantage of the latest technologies as fast as possible in order to produce equipment which has a short design lead time, has good performance and which will sell at the right price. To satisfy and improve our customer base, and also to handle maintenance costs of the machines on site, we need to improve system reliability. Packing more logic into a single gate array reduces the number of components such as printed circuit boards and back planes that are required: this considerably reduces the number of soldered joints which are one of the main causes of hardware faults. Thus, just by moving our design implementations into gate arrays we move a step nearer our objectives.

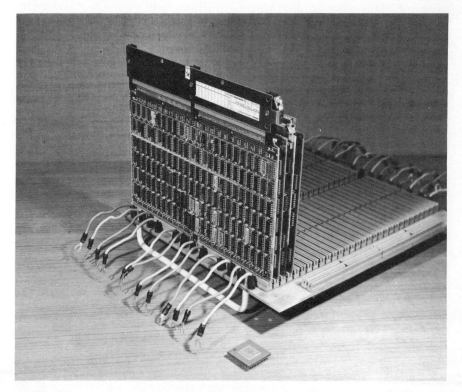

Fig. 8.9 The logic function of four MSI/SSI logic PCBs can be packed into one Fujitsu 8000 gate CMOS array

8.16 Criteria for choosing the array and vendor

There are many aspects of the array and the vendor that need careful evaluation before a commitment is made since the product may well depend on the one vendor and the array they supply. These will be discussed in turn although not in any particular order as specific products will have different priorities.

VENDOR: Commitment to the gate array is one of the main criteria in assessing the vendor as the complete project will depend on the one gate array. Past performance and commitment will obviously be evaluated.

GATE/PIN COUNT: As the gate count increases so does the requirement for more pins until the functional entity can be contained in one device. In complex mainframe systems, however, the functional entity tends to increase in size. Thus we normally require a higher pin to gate count than the rest of the electronics industry. This also applies to new designs, whichever technology is chosen. For cost reductions the required gate and pin counts are very dependent on how the existing design can be partitioned. The trend here also tends to be for more pins for any given gate count.

When reviewing vendors' specifications with regard to the number of gates in the array, it must be remembered that the design engineer is not so much interested in how many gates there are in the array, but how many he can use. Thus gate utilisation, (and the number of allowed input pins, output pins and bidirectional pins), needs to be evaluated.

MACRO-LIBRARY: These are the logic building bricks that the engineers use to build their designs up onto the array. The library should have a section which can contain the required functions; if not the vendor should be willing to include such a section in the design. It must be noted that a good macro-library will allow a more efficient use of gates in implementing the design onto the array.

PERFORMANCE: Gate array performance is used as a means to achieve the required overall system performance. The critical machine timing paths may not be contained on one device but may of necessity span two or three. Thus, apart from the intrinsic gate delay, the output buffer drive capability and the input buffer capacitance also need careful evaluation. In bus-structured designs the ability of the array to drive a large number of outputs simultaneously is also a requirement.

The design engineer needs to ensure not only that his array design will work functionally in the overall system, but also will work parametrically. If the vendors do the physical placement and tracking of the design, they will very often not guarantee the dynamic performance of the design and will only quote statistical delays. On some of our designs we were able to specify the critical paths and, when given this information, the vendor was willing to guarantee the chip performance and tolerances. However, in another situation we were totally unable to get the vendor to guarantee adequate chip performance and we were thus forced to withdraw from the collaboration.

DESIGN INTERFACE: Once the requirement for a gate array is established the first action is to check which gate arrays the company has used and which design interfaces are already in place and validated. There is obviously a strong motivation to use a validated and known route if available.

The interface between the gate array user and the semiconductor manufacturer is very dependent on the number of different designs that need fabricating rather than the type of computer product or any particular technology. In one case ICL had over forty array designs all of which needed to be produced within a short time-scale. In this situation we needed to find a vendor who, as well as having the required technology, also had adequate validation software and computing power coupled with a good design interface to which we could input. In many other cases we have only required one design on a particular array and in these situations it is not cost effective to produce a very formal interface: logic diagrams coupled with the validated test patterns will suffice as the interface. Close liaison between the two companies at an engineering level is then required to resolve the many problems that can occur in this type of interface.

COSTS: The total cost of buying gate arrays in volume consists not only of the volume piece-part cost but also the development cost incurred from inputting the design to the vendor through to engineering samples. If any design remakes are required for a low final volume requirement then this development cost can become large when amortised across the total required volume.

Gate arrays are considerably more expensive than the equivalent numbers of SSI/MSI parts and the break point where the savings in

PCBs, backplanes, cabinets, power supplies etc. needs evaluation when costing a project using a particular gate array.

As with most items, particularly semiconductors, the higher the volume of devices of one type that are required the lower the price that can be negotiated.

SECOND SOURCING: In common with other semiconductor users the gate array user needs to ensure security of component supplies. One way of ensuring this is to obtain two separate sources for the identical gate array and split the volumes between the two. This method is difficult because it incurs cost penalties as the development cost is doubled and the volume per supplier is reduced resulting in higher per-unit prices from the suppliers. Another method is to choose a source which is capable of manufacturing the array in different plants so that if a natural disaster hits one plant then manufacturing can be quickly transferred to the other. We would obviously not choose a vendor who had both plants on the San Andreas fault!

8.17 Resolving the interface and problems

There are two main problems that we have come across in the interface specification which is available from the vendor. The first of these is in the definition of the available cell library. The functionality is normally expressed as truth tables or a gate equivalent drawing or a combination of both. For the simpler functions such as AND-OR gates this is perfectly adequate. However, for some of the more complicated functions such as multiplexer master-slave latches misunderstandings can occur. Errors in the cell library may also occur as a result of mistakes made during the manual transcription of the cell-performance figures from the manufacturer's data sheets into our data bases to allow timing validation to be done on our designs.

The second problem that can occur with the interface definition is with ambiguities in the file format specifications. The major problem we have experienced in this area is with test data file formats where it is necesary to know and understand the restrictions of both the vendor's test equipment *and* the vendor's simulator, which will be used to validate the test data. This problem is exacerbated when bidirectional pins are required as there are not only further technology and tester constraints, but the simulators need to check for open circuit inputs and/or electrical conflicts as well.

If there is only a small number of designs which need implementing on the array it is normally quicker and more cost effective to use as much of the semiconductor manufacturers build and validation software as possible. In these cases the design is logically captured in-house and comprehensive validation patterns produced which are fully simulated against the design. This can be done in two ways. The logic design can be captured in MSI/SSI descriptions with the manufacturer then converting the design into the available cells in his macro-library. The other method is for the design engineer to capture his design using the vendor's cell library functions having first produced the cell description in his logic capture system. However in this case gate level models would also have to be written so that the simulations could be done. In either case the 'definition' of the design must ultimately be the test data, i.e. we will buy devices that satisfy the test data that has been supplied.

If we want to input a large number of designs within a short timescale then the complete design route and our usage of the macrocell library need full validation before the actual product designs are input.

When the in-house software has been produced for interfacing all the required data into the specified file formats and all the attributes of the vendor's macro-library have been fully captured we need to prove the route. We do this by producing a software pilot. This is an array design which is not for manufacture but is used to validate the design process. It must therefore contain all the required functions of the interface that the product designs will use.

When the interface route is operational and the macrocell library is in place an evaluation design is produced right through to samples. The purpose of this is to further verify the design/interface route and also to validate our use of the macro-library. If the gate array is new then this device will also be used to validate the performance of the complete cell library. Careful design of this device is imperative to obtain maximum validation benefits.

Real designs are now input. However, it is a mistake to assume that problems due to software bugs, both in the customer's and the vendor's software, will not occur. A lot of thought and discussion is necessary to find these faults and to minimise the delays that arise when they are discovered. Physical and logical faults are often discovered when simulating the test pattern as, of course, are faults in the test patterns themselves. It is thus of considerable benefit if the test data can be logically structured so that faults and discrepancies can be quickly identified. It is also a primary requirement that the vendor and customer can correlate equivalent failing patterns in each other's simulators.

It must be noted that any problems encountered when actually testing the wafers are extremely difficult to diagnose because of the large number of variables.

We have discussed briefly the benefits that a computer designer obtains by using gate arrays and the requirements that he has of the vendor and the gate array, and if sufficient emphasis is placed on the interfaces between the two companies then no real problems should be encountered.

8.18 References

8.1 Hurst, S.L. (1982) 'Commercial applications of semi-custom IC design'. *Proceedings of the 2nd International Conference on Semi-Custom ICs*. Prodex Ltd: London.

8.2 Grierson, J.R. (1984) 'Selection of semi-custom technique, supplier and design route'. *Semi-custom IC design and VLSI*. ed. P.J. Hicks, Peter Perigrinus: London.

8.3 Jack, M.S. (1983) 'Semi-custom integrated circuit design in the UK – a capability profile'. *IEE Electronics and Power*. pp. 217-221.

8.4 Mavor, J., Jack, M.A. and Denyer, P.B. (1983) *Introduction to MOS LSI design*. Addison-Wesley: Reading, Mass.

8.5 Mead, Carver and Conway, Lynn (1980) *Introduction to VLSI systems*. Addison-Wesley: Reading, Mass.

8.6 'The challenge of managing complexity' *Electronics Weekly*, 1981.

Chapter 9

Future Trends

JOHN W. READ

STC Telecommunications Ltd

In the preceding chapters, the various authors have given detailed background information on a variety of aspects of gate array technologies, design, manufacture, testing and use, together with occasional views on where the future lies in each of these areas. It is the purpose of this short chapter to take a broad look at the future of semi-custom techniques and to put the role played by gate arrays into perspective.

9.1 Logic arrays — the limitations

As refinements in lithography and wafer processing allow dimensions of 1 μm and below to be achieved, it will be possible to continue to offer ever larger arrays of gates for interconnect on a semi-custom basis as described in this book. However, there is a serious question about the usefulness of such arrays. At the time of writing, arrays as large as 20K gates have been proposed. Although arrays of the order of 8K gates per chip have been used quite extensively by some systems houses (for example, see chapter 8), the maximum volume of interest appears to be at around the 1 to 1.5K gates per chip complexity level and tails off rapidly above 2K gates per chip. The basic reason for this is that, except in mainframe computer terms, a system with 2K gates is quite large. In many cases the requirements of such a system can be met economically and flexibly by a microprocessor minimum-chip solution or even a single-chip micro-computer. Even where this is not the case, large gate arrays are of limited use and economic viability because they require memory within a system, either RAM (static or dynamic), or ROM, in various forms. In general, memory and memory address/decode functions can only be performed inefficiently on a gate array, thus consuming large numbers of gates and a considerable area of silicon. The alternative option, using off-chip memory, is expensive on package pins because of the need for parallel addresses and byte- or word-wide data buses to achieve sensible instruction speeds. The ideal solution could be to offer pre-configured memory blocks on chip along with the sea of gates. This, however, only raises more questions like: 'What type of memory?' 'How much?', 'What configuration?', 'Speed?', 'Where on chip?', etc. To such questions every system designer has a different answer for each system. To some extent pre-configured memory is one of the key features of microcomputers – but we have microcomputer families with varying amounts of ROM and RAM just because of this problem. While such memories are accessed and used in standard, predefined ways in a microcomputer, it could be less easy to define such components acceptably for a gate array. Furthermore, the interface to the real world, at either inputs or outputs to the system, often also demands analog capability.

9.2 Analog functions

While a limited number of analogue interface options can be catered for by rewiring a TTL or MOS buffer in conjunction with some internal gates or transistors, it is nevertheless impossible to cater directly for the wide range of requirements possible and limitations must be imposed on the range of choice available to the system designer. Analog/linear functions are still usually provided by separate chips as discussed in chapter 4 except for very limited instances such as VCOs and simple D to A or A to D functions of limited resolution for example. Other such examples were given in chapters 2 and 3.

There are several problems associated with offering on-chip analog functions to the system designer. Basically, these are:

* compatibility of optimum technology with the preferred digital gate array technology;
* flexibility of choice;
* modelling and simulation tools plus characterization data, i.e. support.

In general, the technologies chosen for purpose-designed wholly-digital or wholly-analog ICs are different. They are optimised for different parameters in order, in each case, to squeeze the ultimate in performance out of that technology for that particular function. Where some mixture is achieved such as in the use of switched-capacitor filters (basically digital to achieve an analog result) the fabrication process is often made more complicated (and therefore more expensive) to achieve the result. In this case such a mixture of complex digital and sophisticated analog requirements has proved viable and the results in terms of codecs, filters, modems, etc., are widely available today. The convergence towards double-poly (for accurate capacitors) double-level-metal (for flexibility of inter-connect) CMOS (for low-power) offers the best opportunity for the ultimate realisation of systems comprising both digital and analog functions on a single chip.

9.3 Cell techniques

One solution to the problems outlined in sections 9.1 and 9.2 is to offer the systems designer a library of functional cells which have been predefined, predesigned, built and characterised. A drawback to using this approach is the consequent loss of a major advantage associated with gate arrays, ROMs and microcomputers where only 1 to 3 levels out of 10 to 15 are customised – all photomask layers would now be unique for each chip design unless the semi-custom user has a number of similar but slightly different requirements and the ability to build into his design a second, nested layer of customisation.

This approach has in fact been on offer for a number of years for logic designs. Libraries of cells of simple logic functions in proven technologies have been available from several large semiconductor manufacturers. In general the cells have emulated TTL-type functions, including buffers with the requisite drive capabilities, operated from 5 V supplies and have been designed to a fixed height, variable width philosophy, (fig. 9.1). Chip layout is done with rows of such cells with interconnect channels between them and tends to look rather like a 'Snakes and Ladders' board, (see fig. 9.2).

Until fairly recently such approaches have been limited in their usefulness as designs have required a great deal of expertise with integrated circuitry and a high level of engineering manpower; consequently they have been almost as expensive as a full-custom design.

The functional density achievable has also been less than that

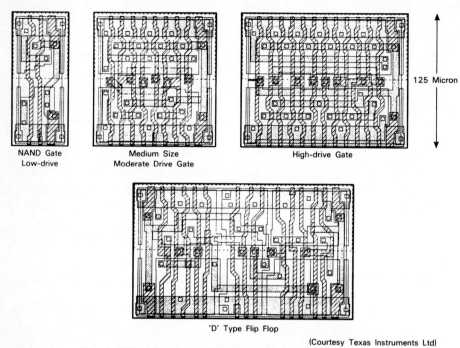

NAND Gate
Low-drive

Medium Size
Moderate Drive Gate

High-drive Gate

125 Micron

'D' Type Flip Flop

(Courtesy Texas Instruments Ltd)

Fig. 9.1 Relative sizes of fixed-height variable width cells

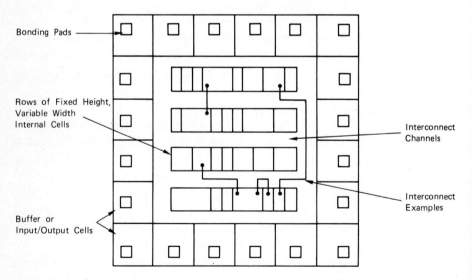

Bonding Pads

Rows of Fixed Height,
Variable Width
Internal Cells

Interconnect
Channels

Interconnect
Examples

Buffer or
Input/Output Cells

Fig. 9.2 Block diagram of first-generation cell-based semi-custom chip

achievable with a full custom design due to both the highly structured layout approach and its inefficiencies and also to the technology lag inherent in the provision of a fully characterised cell library and support tools for use by non-IC designers. The 'cut and strap' modification techniques applicable to TTL designs on PCBs have no equivalent in silicon technology. To satisfy the demand for chip designs we need a new breed of IC designer who does not need to understand the detailed process and device intricacies. Also, the larger and more complex the cell (e.g. an ALU), and perhaps therefore the more generally useful, the more difficult it is to support with CAD tools.

Prior to the advent of CMOS, the parasitics associated with series resistances, the capacitance of long interconnects and the effects of widely variable and large fan-outs were problems requiring skilled IC expertise.

With the advent of CMOS technology and all its advantages as explained in chapter 3, together with increasingly sophisticated CAD tools and engineering workstations, it has now become possible to provide cell libraries and design and verification tools which enable designs to be executed in the same manner, and with the same basic knowledge and skills, as previously required for PCB design using building blocks of TTL and linear from a semiconductor supplier's catalogue but with the one limitation expressed above.

Although there is still a long way to go with the development of this approach, the path is clear and the role of gate arrays as described by the main body of this book is clearly bounded in its upper band by the limitations discussed above, and the solution to those limitations will be provided by 'cells'. This does not mean that gate arrays are not important, just that they have their place and are not the solution to everybody's problems. Clearly, where cell-based approaches do not offer lower total cost, at low complexities for low volumes (a few thousand parts a year) for example, then gate arrays will be the preferred solution. It should also be noted that cell techniques overcome the silicon area wastage involved in unused gates on an array. Typically 70-80% utilisation of the available gates is good. This also leaves some gates available for later design improvements on the base design!

To increase the packing density on the silicon, attempts are being made to abut cells in both X- and Y-directions with cell interconnect overhead instead of in channels, (see fig. 9.3). This leads to chip layouts more closely akin to full custom and reduces the dis-advantages of the cell approach. Structured logic approaches using

PLAs instead of random logic gates can also give increased functional density.

The usefulness of cell libraries is very dependent on good characterisation, good CAD-support tools, availability of state-of-the-art technology and commitment of the semiconductor manufacturer to support these areas and upgrade them as dictated by technology changes. Above all, the success of any individual project will depend on a well-defined interface between vendor and customer and the ability to sort out problems when they arise and make sure that the same problems do not recur.

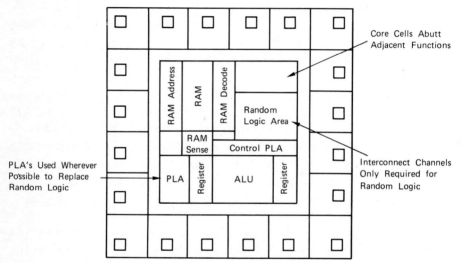

Fig. 9.3 Chip layout using abutted cells – second generation design

9.4 The silicon compiler

The ultimate answer to the systems-design need is the silicon compiler[9.1] where a functional, or even behavioural, definition of the system's requirement is presented to a computer which then draws on a set of design rules and prior art to design a chip. A model is developed which allows simulation of the system to check for conceptual or design errors and once this is completed, a manufacturing data base is prepared complete with mask information, process instructions, test tapes and assembly, symbolisation, packing, shipping and invoice information. This is really just another expert system made feasible and viable by the rapid advances in semiconductor technology! There is no reason why systems like this cannot be done right now – just time, cost and manpower – and key to the whole affair is defining an acceptable set of constraints or boundary conditions. To develop such a system for the general case – any process technology, any package, any manufacturer, etc. – would be unnecessarily large and costly but what is the minimum set of capabilities that are acceptable?

Some basic systems along these lines are available, primarily as a result of University research, but given the learning capabilities inherent in the kernel of expert systems it is strange that more basic systems along these lines are not available from semiconductor suppliers; these could be built on as demand and capabilities change and grow.

Silicon compilers as well as cell design techniques are beyond the scope of this book and will be the subject of many new books in the future. At least 2 magazines provide specific articles and information related to the state of the art in VLSI[9.2] and semi-custom technology.[9.3]

Design methodology is not the only challenge for the future, other factors will be the supplier/customer interfaces, manufacturing changes to shorten cycle times, testing and last, but not least, what will these chips and systems do?

9.5 The supplier/customer interface

The requirement for all sorts of different exchanges of information between the semi-custom supplier and the customer, i.e. the systems house, has been mentioned in nearly every chapter of this book. The situation can be further complicated by the interposition of a third party design house where required. A simple overview of the exchanges of data is shown in fig. 9.4. We do not need to go into detail. It is sufficient to understand that for a successful outcome of the development each set of data has to mean the same thing to both sides; it has to be intelligible to each side's suites of design programs, hardware and engineers! It must contain all of the information in a consistent fashion and be unambiguous. These conditions must hold for each interface for a successful outcome.

The catch is that a single supplier can set up all of his programs and requirements and work with any individual customer to resolve differences and for a large customer he will, of course, be only too willing to do this. But, this is not what semi-custom is about, especially for arrays. It's about reaching the widest possible customer base of all sizes of demand. From a customer's point of view it's also

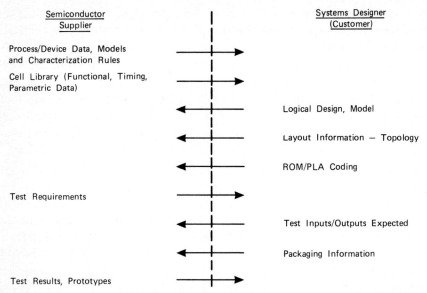

Fig. 9.4 Exchanges of data between silicon supplier and customer (systems design house)

about being able to second-source a design for security of supply and competitive pricing without having to go through a second set of design and development procedures with a different library, set of tools, and so on, with the attendant extra costs and delays.

In the past, each vendor has regarded his set of CAD tools and interfaces as key to his business and kept them to himself. Some second-source arrangements of a limited nature have been set up but even where base arrays and processes have been cross-licenced, it has sometimes been necessary for the customer to redo the simulation and design and re-input the database for the second source.

It is, therefore, encouraging that a number of companies have recently got together to try and arrive at an agreed standard interface specification, called EDIF (Electronic Design Interface Format), and that they have done this in open forums soliciting input and comments from other companies to attempt wider agreement. While it is unlikely that this will provide the final answer, and there will still be suppliers who feel that the proposals for EDIF do not meet their needs for whatever reason, one can only wish those well who attempt such standardisation and hope that their efforts will meet with the success they so clearly deserve.

Given such a common format, it is then possible for the various CAD tools on both sides of the interface to be modified and further developed for individual commercial advantage and increased competitiveness while still preserving the ability to exchange data between a wide number of customers/suppliers. One therefore expects that among both semiconductor houses and workstation suppliers their efforts will be concentrated on providing better technologies, libraries and support tools around the common interface. The engineering manpower and creativity that is presently tied up in solving interface problems can then be released to provide further leaps forward in design methodology.

9.6 Manufacturing changes

One of the main enabling forces behind the rapid increases in chip functional densities has been improvements in the manufacturing process giving higher yields and finer linewidths. As linewidths further reduce from the present 3 and 2 μm production processes to the 1.5 and 1.25 μm processes of the mid-80s it is generally accepted that optical technology will be limited to this level by diffraction effects and the basic wavelength of light. Considerable efforts have been expended to explore the uses of electron beams and X-rays for lithography because of their shorter wavelengths and hence reduced diffraction effects compared with the sub-micron dimensions of interest.

X-rays have a considerably shorter wavelength than light and are therefore very attractive for this purpose. However, it is not yet possible to focus and deflect X-rays to write a pattern on photo-resist as required. The use of X-rays therefore requires a thin metal mask to define the photo-resist exposure (and hence final pattern) under a flood of X-ray radiation. The fabrication and handling of such masks is difficult and expensive.

Although e-beams can be focussed and scanned to write patterns directly on to photo-resist, the trade-offs that have to be made mean that the wavelengths of interest are only an order of magnitude less than the optical wavelengths. However, there are significant advantages in using direct e-beam writing despite it being a slow process – typically, 10 minutes per slice compared with, say, 1–2 minutes for DSW (Direct Step on Wafer) optical technology. In addition to increased resolution, i.e. better than 1 μm, it is possible to use the e-beam to look at the pattern of the previous layer and provide electronic alignment of the new mark level to previous pattern levels of better than 0.1 μm. This compares with a mechanical tolerance closer to 1 μm for inter-level alignments in optical technology. The repercussions of this on the original design are tremendous as significant amounts of the total device and chip sizes are consumed by the need to ensure that manufacturing mis-alignment tolerances are adequately compensated for.

The electron-beam machine can also be driven directly from the CAD database containing the topological layout data. No glass masks are required and the delay of several days presently required for mask manufacture can, therefore, be eliminated from the manufacturing process. This is particularly important for the initial verification of a new design and in semi-custom prototyping.

It is also possible to mix optical and e-beam techniques on different layers if one is willing and able to put up with the grosser dimensions, linewidths and tolerances on the optical layers in the same way as is presently done using optical techniques of widely differing costs and capabilities.[9.4] This is important because e-beam machines are three to four times more expensive than steppers and have a lower throughput, resulting in a higher wafer cost. In any case, e-beam technology provides the means for significant improvements in prototype turn-around time and we can expect to see several manufacturers commit themselves to the use of this technique, at least for the customisation levels, over the next few years. In this respect there is a significant convergence of the needs of standard VLSI and semi-custom. There will be many other significant changes in manufacturing technology but the discontinuity provided by the move from optical to e-beam techniques seems to be the most important.

Coupled with the move to e-beam for pattern definition will be the use of e-beam machines in voltage contrast mode for VLSI testing, analysis and characterisation. Electron microscopes will be needed just to look satisfactorily at sub-micron geometry devices because of the same diffraction limitations described before. However, the use of an e-beam microscope in voltage contrast mode allows examination of the operation of internal circuit nodes at speed without the significant loading imposed by a mechanical probe. In this way, VLSI circuits can be more easily checked during development and operating margins analysed. This will become an important technique for suppliers of ICs.

9.7 Testability

The subject of design-for-testability has been dealt with in chapter 7 but is still in its infancy as far as most semi-custom users are concerned. Dave Tonge has outlined the development of more sophisticated techniques for testing but the increasing complexity of VLSI standard and semi-custom will depend on the ability to maintain high chip yields. In the supply of DRAMs, more manufacturers are incorporating the concept of redundancy and repair or replacement of defective rows and columns of the array by the redundant on-chip elements. It is also said that 1 Mbit and larger DRAMs will not be achievable without this technique.

Presently, address-decode reprogramming, which is done to allow redundant elements to be used in place of defective ones, is accomplished at test with laser trimming of poly-silicon fuse links. Much work is being done with EAROMs on electrically alterable elements that could be used instead. It is, therefore, likely that redundant logic blocks (at higher than gate level) will be feasible on-chip in the near future and it may be possible for them to be wired-out if defective and replaced by other blocks entirely by electrical programming. If this becomes possible then this technique could be used to increase yields in commercial applications and, also, improve reliability and operating life by built-in testing and built-in repair. This would be of particular importance initially in military, avionic and medical applications.

9.8 Applications of semi-custom VLSI

Increasing complexity brought about by VLSI and the increasing diversity made possible by the discontinuities in design methodology represented by present and projected semi-custom techniques do pose the questions: 'where will such large chips be used?' and, 'won't they all be standards if they are infinitely programmable and incredibly cheap?' There are, of course, no simple answers, except to make the point that most of the big end-product changes brought about by semiconductors have been in high volume production only three to four years after conception; many of the main uses of semiconductor technology today were not conceived of five or so years ago.

It is easy to project the cost reductions of present-day complex electronic systems – more powerful personal computers and personal communications, breakthroughs in voice input/output technology, improved video techniques for easier user interfaces, fifth-generation computers and expert systems. It is, however, the discontinuities that provide the biggest breakthroughs and whoever can predict those will probably not be writing about them but trying to make them happen.

I wish you success in your use of semi-custom technology and I hope that this book has helped you along your way in understanding the basic concepts and techniques of logic arrays.

9.9 References

9.1 Mead, C. and Conway, L. (1980) *Introduction to VLSI Systems.* Addison-Wesley: Reading, Mass.

9.2 *VLSI design.* CMP Publications Inc: Manhasset, N.Y.

9.3 *Journal of semi-custom ICs.* Benn Electronic Publications Ltd: Luton, UK.

9.4 'Mix and match alignment: Cost effective for VLSI' *Semiconductor International* (April 1983) Denver, Colorado, pp. 59–66.

Index

Index